Justice for Girls?

A volume in the series

Adolescent Development and Legal Policy

EDITED BY FRANKLIN E. ZIMRING

Also in the series:

Changing Lives: Delinquency Prevention as Crime-Control Policy
by Peter W. Greenwood

Double Jeopardy: Adolescent Offenders with Mental Disorders
by Thomas Grisso

An American Travesty: Legal Responses to Adolescent Sexual Offending
by Franklin E. Zimring

Justice for Girls?

Stability and Change in the Youth Justice Systems of the United States and Canada

Jane B. Sprott and Anthony N. Doob

WITH A FOREWORD BY FRANKLIN E. ZIMRING

The University of Chicago Press | *Chicago & London*

Jane B. Sprott is associate professor of criminal justice and crimi-
nology at Ryerson University. **Anthony N. Doob** is professor at the
Centre of Criminology at the University of Toronto and coauthor of
Responding to Youth Crime in Canada.

The University of Chicago Press, Chicago 60637
The University of Chicago Press, Ltd., London
© 2009 by The University of Chicago
All rights reserved. Published 2009
Printed in the United States of America

17 16 15 14 13 12 11 10 09   1 2 3 4 5

ISBN-13: 978-0-226-77004-8 (cloth)
ISBN-10: 0-226-77004-4 (cloth)

Sprott, Jane B.
   Justice for girls? : stability and change in the youth justice
systems of the United States and Canada / Jane B. Sprott and
Anthony N. Doob ; with a foreword by Franklin E. Zimring.
       p.   cm.
   Includes bibliographical references and index.
   ISBN-13: 978-0-226-77004-8 (cloth : alk. paper)
   ISBN-10: 0-226-77004-4 (cloth : alk. paper)   1. Female juvenile
delinquents—United States.   2. Juvenile justice, Administration
of—United States.   3. Female juvenile delinquents—Canada.
4. Juvenile justice, Administration of—Canada.   I. Doob,
Anthony N.   II. Zimring, Franklin E.   III. Title.
   HV9104.S676 2009
   364.36082'0973—dc22

                                        2009009306

♾ The paper used in this publication meets the minimum re-
quirements of the American National Standard for Information
Sciences—Permanence of Paper for Printed Library Materials,
ANSI Z39.48-1992.

Contents

Foreword by *Franklin E. Zimring* | vii
Acknowledgments | xi

Chapter 1   Criminal Girls and Girls in Youth Justice | 1

Chapter 2   Are Sugar and Spice Really Evolving into Snips and Snails and Puppy-Dog Tails? | 19

Chapter 3   Paternalism and the Social Control of Adolescent Girls: Juvenile Justice Reform in the United States | 44

Chapter 4   Paternalism and the Social Control of Adolescent Girls: Juvenile Justice Reform in Canada | 74

Chapter 5   The Impact of Law Reform: Deinstitutionalization in Law and Practice in the United States | 98

Chapter 6   The Impact of Law Reform: Deinstitutionalization in Law and Practice in Canada | 128

Chapter 7   Continuity and Change in Justice for Girls | 158

Appendixes | 175
Notes | 191
References | 199
Index | 209

Foreword

Franklin E. Zimring

Males have always been the dominant gender in both the theory and practice of juvenile justice in the United States and in every other developed nation where statistics are kept. This is understandable as an emphasis, yet the paucity of data and analyses about girls in juvenile justice is both inexcusable and dangerous.

Girls in the juvenile justice system are, to begin with, an important and intractable practical problem. Females under the age of 18 enter the U.S. juvenile justice system by the hundreds of thousands and present issues substantially different from male offenders. Their proportional impact elsewhere in the developed world is similar. A substantial fraction of cases involving girl offenders also involve family conflict and status offenses, difficult situations that reformers have been trying to resolve for more than a generation without resorting to secure confinement of the girls. The concentration of noncriminal misbehavior of girls was so great that more than 20 percent of all juveniles in custody were females in the early 1970s, six times the percentage of females in adult prisons. Have three decades of reform efforts made a dent in this problem? The best way to answer this question is to carefully assess trends in the juvenile court processing of young women.

A second important issue that requires careful analysis of trends in female youth crime is whether the removal of traditional sex role constraints has produced increases in female rates of serious crime. The theory is that freedom will push toward equality of crime rates by gender. But this question has not received the careful attention it deserves. Have the enormous social changes in sex roles in the developed world in the past generation produced fundamental criminological change as well?

The editorial board of this series was eager to launch a sustained study of girls and juvenile justice, and we were fortunate to persuade Jane Sprott and Anthony Doob to undertake an ambitious two-country study of juvenile crime and juvenile justice. The volume they have produced uses an eclectic portfolio of empirical methods to put a generation of social and legal changes in perspective. Trends over time for young females are compared with those for young males, and case processing for younger girls is compared to dispositional profiles for older females. Legal, institutional, and criminological developments in the United States are compared to parallel and contrasting patterns in Canada.

After a careful and balanced analysis, three significant findings emerge from this study. First, the long-awaited expansion of serious criminality among young women hasn't happened in either the United States or Canada. Although isolated and misleading statistical sound bites make the news, the long-term stability of low rates of serious crime by females is a rule with very few exceptions. As of 2008, the girl crime wave is properly classified as an urban legend.

The second major theme to emerge from the study is the persistence of family conflict and status offending as major issues in juvenile justice for girls in the United States and Canada. For three decades after 1970, some progress was made in both countries toward reductions in the use of custody for noncriminal misbehavior by girls and by boys, but custodial outcomes in such cases remained by no means rare. At the turn of the 21st century, the overcontrol of noncriminal misbehavior was still a major problem in both nations, and Canada and the United States had comparable levels of success in custodial reduction.

New Canadian youth justice legislation of 2003 produced swift and sharp reductions in the use of secure confinement for both boys and girls. Three years after this Canadian legislation, a wide gap opened between the decarcerative successes in Canada and the United States. What made the Canadian policy such a powerful influence was its broad sweep—an attempt to reduce sentences of secure confinement across the board. By contrast, the reforms in the United States are an attempt to fine-tune custodial policy—to release noncriminal juveniles while allowing substantial rates of custodial confinement for other types of delinquency. That mixed system is easier to cheat, and the faith in custody that animates so much of current U.S. policy also restrains the enthusiasm that many in the system show toward keeping any class of children out of custody.

This fine book follows a few other pioneering efforts at comparative juvenile justice (see Bottoms, 2002; and Tonry and Doob, 2004). I can only hope that the solid contributions of this effort will inspire a larger number of comparative studies.

Berkeley, California
May 2008

Acknowledgments

This book would never have happened had it not been for Professor Franklin E. Zimring. A number of years ago, in connection with his participation in the MacArthur Foundation's Research Network on Adolescent Development and Juvenile Justice, Frank asked us—two Canadians who had been doing research on the Canadian youth justice system—if we would be willing to consider doing a study of "girls in the youth justice systems of the United States and Canada." We knew that one of the major challenges would be to find adequate data on this issue in Canada. One of us (J. S.) had worked with the U.S. data and knew—notwithstanding the data that are housed in the National Center for Juvenile Justice—that it would also be a challenge to get adequate data for the United States.

Our initial inclination—and our response to him—was that it was probably something that was best carried out with respect to one country rather than two. At that time, Frank was just completing his work on *The Great American Crime Decline,* and we expect that was why he told us that we were almost certainly wrong. He had found—as readers have done since then—that his comparative analysis in chapter 5 of that book of the largely similar decline in Canadian crime (not as widely noticed in Canada as the comparable crime decline in the United States) was very useful as a tool for evaluating American explanations for the American crime decline. He was, therefore, an advocate for comparative analyses, arguing that each country could, in effect, act as a lens through which the events in the other could be seen.

We hope that readers will agree that looking at these two countries simultaneously does shed additional light on what happened in both. The similarities and differences between the two systems and the manner in which different legal regimes responded to girls tell a story that could not be told had we prevailed over Professor Zimring. We hope that the reader will agree that these two stories, taken together, do, in fact, add up to more than the sum of their parts.

Those who know Frank Zimring know that he can be very persuasive. Having looked, some years earlier, at the issue of the relative growth in the number of girls in the Canadian youth justice system, we were, of course, interested in the topic. Frank's enthusiasm for the topic and his promise to be available to give us advice convinced us to take on the task. At certain times in the process—for example, when we discovered that certain data we thought we needed simply were not available—we wondered what we were thinking when we took this task on. But Frank read numerous versions of all chapters and gave us enormously helpful and detailed suggestions on all aspects of this book. Those familiar with Frank's own work on the American juvenile justice system will—we hope—see his influence on some aspects of our analysis. We are, therefore, enormously grateful for the help that he generously and repeatedly gave us. It is not an exaggeration to state that this project would never have been started, let alone been completed, without Frank Zimring's help.

We also wish to thank Howard Snyder and the National Center for Juvenile Justice not only for giving us access to detailed youth court data but also for patiently responding to all of our questions. Robert Schwartz from the Juvenile Law Center also gave us valuable feedback on aspects of the American juvenile justice system. In the end, of course, any errors or omissions are our own, despite everyone's best efforts.

Finally, we are grateful to the John D. and Catherine T. MacArthur Foundation and its Research Network on Adolescent Development and Juvenile Justice, which commissioned this study. We were also aided by grants to each of us from the Social Sciences and Humanities Research Council of Canada and by the broad support that our two institutions—Ryerson University and the University of Toronto—have provided to us.

Jane B. Sprott
Anthony N. Doob
Toronto, November 2008

Chapter 1

Criminal Girls and Girls in Youth Justice

Overview of the Book

For more than a century, concerns have been expressed repeatedly about a "crime wave" involving women and girls, one of the main causes of which was thought to be women's increasing freedom. As society changed and women were afforded greater freedoms—most notably in the 1960s and 1970s—a crime wave seemed to be looming on the horizon or was even assumed already to have arrived in various communities. In the past 10 years in the United States and in Canada, concerns about increased involvement of girls in crime—especially violent crime—have grown, with equality and equal opportunity seen once again as the culprits. The only problem is that credible evidence of a crime wave involving young girls does not exist. The long-awaited crime wave simply did not happen.

A different but related issue relates to boys and girls in the youth justice system. Credible data demonstrate that girls are being treated differently from boys by the youth justice systems of these two countries. This different treatment of girls and boys is not the inevitable result of the decisions in these two countries to set up separate justice systems to respond to youth crime. Indeed, in the early days of the youth justice systems in both Canada and the United States, the different treatment of boys and girls was dismissed, in large part because of the perception that girls were more in need of treatment than boys, especially for offenses such as "sexual immorality" and "incorrigibility" (Knupfer, 2001). The treatment of girls—specifically, concern about the offenses that brought them into court and the use of custody—became an important policy topic within youth justice only when more general concerns about due process became salient in the latter part of the 20th century. The manner in which girls have been treated by the youth justice systems of Canada and the United States is the focus of this book.

Focusing a study on the manner in which girls are treated by youth justice systems can be justified in the same way in which the study of women in the adult justice systems is justified: if girls aren't singled out as the focus of their own study, their relatively low numbers mean that differences between the treatment of boys and girls will simply not be noticed. Said differently, in understanding overall trends, girls, in a statistical sense, become error variance. Given that thousands of girls do find themselves in contact with the justice system, to ignore their special treatment by the youth justice system is a bit like saying that in a study of violence, homicide can safely be ignored because the numbers do not warrant a special study.

The study of girls in the youth justice system is useful for a completely different reason as well. Girls and boys are in many, often subtle ways treated differently by the youth justice systems of these two countries. By looking at the different treatment of girls and boys, we can study the sometimes conflicting purposes of the youth justice systems of these two countries. Girls then become a lens through which one can better observe, and thus understand, the system as a whole.

Why, then, study the treatment of girls and boys in the justice systems of these two countries? Why not simply study one country on its own, or one country in relation to some other subset of the 192 countries in the world?[1] Indeed, why treat these two federal states as countries, rather than as a set of 51 separate youth justice systems in the United States and an additional 10 or 13 in Canada?[2] Comparing the United States and Canada is interesting because the separate youth justice systems in these two countries were established almost simultaneously at the end of the 19th and the beginning of the 20th centuries. Those responsible for the establishment of the two systems were in more direct contact with each other than youth justice reformers probably are today in the two countries. More important, the problems that the youth justice systems were designed to address were seen as being quite similar. Both were intent on finding a place to deal with youth crime away from the adult criminal courts. Also, however, the basic structure that was established at the end of the 19th century—a juvenile court operating under legislation that separated youths from the adult justice system—was, and was seen to be, quite similar in its orientation in the two countries. At the same time, there are important differences that make the contrast between these two systems more interesting than simply the contrast between two relatively similar and contiguous countries.

In the first place, the American youth justice model typically is explicitly established by the states under laws that are not explicitly criminal. When Canada established a separate youth justice system, however, it was as part of the criminal-law jurisdiction of the federal government.

But given that the law and the administration of it in the United States is largely the responsibility of the state rather than of the federal government, and that in Canada the administration of the law in the ten provinces and three territories is the responsibility of the province or territory rather than of the federal government, why would one look at national data rather than state or provincial data in either country? Aside from the practical issue of trying to describe and make sense of the historical development of youth justice systems in 64 jurisdictions, there are two simple justifications, one historical and the other legal. In the first place, in the United States, the model of the juvenile court that was developed in Chicago at the end of the 19th century spread across the country rather quickly. Although there are numerous ways in which the laws vary (e.g., how open the court is, how transfers take place, the age jurisdiction of the court, the resources associated with the court), the broad structure of the juvenile justice systems in the U.S. states are relatively similar. In the second place, in recent years factors such as the often-cited Supreme Court cases of the 1960s and 1970s and national standards encouraged through the transfers of funds (e.g., the Juvenile Justice and Delinquency Prevention Act of 1974) applied to—or at least were encouraged in—all the states.

In Canada, there is only one juvenile justice law covering all ten provinces and three territories, though it is clear that the administration of this law varies considerably across provinces (and, almost certainly, across locations within provinces).[3] As in the United States, however, the influence of the federal government is broad and often related to money: at various points in time the federal government has offered the provinces money to move in particular directions that are seen as consistent with federal youth justice policy.

In both countries, therefore, there are fairly straightforward justifications for focusing on the countries as a whole at the outset. The focus on individual states and provinces, and the manner in which they have treated girls in their youth justice systems, is a separate and interesting topic that we will for the most part leave for another day.

We begin our story by looking at the way girls' offending, in particular violent offending, has been discussed and portrayed both in the media and in traditional criminology. We then present trends of girls' offending, looking at both self-reported data and court data, to explore whether there is any evidence of a "girl crime wave" (chapter 2). After placing girls' offending in context and in particular determining whether there has been a rise in violence by girls, we then turn our attention to legislative changes. The next two chapters focus on juvenile justice policy developments in both the United States (chapter 3) and Canada (chapter 4). The impacts of such developments are then explored for both the United States (chapter 5) and Canada (chapter 6).

In the end, we hope to present a single story that consists of two separate but related subplots. The first subplot is about the girl crime wave that did not happen. The second subplot tells the story of how two different youth justice systems were created at much the same time without much focus on gender issues but developed practices that resulted in different treatment for girls and boys. The laws governing youth justice in the two countries, while initially quite similar, evolved differently over time. One could easily expect, therefore, to find that gender issues played out differently in the two countries. In the end, however, we will see that the issues surrounding the manner in which girls are treated by these two systems are remarkably similar, notwithstanding quite different histories during the past century. The study of the treatment of girls who come in contact with the youth justice systems of these two countries is, therefore, a story that tells us not only about the way in which we view the misbehavior of girls, but also about the manner in which these systems respond to both girls and boys.

Some readers will no doubt notice that we have not mentioned the issue of race or ethnicity in this overview. This absence reflects the subject's near-absence in the rest of the book. The reason is both simple and unfortunate. As will become quickly apparent, we found the gathering of adequate data on gender to be a challenge, especially if we wanted these data broken down by other factors. But in addition, in Canada, there are almost no data on race published on people of any age at any stage of the youth or adult criminal justice system. At various points in time, data on Aboriginal people in the justice system have been reported. And, more recently, for Canada's federal penitentiaries, information about race and ethnicity has sometimes been published. But even then, race or ethnicity and gender do not appear in the same tables. Hence, with the exception of very specific individual studies, we could not find any relevant information on this issue for Canada. In the United States, though we were able occasionally to find some data on race or ethnicity, we were not able to find sufficient data that were broken down simultaneously by gender and race or ethnicity. For our purposes, the separation of race and gender in the presentation of justice-system data meant that the data on race or ethnicity were of little value to us. The problem of race and ethnicity is but one example of the primitive nature of youth justice data in the two countries across any reasonable period of time. It was rare to find consistent data over time that were broken down by gender on variables more complex than factors such as offense. Where possible, we will speculate on how the systems in both countries respond to issues around race or ethnicity.

Concerns about Girls' Offending:
The Media and Traditional Criminology

> It is, therefore, to be expected that as woman's position becomes more like that of man, her criminality will increase. That this has already happened has been illustrated in the statistics.
> —M. Parmelee, *Criminology*, 1918

Throughout the 1990s and 2000s there was discussion in both Canada and the United States about trends in girls' involvement in crime generally and in violence specifically. Almost invariably, the implication was that girls were becoming more violent, or that their violence was becoming more serious. Headlines from newspapers in both countries revealed the concern and belief in the rising levels of violence among girls.

- Girl-vs.-girl fighting up in city schools: But overall violence is down 10 percent over last year (*Chicago Sun-Times*, February 15, 2006)
- Violence raging among teen girls (*Boston Globe*, June 20, 2005)
- Bad girls go wild; A rise in girl-on-girl violence is making headlines nationwide and prompting scientists to ask why (*Newsweek*, June 13, 2005)
- Mean girls getting younger (*National Post*, (Canada) May 5, 2005)
- Behind the surge in girl crime (*Christian Science Monitor*, September 15, 2004)

The media in both countries have tended to focus on isolated events of violence committed by girls and tried to understand these events in a broader context (see also Chesney-Lind and Irwin, 2008, for a discussion of the media depiction of girl violence). The questions of why these events were happening and what explained the perceived change in girls' behavior were often asked with respect to serious offending by girls, but less so about serious offending by boys.

In Canada, in November 1997, a 14-year-old girl, Reena Virk, was brutally beaten and eventually drowned. The culprits were said to be eight other teens, seven of them girls. Ten years later, Reena Virk's name is almost certainly still recognized by most Canadians. The case shocked the country and sparked much debate around the trends and causes of girl violence. What is happening to girls, people asked, that they would do such a terrible thing? Many stories presented this case as part of a growing trend of girl violence. Criminologists like us were called upon by television, radio, and the newspapers not to put this event in context, but rather to explain why such crimes were becoming more common. To argue that they were rare and were *not* becoming more common was to be ignored. "Everyone knew" that "crimes by girls" were increasing in number and becoming more brutal. The lack of evidence to support this assertion was seen as just that: a lack of evidence to support what was "known" by all.

The only national newspaper at the time in Canada, the Toronto *Globe and Mail,* presented a number of stories on this case, linking it to broader trends.

- What is different about last week's murder in Victoria of the 14 year old Reena Virk is that it forces us to create a new image of the youth who disturb us. Alongside the boys, now the girls. Girls are the fastest growing group of violent offenders in the country. (Patricia Pearson, Toronto *Globe and Mail,* November 29, 1997)
- The problem is that while the killing of Reena, who was repeatedly brutalized the night she died and was finally drowned, has many dreadfully unique features, it is one of a series of similar incidents of shocking girl violence that have come to light in recent years. . . . It is clear both in Canada and the U.S. that violence is rising among girls. (Alanna Mitchell, Toronto *Globe and Mail,* November 28, 1997)
- Assault charges against young women in Canada have tripled since 1986, Dr. Artz said, and although teenage boys are still 2½ times more likely to commit an assault than girls of the same age, that gap has narrowed. (Michael Grange, Toronto *Globe and Mail,* November 24, 1997)
- The "horrifying" torture and beating of a teenager in Kitchener, Ont., on the weekend is yet another example of what law-enforcement officials and experts say is an alarming wave of violent crimes by girls across Canada. The incident . . . occurred just two months after the vicious beating of 14 year old Reena Virk. "There's no question that violent crimes by girls are on the increase," said Patricia Pearson, a journalist and author of *When She Was Bad,* a recently published study of female violence. "Girls have been doing this with increasing frequency over the last five years, probably because there is an increase in their comfort level with the use of weapons

and a sense of empowerment with the tactics that have been traditionally dominated by males." In addition to a rise in the use of weapons by girls, she said, violent acts such as torture, extortion and assault have increased markedly. (Isabel Vincent, Toronto *Globe and Mail,* January 20, 1998)

The theme, of course, was that serious crime by girls was a new phenomenon and that we were witnessing a dramatic increase in the involvement of Canadian girls in brutal acts of violence. Various theories were suggested to explain the death of Reena Virk. The stories tended to highlight gangs, the effect of increasingly violent television shows and role models for young girls, racial tensions, or some combination of all of these issues.

- That last, nightmarish night of Reena, a pudgy East Indian girl trying desperately to fit into a teen subculture where girls pretending to be members of L.A. street gangs fight each other, has been elevated into a national tragedy. Dozens of interviews have begun to show that in a period of hours a teenage spat over name calling spiraled into the sort of brutality those young, wannabe gangsters worshipped on their TV screens and listened to on their gangsta-rap CDs. (Miro Cernetig, Brian Laghi, Robert Matas, and Craig McInnes, Toronto *Globe and Mail,* November 12, 1997)
- Many students like to pretend to be gang members, modeling themselves loosely on L.A. gangs like the Bloods and Crips. Police say there are no real gangs in Victoria, but some teenagers have adopted the gang culture and look. (Brian Laghi, Craig McInnes, and Robert Matas, Toronto *Globe and Mail,* November 26, 1997)
- Reena Virk, like many 14 year old girls, had a hard time fitting in where she grew up. . . . It didn't help that she was slightly overweight and the dark-skinned child of immigrants who were not well-to-do. (Andrew Purvis, *Time,* Canadian ed., December 8, 1997, p. 68)

The potential reasons for the crime were discussed and debated in the media, but the suggestion that the very nature of girls was becoming more violent was largely accepted as unquestioned fact. The death of Reena Virk tended to be seen as but one example of the growing violence among girls.

Although attention in the United States may not have focused on a single case like Reena Virk's in Canada, the press there has nonetheless published several stories on the changing behavior of girls and concern over rising rates of girl violence. As has been done by the Canadian media, the violence in these cases is typically explained by the girls' desire for some combination of popularity and respect, an increasingly violent culture, and growing equality between men and women.

- "This is a recent phenomenon, the increase in the amount and intensity of violence committed by girls," said Loren Simmons, director of sexual violence and support services for YWCA Metropolitan Chicago. In movies, video games and television, "They're showing us women who are not only fighting each other, but fighting men, and they're not presenting it as a bad thing, but that it's a good thing that she can 'kick-butt'—a way to earn popularity and respect." (Leslie Baldacci, *Chicago Sun-Times,* February 15, 2006)
- John Sisco, chief of Boston schools police, and his officers also are recording a 5 percent to 10 percent increase in fights among girls and a surge he said is a result of popular culture influences. "Girls of the 21st century are affected by the same music videos and video games that boys are," Sisco said. "We do see a reflection of that in how the girls act. . . . We have more and more girls willing to be physical." (Suzanne Smalley and Ric Kahn, *Boston Globe,* June 20, 2005)
- Part of the spike in violence is related to evolving sex roles. . . . The women's movement, which explicitly encourages women to assert themselves like men, has unintentionally opened the door to girls' violent behavior. (Julie Scelfo, *Newsweek,* June 13, 2005, p. 66)

It is hardly surprising that people believe violence by girls is increasing at an alarming rate. To the extent that Google determines what we know about the world, it is interesting that the first (unsponsored) link on a Google search for the words "girl" and "violence" found that

> 1 out of 4 violent episodes are being perpetrated by teen girls, up from just a generation ago when it was 1 girl–10 boys. As can be seen, girl violence is increasing from 1–10 and now 1 out of every 4 violent episodes involves girls carrying it out. According to the Justice Department, it is not just boys any longer, violence among girls is on the rise. Schools report a similar pattern in the number of girls suspended or expelled for fighting. Around the country schools, polices [*sic*] and teachers are seeing a growing tendency for girls to settle disputes with their fists. They are finding themselves breaking up playground fights in which girls are going at each other at an alarming rate.[4]

The second Google hit had a similar message:

Reports last week that three Mount Vernon middle-school girls jumped a schoolmate and beat her senseless at a dance for honor students left him stunned. "Maybe it's sexist," he said. "Maybe girls like the ones I'm seeing are just challenging my assumptions that young women shouldn't be threatening each other with brass knuckles, but it troubles me. A lot." The Mount Vernon incident left 14-year-old Anahi Espinoza badly bruised and emotionally scarred. The three accused assailants, two of whom are sisters, have pleaded not guilty to assault charges. Washington state doesn't track school discipline incidents by gender, but educators around the region say they can't help noting a trend. "We have seen an uptick in violent behavior—fighting— among girls," said Catherine Carbone, spokeswoman for the Highline school district. "In the last five or 10 years, the same kinds of things that have always caused taunts or teasing before, now are more physical." (Claudia Rowe, *Seattle Post-Intelligencer,* May 13, 2004)

The changing gender roles, or more generally, the "liberation hypothesis"— that girls are becoming increasing violent owing to the greater freedom now afforded them—is not new. It is, however, routinely discussed in the media and popular press. Indeed, it appears to be one of the more popular theories advanced in newspaper articles (DeKeseredy, 2000). Moreover, many of the books highlighted in the popular press that discuss an apparent increase in girl violence tend to focus on various forms of this liberation theory. A recent example—which received press in both Canada and the United States—is *See Jane Hit: Why Girls Are Growing More Violent and What We Can Do About It,* by James Garbarino.

In his book, Garbarino explores changes in culture—television and role models—that may glorify violence in messages aimed at girls. More generally, however, his themes invariably return to ideas of more and greater freedoms for girls and women, which, in turn, change their behavior:

Girls in general are evidencing a new assertiveness and physicality that go far beyond criminal assault. . . . We should welcome the New American Girl's unfettered assertiveness and physicality. . . . But I believe that the increasing violence among troubled girls and the generally elevated levels of aggression in girls are unintended consequences of the general increase in normal girls getting physical and becoming more assertive. All this, the good news of liberation and the bad news of increased aggression, is the New American Girl. (Garbarino, 2006: p. 4)

The publicity Garbarino's book received in Canada made it clear that this growing violence among girls was seen as a problem there. A review in Canada's newspaper of record, the Toronto *Globe and Mail,* highlighted the idea that "[Garbarino] argues [that there] is a dramatic and real rise in aggression among young girls, one borne out both by his own case studies and crime statistics (in Canada, during the 1990s, the number of crimes committed by girls increased 68 percent)" (Rebecca Godfrey, Toronto *Globe and Mail,* March 11, 2006). Clearly, then, in both Canada and the United States, the message was one of changing behaviors of girls, brought on, in large part, by the freedoms girls now enjoyed.

What was unquestioned, of course, was the "fact" that the increase for girls was somehow special. For it to be special, a comparison—with boys, presumably—needed to be made. The assertion of a notable increase, however, apparently did not need careful analysis. The Toronto *Globe and Mail* reviewer found it sufficient to assert only that the "number of crimes committed by girls increased by 68%." A criminologist might find such an assertion noteworthy, not because of the increase but because the question "How many crimes have been committed by girls?" is known to be unanswerable. Not only do we not have reliable self-report data for youths in Canada for this period, but any criminal-justice data are known to be inadequate for estimating the number of crimes *committed* by any subgroup in the population. After all, for a crime to be attributed to a particular subgroup in the population in official crime statistics, it is necessary, among other things, to have a likely suspect. One typically has suspects for a very high proportion of some crimes (e.g., shoplifting) recorded by the police. But for other crimes (e.g., burglaries) few offenders are ever apprehended. Since apprehension rates vary across subgroups of the population (e.g., youths appear to be more likely to be apprehended than adults; see Snyder, 1999), comparative arrest figures may not be valid indicators of relative offending rates. In reporting crime and criminal-justice events and trends, however, detailed facts are not as headline grabbing as are unsubstantiated assertions about these facts.

In 2005 another book that received considerable attention in the U.S. press—and includes a foreword by the former U.S. Attorney General Janet Reno—was *Sugar and Spice and No Longer Nice: How We Can Stop Girls' Violence,* by Deborah Prothrow-Stith and Howard R. Spivak. The main arguments from this book again returned to the similar themes of the dark side of women's liberation: "Girls continue to break down barriers and diminish the differences between their level of achievement and that of boys in many areas, and violent behavior is no exception. . . . Girls have become a part of the epidemic of youth violence" (Prothrow-Stith and Spivak, 2005: pp. 1–2).

Clearly, then, the idea that women and girls' greater freedom has a dark side that explains increasing crime and violence is a popular one in the press and among the public. Interestingly, however, this liberation hypothesis has a rather lengthy history.

The Liberation Hypothesis in the 1800s and Early 1900s

People have been issuing warnings about the unintended consequences of the emancipation of women for more than a century. For example, Pike, in his 1876 book on crime in England, stated that "every step made by a woman towards her independence is a step towards that precipice at the bottom of which lies prison" (Pike, 1876: p. 527). Early criminology texts also sometimes espoused this same theory. The epigraph above came from a 1918 criminology textbook, so not only was this view being expressed, it was being taught to undergraduates.

These early discussions about the dark side of women's liberation typically examined trends in arrests. If evidence could be found supporting the assertion that there were increases in arrests of any kind among girls or women, the link was made to the emancipation of women, however weak any such feminist movement might have been by today's standards. Concerns about the validity of arrest data as indicators of actual behavior of girls were rarely mentioned. In other words, commentators of the day ignored the question of what arrest data were actually measuring. The possibility that changes in arrests could reflect changes in policy on whom to arrest and whom to deal with informally was rarely, if ever raised. In a similar vein, we were unable to find anyone who had seriously even explored the apparent correlation across jurisdictions between an apparent increase in crime by girls and the relative liberation of women. Additionally, aside from a few publications that briefly mentioned concerns over the relationship between women's or girls' liberation and crime, the majority of the writings never even acknowledged the possibility that crime by girls and the response to it were different phenomena. For the most part, however, talk about crimes by youth focused solely on boys.

The Liberation Hypothesis in the 1960s and 1970s

In the 1960s the U.S. government expressed concerns over increases in delinquency and violence, especially among females. For example, in a 1969 report submitted to the U.S. National Commission on the Causes and Prevention of Violence, the authors stated: "It is also the case that the 'emancipation' of females in our society over recent decades has decreased the differences in delinquency and criminality between boys and girls, men and women, as cultural differences between them have narrowed" (Mulvihill, Tumin, and Curtis, 1969: p. 425). In contrast, a very important Canadian report on juvenile delinquency published just a few years earlier—a report that influenced the development of legislation for nearly two decades—did not mention concerns over rising rates of delinquency and girls' increasing freedoms. In fact, this Canadian report never even mentioned girls' involvement in delinquency and instead focused on delinquency generally or by males. Interestingly, however, the report did discuss the liberation hypothesis with respect to the effect working mothers had on their children's delinquency:

> Some observers think that a prominent cause of delinquency in the young stems from the emancipation of women. The issue of the "working mother" is one that has been much debated over the years. Studies of the negative effects of working mothers on their children are far from conclusive. Many persons would argue that a more significant influence on the child occurs by reason of changes in parental functions and family relationships of a much more general nature, reflecting such factors as the increased economic independence of family members and the lack of quite so clear-cut a masculine role for a large number of fathers to assume in present-day society. One view forcibly expressed to the Committee is that to prolong discussion of the "working mother" as an explanation for delinquency only serves to hinder and delay consideration of questions of far greater importance relating to the provision of services to assist family adjustment and to ensure proper standards for the care of children. (Report of the Department of Justice Committee on Juvenile Delinquency, 1965: p. 18)

Thus, in Canada in the mid-1960s, there did not appear to be any official support for the direct liberation hypothesis (i.e., that liberated girls act like boys)—indeed, it was not even mentioned. Nor was there any support for its companion theory of delinquency—that mothers working outside their homes was related to an increase in their children's (boys' and girls') delinquency. Instead, changing family structure more generally was seen as a challenge that service providers needed to recognize and respond to.

However, in the 1970s a number of academic journal articles and books were published, in both Canada and the United States, that attempted to draw a causal link between women's liberation and the apparent increase in the proportion or rate of women and girls arrested (see, for example, Adler, 1975; Austin, 1982; Balkan and Berger, 1979; Bruck, 1975; Deming, 1977; Nettler, 1974; and Rosenblatt and Greenland, 1974). Even the Canadian media, using U.S. data, published stories under such headlines as "Serious crimes by women rise 80 per cent, liberation movement blamed" (Toronto *Globe and Mail,* March 1, 1973). And the limited data in Canada did not stop academic researchers from assuming that the trends were similar in both countries and that women's emancipation was the blame:

> Today, with an increasing variety of roles opening to women, their criminal violence might also be expected to increase. In fact that seems to be the case, although in Canada there is as yet little statistical evidence available to confirm the size of the trend. . . . In the United States, police reports indicate that violent crime by women is definitely increasing at a faster rate than that by men. (Rosenblatt and Greenland, 1974: p. 173)

However, perhaps the most well-known research, in both Canada and the United States, was Freda Adler's book *Sisters in Crime: The Rise of the New Female Offender.* Adler suggested that the newly liberated females of the 1960s were becoming more involved in crime than were previous generations. As evidence for her theory she used interviews and FBI arrest data. Although the main focus of her book was on women, she did have one chapter on girls. With respect to girls specifically, she argued that

> the emancipation of women appears to be having a twofold influence on female juvenile crimes. Girls are involved in more drinking, stealing, gang activity, and fighting—behavior in keeping with their adoption of male roles. We also find increases in the total number of female deviances. The departure from the safety of traditional female roles and the testing of uncertain alternative roles coincide with the turmoil of adolescence creating criminogenic risk factors which are bound to create this increase. These considerations help explain the fact that between 1960 and 1972 national arrests for major crimes show a jump for boys of 82 percent—for girls, 306 percent. (Adler, 1975: p. 95)

As others have noted, however, percentage increases can be somewhat deceptive if one is dealing with small numbers (see Chesney-Lind and

Shelden, 2004: p. 127). There are, however, two quite different "small numbers" problems. As has been pointed out by others, when Cain killed Abel, the world's homicide rate increased an infinite amount as a result of one murder—from zero to 250,000 per hundred thousand in the general population (the world, according to Genesis, had only four people, one of whom was the victim). One might suggest this rate of increase and the homicide rate itself have been unmatched since. Small numbers of events can create large rate changes. The second—and quite independent—problem with small numbers is that they are more likely to be unstable.

Crime by girls—in particular serious violent crime by girls (which is relatively rare)—is obviously vulnerable to the first of these small-numbers problems. If a crime rate for boys increases from 10 to 14 per one thousand boys, we might describe that change as a 40 percent increase. If, at the same time, the rate for girls increased from 4 to 6 per one thousand girls, we might describe that increase as a 50 percent increase. Was the increase of 2 really larger than the increase of 4? At time 1, the difference between the rate for boys and girls was 6. At time 2, the difference was 8. However, at time 1, the rate for boys was 2.5 times that of girls. At time 2, it was only 2.3 times that of girls. In this example, are girls really becoming more like boys?

Because the starting points are different, it is not clear exactly what to make of comparisons of percentage changes. After Cain killed Abel, the homicide rate for boys obviously decreased. The homicide rate for girls, however, was obviously zero, and hence, from that starting point, only increases in girls' homicide rates were possible.

Adler's data comparing the number of arrests for index offenses (violence and property) in 1960 and 1970 raises quite similar issues.[5] Arrests of boys increased by 139,584 (from 171,036 in 1960 to 310,620 in 1972—an 82 percent increase), and arrests of girls increased 49,933 (16,311 in 1960 to 66,244 in 1972—a 306 percent increase). Is an increase of 49,933 more substantial than an increase of 139,584? Putting these numbers into rates per ten thousand 10-to-17-year-olds, for boys we see a rate increase of 49.33 (from 132.79 in 1960 to 182.12 in 1972), whereas for girls we see a rate increase of 27.30 (from 13.06 to 40.36). These data are presented in figure 1.1. One can immediately see from the figure just how small the rate of girl crime was compared to that of boys. (Comparisons of changes can, in fact, be presented in many different ways; see Appendix A for some examples.)

Increases in violence were of particular concern. Adler noted that "in the growing repertoire of female delinquencies, violence is becoming a more frequent option" (Adler, 1975: p. 96). She provided numerous quotes from various police officials, all citing perceived increases in violence among girls:

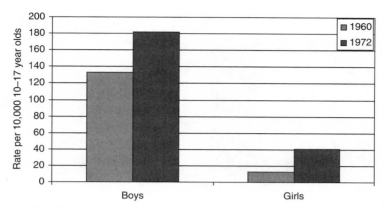

Figure 1.1. Rate (per ten thousand 10-to-17-year-olds) of arrests for index offenses (violent and property)

Sources: Arrest data: U.S. Department of Justice (1972). *Crime in the United States, 1972*, Uniform Crime Reports (Washington, D.C.: Government Printing Office), p. 124.

Population estimates in 1960 and 1972 (for calculation of rates): http://www.census.gov/popest/archives/pre-1980/PE-11.html

"Now, you don't get the name-calling, hair-pulling that used to go [on] between girls . . . you get vicious physical assault" (youth aid worker in a New York police department, cited in Adler, 1975: p. 97). And:

> I push my way through the crowd—they're going crazy like it is really a mean fight—and when I get to the middle . . . I like fell over. Here are two husky broads and they are fighting . . . now I don't mean any hair-pulling face-scratching kind of thing; I mean two broads squared off and duking it out. Throwing jabs and hooking in at each other and handling themselves like a couple of goddamned pro sparring partners. I mean, I got to ask myself, What the hell is going on? What in the name of God is happening to these girls any more? (Washington police sergeant, cited in Adler, 1975: p. 96)

Using FBI Uniform Crime Reports and comparing percentage increases in arrests between boys and girls—and using some indexes but not others—one *could* argue that *serious* violence was increasing more among girls than boys during this time. For example, among *index* violent crime, boys saw a 203 percent increase (13,811 arrests in 1960 and 41,875 in 1972) whereas girls saw a 388 percent increase (from 1,013 to 4,946). Alternatively, one could also look at rates per ten thousand 10-to-17-year-old boys and girls in the population (fig. 1.2). Boys were arrested for index violent crimes at a rate

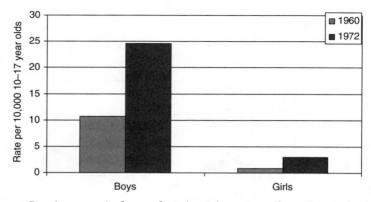

Figure 1.2. Rate (per 10,000) of arrests for index violent-crime offenses (boys and girls)
Sources: Arrest data: U.S. Department of Justice (1972), *Crime in the United States, 1972.* Uniform
Crime Reports (Washington, D.C.: Government Printing Office), p. 124.
Population estimates in 1960 and 1972 (for calculation of rates): http://www.census.gov/popest/archives/
pre-1980/PE-11.html.

of 10.72 (per ten thousand 10-to-17-year-olds) in 1960 and by 1972 that rate
had increased 13.83 up to 24.55 per ten thousand. Girls, on the other hand,
saw a rate increase of 2.2, from 0.81 in 1960 to 3.01 in 1972. Is a rate increase
of 2.2 a greater cause for concern than a rate increase of 13.83?

Critiques of Adler's theory and supporting data with respect to juveniles
specifically were not long in coming. For example, Steffensmeier and Kramer
(1979), after examining youth court data for Pennsylvania in 1970 and 1976,
argued that if substantial gains had been made by women during the late
1960s and early 1970s, the effect of women's liberation on girl crime should
have been seen during the 1970s. Instead, they found rather remarkable
stability. The only differences between boys and girls emerged in offenses
involving drugs or drinking, where there was a slight increase in the number
of girls referred to court (a 0.1 rate per 10,000 increase) but a slight *decrease*
in the number of boys referred to court (a 0.93 rate decrease) for those same
offenses. The authors concluded that "female delinquency has not changed
much in recent years . . . females continue to be referred to court . . .
for traditionally female crimes such as petty theft, use of drugs and status
offenses" (Steffensmeier and Kramer, 1979: p. 766). Later studies that examined arrests, court referrals, and self-reported offending and victimization
came to similar conclusions (Steffensmeier and Steffensmeier, 1980). Girls
were not "catching up" with boys in the commission of violent offenses.

While some continued to argue that the arrest data did indeed show a
more substantial increase in girls' violent offending than in boys (see, for

example, Austin, 1982; Balkan and Berger, 1979; and Wilson, 1981), others argued that percentage increases were deceptive given the starting point for these calculations for girls (see, for example, Datesman and Scarpitti, 1980; and Steffensmeier and Steffensmeier, 1980). Studies using longer time periods or different time periods, as well as arrest data, court data, or self-reported data, all tended to reveal similar findings (see, for example, Ageton and Elliott, 1978, cited in Berger 1989; Canter, 1982; Chesney-Lind and Shelden, 1992; Datesman and Scarpitti, 1980; Gold and Reimer, 1975; Steffensmeier and Cobb, 1981; and Thornton, Voigt, and Doerner, 1987, as cited in Berger 1989). National arrest rates and court referrals were tending to rise for girls, though this was predominantly concentrated in the less serious property and status offenses (offenses that would not be crimes if an adult committed them, e.g., incorrigibility, disobedience, truancy, curfew violations, etc.) in the 1960s, with a general leveling off in the 1970s. Self-reported delinquency, on the other hand, showed increases for girls in drug use (alcohol and marijuana), while involvement in other offenses tended to stay relatively stable and may have declined slightly for boys.

Some research was conducted that attempted to test Adler's theory that women's emancipation led to more involvement of women and girls in crime. Some studies focused specifically on girls or young women and assessed their attitudes toward feminism or nontraditional female behavior and their self-reported delinquency (see, for example, Figueria-McDonough, 1984; Giordano and Cernkovich, 1979; and James and Thornton, 1980). These studies found either no relationship or a negative relationship between feminist views and involvement in delinquency (those with stronger feminist views tended to be *less* likely to be involved in delinquency). Thus, there has been no convincing empirical support for the theory that the women's movement in the 1960s and 1970s lead to increased delinquency, and in particular violence, among girls.

Summary: 1900 to the Early 1970s

From about 1900 on, then, concerns have been expressed repeatedly about the effect of women's liberation on women's and girls' involvement in offending. Despite the debates in the 1960s and 1970s about whether or not girls saw larger increases than boys in their involvement in crime, and, specifically, violence, the majority of the literature suggests that whatever increases there were among arrest and court data, they were generally not substantiated in self-reported data. Moreover, research failed to find any positive correlation between girls' feminist attitudes and their self-reported delinquency. Nonetheless, the idea that girls' behavior is changing and becoming more violent as a result of increased freedoms afforded to women persists to the present day. And thus, as in the early 1900s, there is still concern that in the later 1990s girls were becoming more involved in violence. We explore the evidence for this perception in the following chapter.

Chapter 2

Are Sugar and Spice Really Evolving into Snips and Snails and Puppy-Dog Tails?

Nobody needs to be told that boys are different from girls. And almost nobody needs evidence that girls are less involved in crime than are boys. That most crime is committed by boys is listed by John Braithwaite (1989) as the first of the "Facts a theory of crime ought to fit" (p. 44). But is the dominance of youth crime by boys universal across offense categories and time? As we noted in the previous chapter, one would have the feeling from reading some mass-media reports that girls were increasingly becoming not just more crime prone, but that they are becoming just like boys.

A necessary starting point in any investigation of the manner in which youth justice systems respond to crime is to have a reasonably clear picture of the differences in the kinds of things girls and boys do that might bring them in contact with the youth justice system. There is no reason to expect that different rates at which given crimes are committed would be consistent over time. And, of course, when one turns from "crime" to "youth justice processing," there is even less reason to expect that those cases seen as deserving of court attention would occur at the same rate for boys and for girls.

In this chapter, therefore, we will be attempting to answer a set of closely related questions: What is the evidence related to the assertion that girls are becoming more and more like boys in the nature and rate of their offending? How do the differences that do exist in Canada and the United States translate into court processing? Put differently, do the most salient data on "youth crime"—official court processing of youths—reflect the differences that we see in self-reported offending? Answering these questions with data from both Canada and the United States is useful in part because the laws that deal with offending by youths developed, in the latter part of the twentieth century, in quite different ways. In addition, as we will see, the official view of how youths who offend generally—both boys and girls—should be treated was quite different by the beginning of this century.

This chapter looks at the following issues:

1. How girls and women are underrepresented as offenders. We will be relying in large part on arrest data, but will also look at self-reported offending.
2. Trends in estimates of the amount of crime apparently attributable to girls and boys.
3. Trends in the use of court for girls and boys. These data need to be thought of as being quite different from "crime" data because large numbers of youths are dealt with informally rather than being brought to court.

Girls' and Women's Involvement in Offending

One of the most obvious facts about crime is that males are greatly over-represented as offenders. For example, self-report data not only from the United States, but also from other countries such as Canada, England, the Netherlands, Australia, Greece, and the Philippines, reveal that boys are consistently more involved in offending, especially serious violent offending, than girls (Chesney-Lind and Shelden, 2004; Fergusson and Harwood, 2002; Junger Tas, 1984; Kotsopoulos and Loutsi, 1977; LeBlanc and Biron, 1980; Mawby, 1980; Shoemaker, 1994; and Sprott, Doob, and Jenkins, 2001). Even in less serious forms of offending—and in traditionally "female" crimes such as status offenses—boys self-report more involvement than do girls (Canter, 1982; and Leblanc and Biron, 1980). Overall, then, "self-report studies suggest . . . that female delinquency is more prevalent than official statistics lead one to believe. . . . But girls commit offenses far less frequently than do boys" (Chesney-Lind and Shelden, 2004: p. 22).

Thus, no matter what measures one looks at, whether they are self-reports (Pastore and Maguire, 2004; Snyder and Sickmund, 2006; and Sprott, Doob, and Jenkins, 2001), arrests for crime generally, suspects for serious crimes such as homicides (Pastore and Maguire, 2004; Snyder and Sickmund, 2006; and Wallace, 2004), or prison or penitentiary sentencings (Beattie, 2005; Calverley, 2006; Pastore and Maguire, 2004; and Snyder and Sickmund, 2006), one is almost certain to find substantially more men involved in crime than women. Although the extent of the underrepresentation of women and girls involved in crime and the criminal justice system varies from measure to measure, from offense to offense, and from age group to age group, it is rare to find more women involved as offenders than men. Though there has been an enormous amount of theorizing and speculation about the reasons for these variations, the difference is widespread enough that it might be considered to be, for all practical purposes, universal.

Looking at Canadian police-reported crime in 2006 (from Canada's Uniform Crime Reports [UCR]), women, compared to men, are under-represented in all but three of the more than 80 independent groupings of crime incidents (defined by the most serious offense within the incident). The exceptions are, not surprisingly, prostitution offenses and infanticide (a lesser form of homicide only available to women). The data for youths charged with offenses are quite similar: girls are dramatically underrepresented for all offenses except prostitution offenses. The Uniform Crime Reports from the United States indicate the same kind of disproportion. Using 29 independent offense categorizations from 2006, we found girls were underrepresented in all but two offenses—prostitution and runaways (Federal Bureau of Investigation [FBI], 2006: table 37).[1] Even this latter category (runaways) is problematic, because for a person to be classified as a runaway, someone (presumably the parent or another caregiver) must report that the youth is missing. Reporting differences may reflect a greater concern on the part of parents or other caregivers for the welfare of girls who are away from home than for that of boys.

More important, when one looks more closely at these charge data, an interesting picture appears. Women and girls tend to be especially under-represented among those charged with the most serious offenses. In 2006 in the United States, for example, adult women accounted for 31 percent of index property crime (burglary, larceny/theft, motor vehicle theft, and arson) but only 18 percent of index violent crime (murder, forcible rape, robbery, and aggravated assault; see fig. 2.1). Within the category of offenses involving violence, women constitute about 25 percent of those charged with relatively minor assaults (e.g., assaults other than aggravated assaults) but only 11 percent of those charged with murder or nonnegligent man-slaughter (FBI, 2006: table 42).[2]

A similar picture emerges in Canada.[3] Looking at broad categories of offenses, we see that adult women constitute about 24 percent of those charged with property offenses in Canada in 2006, but only 17 percent of those charged with violent offenses (see fig. 2.2). Within the category of violent offenses, women constitute about 18 percent of those charged with minor assaults, but only 14 percent of those charged with homicide offenses (Canadian Centre for Justice Statistics [CCJS], 2006; data made available to us in response to a special request).

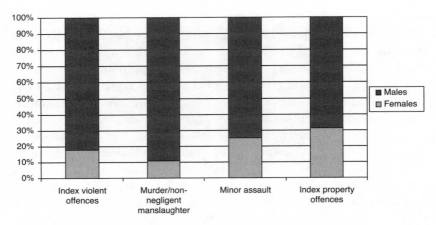

Figure 2.1. Men and women charged with selected offenses: United States, 2006
Source: Federal Bureau of Investigation (2006), *Crime in the United States,* Uniform Crime Reports (Washington, D.C.: FBI, Department of Justice), table 42.

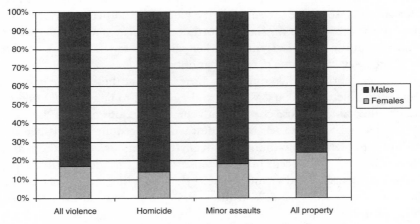

Figure 2.2. Men and women charged with selected offenses: Canada, 2006
Source: Canadian Centre for Justice Statistics (2006), data available on special request.

The data for youth are similar, but not identical. In 2006 in the United States, girls accounted for 18 percent of those charged with index violent offenses and 33 percent of those charged with index property offenses (FBI, 2006: table 37).[4] Once again, girls tended to be more involved in the less serious offenses. For example, only 5 percent of the youths charged with a murder or nonnegligent manslaughter offense were girls, compared to 34 percent of the youths charged with more minor assaults (i.e., assaults other than aggravated assaults). As for property crime, girls constituted 12 percent of those charged with burglary but 41 percent of those charged with larceny/theft (see figs. 2.3 and 2.4).

In Canada, girls constituted 26 percent of those charged with violent offenses and 23 percent of those charged with property offenses (CCJS, 2006; data available on special request). Within categories, however, the relative involvement of girls showed the same pattern: they were less frequently involved in serious offenses than boys (see fig. 2.5). Only 14 percent of the youths charged with a homicide offense were girls, compared to 30 percent of the youths charged with minor assaults. The most serious relatively

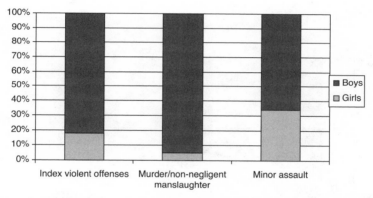

Figure 2.3. Boys and girls charged with selected violent offenses: United States, 2006
Source: Federal Bureau of Investigation (2006), *Crime in the United States,* Uniform Crime Reports (Washington, D.C.: FBI, Department of Justice), table 37.

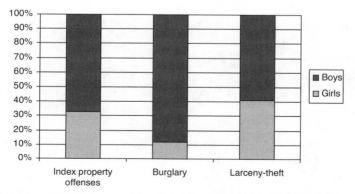

Figure 2.4. Boys and girls charged with selected property offenses: United States, 2006
Source: Federal Bureau of Investigation (2006), *Crime in the United States,* Uniform Crime Reports (Washington, D.C.: FBI, Department of Justice), table 37.

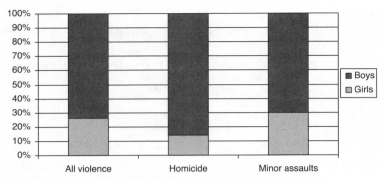

Figure 2.5. Boys and girls charged with selected violent offenses: Canada, 2006
Source: Canadian Centre for Justice Statistics (2006), data available on special request.

Figure 2.6. Boys and girls charged with selected property offenses: Canada, 2006
Source: Canadian Centre for Justice Statistics (2006), data available on special request.

high-volume property crime is usually considered to be break-and-enter. In Canada in 2006, girls constituted 12 percent of those charged with break-and-enter but 34 percent of those charged with theft of property valued at less than $5,000 (see fig. 2.6).

Women generally, and girls in particular, then, are not heavily involved in the most serious kinds of crimes. In the United States, of the estimated 8,068 people charged with murder or nonnegligent manslaughter in 2006, only 40 (fewer than 1 percent) were girls age 10–17 (FBI, 2006: table 37).[5] Similarly, of the 509 people charged with a homicide offense in Canada in 2006, only 12 (2 percent) were girls age 12–17 (CCJS, 2006; data available by special request). One might expect, then, that there would be little concern on the part of authorities and the general public about serious violent crime by women and girls: after all, they don't commit very much of it.

In fact, we suspect exactly the opposite: that the concern about possible increases in crime by girls derives directly from the fact that serious crime committed by girls is very rare. Women and girls may be seen as providing a potential for an enormous increase in crime. How could this happen? It is easy: if women in Canada acted just like men and committed homicide offenses with the same frequency, the homicide rate in Canada would increase by 75 percent. The same would be true in the United States. In other words, unlike the "superpredator" scare of the 1990s (see Zimring, 2005), the potential for disaster is already with us: if American women and girls were to act like men and boys, the rate of serious violent crime in the United States would increase dramatically. Furthermore, the evidence that females are becoming more like males surrounds us in most Western cultures. Women's participation in work generally and "male-oriented" professions in particular has changed dramatically over the past 50 years. If women can become police officers (and police chiefs), then they can become robbers and gang leaders. If women can become aggressive business leaders, what is to stop them from becoming violent criminals? Those millions of women who, if they acted like men, would be capable of dramatically increasing crime in Western countries are in our communities today.

The Crime Wave That Didn't Happen

Steffensmeier and colleagues have investigated trends in the United States in girls' and boys' delinquency using self-reported data, arrest data, and court data gathered during the 1960s and 1970s and again during the 1980s through the early 2000s and found, in all analyses, that increases in official data (arrest or court data) tended not to be mirrored by increases in self-reported data (Steffensmeier, Schwartz, Zhong, and Ackerman, 2005; Steffensmeier and Steffensmeier, 1980; and Steffensmeier, Zhong, Ackerman, Schwartz, and Agha, 2006). Looking at national arrest trends from 1965 to 1977, Steffensmeier and Steffensmeier (1980) found increases in the arrest rates of girls only for minor offenses (minor thefts, running away, liquor-law violations, etc.). Juvenile court statistics revealed a similar pattern of increases in the referral rate of girls for minor offenses (marijuana, drug use, and status offenses such as running away). Self-reported data from a national sample of adolescents in grades 8–12 from 1967 to 1972 revealed stability in girls' involvement in offending, with only a slight increase in the use of marijuana. Steffensmeier and Steffensmeier (1980) also examined 13 other studies that reported findings from various jurisdictions in the United States on boys' and girls' self-reported offending during the 1950s to the 1970s.

There was no evidence of girls' increasing involvement in serious offending, or that involvement in offending by girls was increasing faster than that by boys. As with the national data, any increases in girls' offending appeared to be concentrated in minor offending (e.g., damaging property and theft of property valued at less than $10). In the end, the authors concluded that

> arrest data and studies of juvenile gangs show little increase in female violence or in gang-related delinquencies. Generally, females are not catching up with males in the commission of violent, masculine, or serious crime. . . . Arrest statistics of the Uniform Crime Reports show rising levels of female delinquency mainly in the categories of larceny, runaways, and liquor law violations. Gains in other offences are small and have leveled off in recent years suggesting that earlier gains were partly a statistical artifact of rising arrest rates for both sexes and lower base rates for females than males. Juvenile court statistics and self-report studies reveal a similar pattern of female delinquency with gains for marijuana use also apparent. Notwithstanding female gains in marijuana and drinking, self-report data show generally that the sex differential in delinquency has remained stable over the past decade [mid-1960s to mid-1970s]. (Steffensmeier and Steffensmeier, 1980: p. 80)

More recently, focusing on the 1980s to 2003, Steffensmeier, Schwartz, Zhong, and Ackerman (2005) and Steffensmeier, Zhong, Ackerman, Schwartz, and Agha (2006) explored trends in violence from UCR arrest data and self-reported offending from two national data sets and one national victimization data set. While arrest rates for violence—in particular minor assaults—among girls rose during the late 1980s and early 1990s, there was no such increase in self-reported violence among girls. Data from multiple national self-report surveys (Monitoring the Future, the National Crime Victimization Survey, and the National Youth Risk Behavior Survey) revealed either relative stability or declines in the rates of girls' self-reported participation in violent offending. To illustrate their main findings, we have reproduced two figures from these surveys. Figure 2.7, from the Uniform Crime Reports, shows the clear increase in the arrest rate of both boys and girls for minor assaults. Figure 2.8 shows the self-reported data from the National Crime Victimization Survey, which asked about being the victim of a minor assault. Here one sees declines for boys throughout the 1990s and stability for girls.

After looking at trends in arrest rates for aggravated assaults, minor assaults, and the violent-crime index (homicide, aggravated assault, rape, and

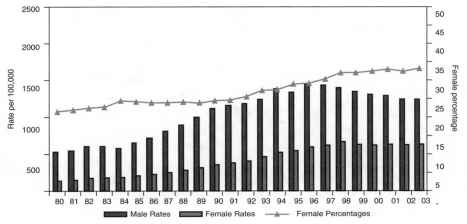

Figure 2.7. UCR arrest data

Note: Rates are adjusted for the sex composition of the population and for changes in UCR coverage over time. The population base includes ages 12–17. Female percentage = female rate / (female rate + male rate) × 100.

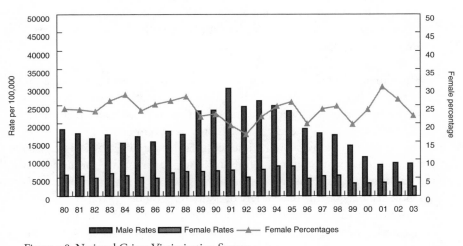

Figure 2.8. National Crime Victimization Survey

Note: Data are adjusted to take into account effects of the survey redesign in 1992. The multiplier is specific to offense and sex and is calculated based only on juvenile data. The formula is: multiplier = (n92 + n93 + n94) / (n90 + n91 + n92).

robbery) and comparing those trends to self-reports of violent offending and victimization, the authors concluded that

> the rise in girls' violence as counted in police arrest data is not born out in unofficial longitudinal sources—victimization data in the National Crime Victimization Survey (where the victim identifies sex of offender), along with self-reported violent behavior in Monitoring the Future and the National Youth Risk Behavior Survey. These sources all show little overall change in girls' levels of violence over the past one to two decades and constancy or very little, if any, change in the gender gap in youth violence. The significance of these findings is underscored, first, by their consistency across the three survey sources that involve national samples from the general youth population and . . . are held in high regard within the social science research community. . . . Second, the finding of little overall change has added credibility because it is observed in the context of heightened perceptions about girls today as being more violent and "male like." These perceptions might sway some victims and citizens to more readily identify girls as violent offenders, and also encourage girls in survey samples to self-report incidents of physical attack or threat. (Steffensmeier, Schwartz, Zhong, and Ackerman, 2005: pp. 395–96)

The violent girl crime wave that people have been waiting for since the early 1900s, then, has simply not happened. Although recurrent concerns involving girls' violence surfaced in the 1960s, the 1980s, and, most recently, the late 1990s and early 2000s, there has never been any credible evidence that girls' involvement in violence has substantially changed (see also Chesney-Lind, 2001; Chesney-Lind and Irwin, 2008; and Chesney-Lind and Paramore, 2001). The increase in some arrest rates among girls for minor violence may be due to a variety of issues ranging from "zero-tolerance" policing to an increase in dealing with family conflict within the youth justice system. In investigating the nature of girls' assault cases, for example, some have found that the overwhelming majority of assaults involve physical fights within the family (Acoca, 1999; Bartollas, 1993; and Belknap, Winter, and Cady, 2001). Based on findings such as these, Chesney-Lind (2002) argues that the "relabeling of girls' arguments with parents from status offenses (like 'incorrigible' or 'person in need of supervision') to assault is a form of 'bootstrapping' that has been particularly pronounced in the official delinquency of African-American girls" (p. 84).

There is, however, another important issue with respect to girls' increased involvement in crime or violence. In the UCR arrest data of youths age 12–17 (see fig. 2.7), we see increases in the percentage of minor assault cases involving girls as accused during the latter part of the 1990s and the early 2000s. This percentage increase is driven not by changes in the behavior of girls, but rather by decreases in the arrests of boys. It is understandable that criminal justice officials, or anyone else looking at arrest data during this period, would say that girls were becoming more violent (at least as measured by simple assaults): the mix of youths in court was becoming more feminized.

Trends in the Use of Court: The United States and Canada

From a legal perspective, being adjudicated delinquent (or, in Canadian terms, being found guilty) is important. These official numbers may also help to further explain the perception that girls are becoming more criminal. Hence, we now turn to American and Canadian court data and present trends in the rates at which boys and girls are adjudicated delinquent for violent, property, and drug offenses. This, clearly, is not a measure of "crime" in society. Instead, it shows how the two countries choose to respond to youthful offending. Given the research of Steffensmeier, Schwartz, Zhong, and Ackerman (2005) and Steffensmeier, Zhong, Ackerman, Schwartz, and Agha (2006) on self-reported offending and arrest trends, it is clear that "increases" shown in the court data suggest a change in policy or in the administration of justice rather than a change in youths' behavior.

U.S. Court Trends

The National Center for Juvenile Justice collects data on delinquency cases handled by U.S. courts (National Center for Juvenile Justice [NCJJ], 2006). The sample of juvenile courts that provide data to the Juvenile Court Statistics series varies somewhat from year to year, and thus national estimates (rounded to the nearest 100th) are computed (Puzzanchera and Kang, 2007). The unit of count used in these court data is the number of cases disposed. A "case" is defined as a youth processed by a juvenile court on a new referral, regardless of the number of law violations contained in the referral. For example, a youth charged with four burglaries in a single referral would constitute a single case. However, a youth referred on one day for three burglaries and referred again the following week in relation to another burglary charge would constitute two cases, even if the court eventually merged the two referrals for more efficient processing. Cases are organized by the most serious offense for which the youth was referred to court intake.

For the most part, trends in youth court rates mirror arrest trends of youths. However, some of the declines seen at the arrest stage are not seen when looking at the rate at which youths are adjudicated delinquent. There are a number of possible reasons for the difference. For example, although fewer cases might be sent to court, a larger proportion might be handled formally (e.g., filing a petition requesting an adjudicatory or waiver hearing). Snyder and Sickmund (2006) found that the proportion of cases handled formally increased from 45 percent in 1985 to 58 percent in 2002. Another factor that may explain the discrepancies between youth court rates and arrest rates is that the youth court caseload can come from sources other than the police. This could explain the discrepancies between arrest data (decreases) and court data (increases) for drug offenses (see Snyder and Sickmund, 2006, for a full discussion).

Looking at the rate at which cases involving girls and boys were adjudicated delinquent, one sees increases until the late 1990s, followed by relative stability (see fig. 2.9). One can also see that girls are adjudicated delinquent at a much lower rate than boys.

The rate of adjudicating delinquent cases involving index violent crimes (murder and nonnegligent manslaughter, forcible rape, robbery, and aggravated assault) increased for boys from the late 1980s to the mid-1990s (see fig. 2.10). From the mid-1900s on, boys saw declines that brought them back down to the 1985 rate. Girls saw slight increases until the mid-1990s and stability thereafter (see again fig. 2.10). It is clear, however, that during this period girls were never as involved in index violent crimes as boys. Thus, with respect to youths being adjudicated delinquent for index violent crimes, girls are not catching up to boys.

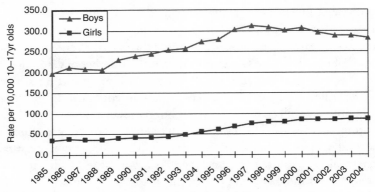

Figure 2.9. Rate of all delinquency cases adjudicated delinquent in youth court

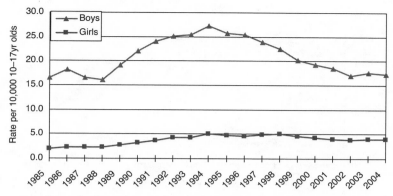

Figure 2.10. Rate of index violent crimes adjudicated delinquent in youth court

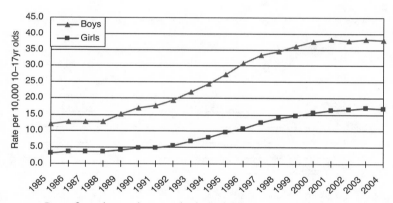

Figure 2.11. Rate of simple assault cases adjudicated delinquent in youth court

While index violent crimes have declined for boys and have been relatively stable for girls, one type of violence has been increasing: simple assaults. This offense typically involves minor pushing and shoving to the extent that injuries, if any, consist of no more than minor bruising. Figure 2.11 shows the increasing rate of simple assault cases (for both boys and girls) adjudicated delinquent. Girls, however, are not "catching up" with boys. In 1985 the rate difference was 9.0 (the boys' rate of 12.2 minus the girls' rate of 3.2), and by 2004 the rate difference was 21.2 (37.9 − 16.7). Thus, the difference between the rates for boys and girls was larger at the beginning of the new millennium than they were in 1985.

Cases of index property offenses (burglary, larceny/theft, motor vehicle theft, and arson) adjudicated delinquent show stability from 1984 until the

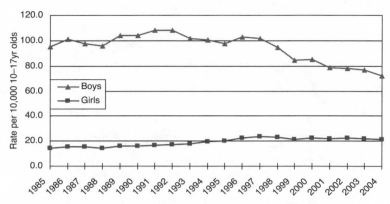

Figure 2.12. Rate of index property crimes adjudicated delinquent in youth court

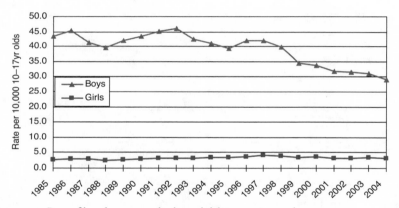

Figure 2.13. Rate of burglary cases adjudicated delinquent in youth court

late 1990s, when the rates for boys started to decline (see fig. 2.12). The rates for girls, on the other hand, were either relatively stable or increased slightly during this time period.

All research is consistent in showing that girls are less likely to be involved in the more serious offenses—such as burglary (see fig. 2.13) as compared to thefts (see fig. 2.14). Although there were declines from the early 1990s on in the rates at which boys were adjudicated delinquent for burglary, the rates for girls remained stable (see fig. 2.13). Moreover, though the rates at which boys were adjudicated delinquent for theft declined from the late 1990s on, the rate at which girls were adjudicated delinquent for theft increased (see fig. 2.14). Once again, however, one must be cautious about drawing inferences with respect to the increase—it is very likely that the change is the result of changing policy or tolerance levels toward the behavior and does not reflect an increase in the actual number of thefts committed.

Both boys and girls saw increases in the rates at which they were adjudicated delinquent for drug offenses (see fig. 2.15). As Snyder and Sickmund (2006) point out, this trend is not mirrored in arrest data. If the increase starting in the early 1990s reflects a delayed war on drugged youths, then it is clear that the war was waged largely against boys: the difference between the rates at which girls and boys were adjudicated delinquent in juvenile court for drug offenses was much larger in 2004 than it was in 1985 (see Appendix B for the proportion of girls in youth court across various offenses).

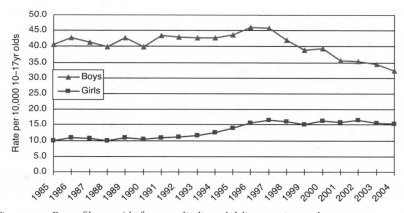

Figure 2.14. Rate of larceny/theft cases adjudicated delinquent in youth court

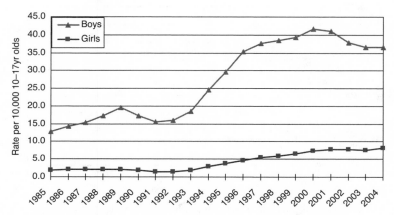

Figure 2.15. Rate of drug law violations adjudicated delinquent in youth court

Canadian Court Trends

Trends in Canadian youth court are somewhat different from those in the juvenile courts in the United States. Although the exact rates cannot be compared between the two countries,[6] trends can be meaningfully compared, as can the proportions of cases in which the most serious charges are violent, property, or drug offenses. Figure 2.16 shows that throughout the period for which we have national data, the rate at which boys were found guilty in youth court declined, while the rate for girls was relatively stable. And when Canada brought in a dramatically different approach to youth justice—the Youth Criminal Justice Act (YCJA), which took effect in 2003–4—there was a substantial one-year decrease in the rate at which both boys and girls were found guilty. These trends stand in contrast to the United States, where this same period saw increases in the rate at which boys and girls were adjudicated delinquent. Nevertheless, even though there were different overall trends in the two countries, boys were always more likely than girls to have been found guilty in youth court.

Canada does not have a violent crime index, so we created a "serious violence" index consisting of homicide, all sexual assaults, robbery, and serious nonsexual assaults. This measure probably captures a broader range of offenses than does the U.S. Violent Crime Index, but it clearly includes the more serious crimes in Canada. Looking at the rate at which guilty verdicts have been rendered in youth court for these cases involving serious violent crimes, one sees relative stability for girls and declines for boys from the late 1990s on (see fig. 2.17)

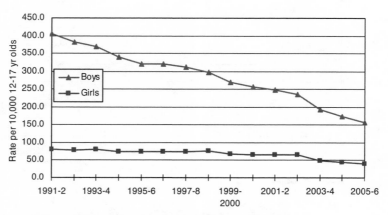

Figure 2.16. Rate of all cases found guilty in youth court: Canada
Note: Excluding traffic offenses.

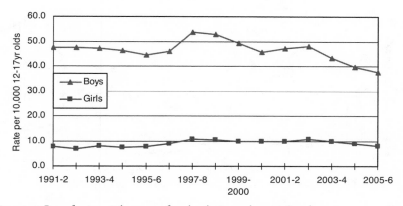

Figure 2.17. Rate of serious-violence cases found guilty in youth court: Canada
Note: Serious violence = homicide, robbery, all sexual assaults, and serious nonsexual assaults.

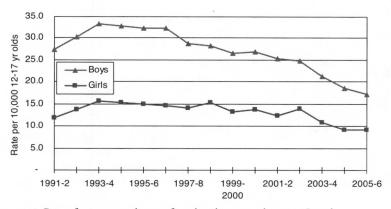

Figure 2.18. Rate of minor assault cases found guilty in youth court: Canada

There was a slight increase from 1991–92 to 1993–94 in the rates at which both boys and girls were found guilty of minor assaults (see fig. 2.18). This increase was followed by stability and then declines for both boys and girls, but (as with youth crime overall) these decreases were larger for boys. For both boys and girls, there was a large one-year decrease in these rates when the new youth justice law came into effect. Here the Canadian trends are different from those in the United States: the United States saw relatively large increases in the rate at which accused were adjudicated delinquent in minor assault cases. However, as in the United States, there is no evidence of an increase in girls' involvement in violence in Canada.

Throughout the 1990s there were decreases for boys and relative stability

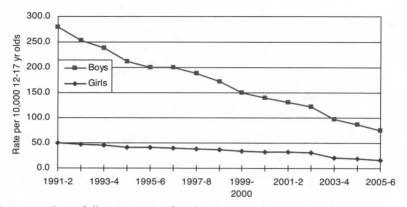

Figure 2.19. Rate of all property cases found guilty in youth court: Canada

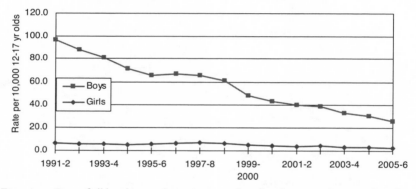

Figure 2.20 Rate of all breaking and entering cases found guilty in youth court: Canada

for girls in the rates at which they were found guilty of property offenses (see fig. 2.19).[7] As with all of the trends presented thus far, girls are far less likely to be found guilty of property offenses than boys. The United States did not start to see decreases (for boys) in the rate of their being adjudicating delinquent for index property offenses until the late 1990s. Girls in the United States, like those in Canada, were adjudicated delinquent for index property crimes at relatively stable rates throughout this period. The "convergence" for boys and girls on this offense (as with the rates for all offenses, shown in fig. 2.16) is due to changes in the treatment of boys, not to changes in girls' behavior or in the treatment of girls.

In Canada, the rate of convictions for breaking and entering has been relatively stable for girls (as in the United States) and has declined for boys (see fig. 2.20). Once again, girls are much less likely than boys to be in court.

Figure 2.21 shows the rate at which boys and girls were found guilty of thefts. Once again, the rate for boys has decreased rather substantially. The rate for girls has also decreased during this period, especially after the YCJA took effect (2003–4). These trends stand in contrast to those in the United States, where the rate at which girls were adjudicated delinquent for larceny/ theft actually increased during the mid-1990s. There were decreases for boys in the United States, but not until the later 1990s. Once again, girls are less likely to be in court than boys, though clearly there is less difference in the most minor offenses such as theft.

The trend in rates at which boys and girls have been found guilty of drug offenses is presented in figure 2.22. Interestingly, in the early 1990s there were increases in the rate at which boys were found guilty of drug offenses,

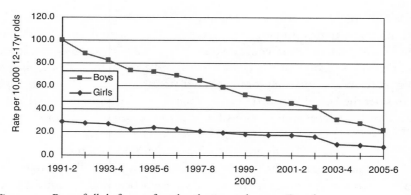

Figure 2.21. Rate of all theft cases found guilty in youth court: Canada

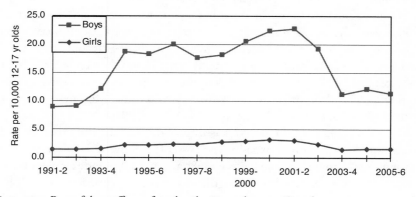

Figure 2.22. Rate of drug offenses found guilty in youth court: Canada

and slight increases for girls as well. These high rates dropped dramatically with the implementation of the new youth justice legislation at the beginning of the 2003–4 fiscal year. Drug offenses—particularly marijuana offenses—in Canada tend not to be seen as serious crime problems and are instead viewed more as a public health issue. Indeed, Canada's new drug laws, which came into force in 1997, made clear distinctions (in the penalty structure) for the first time between "hard" and "soft" drugs. This revised definition of drug offenses is one reason the number of these minor drug cases declined when the new youth justice legislation came into force on April 1, 2003. These trends obviously contrast with the trends in the United States (see Appendix B for more details on the proportions of girls in youth court across various offenses).

Concluding Remarks on Trends

One fact stands out that is common to both the American and Canadian youth court trends. In every case except for Canadian drug offenses, the ratio of the rates of girls' court involvement to boys' was higher at the end of this period (2004 for the United States and 2005–6 for Canada) than it was at the beginning (1985 for the United States and 1991 for Canada). First consider the U.S. data, starting with "total delinquency" (see fig. 2.9)—the ratio of the rate of adjudications for girls to the rate for boys in 1985 was about 0.17 (or 17 girls for every 100 boys). In 2004 both rates had gone up, as had the ratio of girls to boys, which had increased to 0.31 (or 31 girls for every 100 boys). From the perspective of someone who walked into court, or of anyone who worked in the area of youth justice (police, probation officers, and judges, among others), there is no question, then, that there was a higher proportion of girls in court in 2004 than there had been in 1985. Similar trends are found in the other six offense categories (see fig. 2.23). However, the reason for the increased ratio of girls to boys differed across offenses. For property offenses, the increased ratio of girls compared to boys was due, in large part, to the decreases seen in boys' cases, as opposed to increases in girls' cases. For total delinquency, index violent crimes, simple assaults, and drug offenses, the increased ratio of girls to boys was due to the larger proportional increase for girls.[8]

At the same time, however, it is important to remember that for total delinquency and minor assaults, the absolute difference between the rates for girls and boys increased between 1985 and 2004. For index violent crime, the difference between boys and girls was about the same in 2004 as it had been in 1985. Moreover, boys saw larger rate increases (and, for index vio-

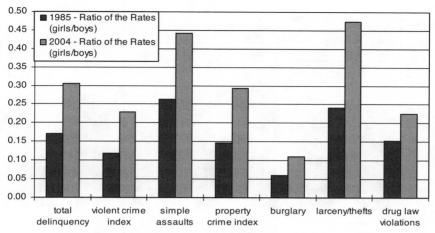

Figure 2.23. Ratio of rates of girls' crimes to boys' crimes: United States

lent crimes, subsequent declines) during this time (for those three offense categories) then did girls. These different approaches to rate changes (e.g., the absolute rate changes or ratios and percentages) are not simply exercises in the use of different indexes. They reflect real and legitimate differences in perspectives on what has happened with the relative rates of youth court delinquency cases involving girls and boys. The measures of rate changes show conclusively that the rates for girls and boys (for these three offenses) will, if they continue in this way, never converge. Girls are, quite simply, not catching up to boys—and where there are convergences between boys and girls, it is due predominantly to the rates for boys declining.

On the other hand, the criminal justice official who, for example, might have to plan what proportion of programs should be designed for boys and for girls will, indeed, have to plan on a higher proportion of programs being designed for girls. In other words, the official in charge of programs with $1 million to spend on programs should be spending a higher proportion of those dollars on girls at the end of this period than he or she was at the beginning of the period.

Looking next at Canada, one can see that for six of the seven offense categories, the ratio is larger (i.e., more girls per 100 boys) in 2006 than it was in 1991 (see fig. 2.24). Only for drug offenses had the relative rates declined—meaning there were fewer girls for every 100 boys charged with drug offenses in 2005–6 than there had been in 1991–2. The increased ratios for the other six offense categories (meaning more girls for every boy) are due, in large part, to declines seen in the rates for boys. That is, the casual

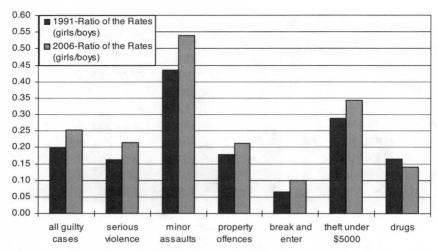

Figure 2.24. Ratio of rates of girls' crimes to boys' crimes: Canada

observers of a room full of youths found guilty in Canada's youth courts in 2005–6 would see more girls than they would have seen in this same room in 1991–92, not because the rate of girls being found guilty had increased, but, rather, because the rates of boys being found guilty had decreased. It is our informal experience that people who work in the youth justice system in Canada talk about the increased involvement of girls, as if the behavior of girls had become more criminal. The figure that appears to drive these perceptions—the relative rates, or the proportion of girls in a random sample of young offenders—is in stark contrast to the actual rates of girls' involvement. Indeed, looking at the Canadian court trends (see figs. 2.16–2.22), one sees general stability or slight declines in adjudicating girls delinquent.

In understanding—and perhaps resolving—the differences between the self-reported trends that show stability, court trends that show that girls are not "catching up to boys," and the perceptions, as discussed in chapter 1, that girls are involved in more crime and violence, these increased ratios of girls to boys must be considered. Because the ratio of girls to boys increased during this period, it gives the illusion—for anyone looking, for example, at a courtroom full of adjudicated youths—that girls were becoming more like boys.

This is not a trick of numbers. It is the ratio of girls to boys that people in the justice system will see. The mistake they apparently make is to assume that an increased ratio of girl offenders to boy offenders meant an increased rate of girls in juvenile court, or that girls were catching up to boys in their offending behavior. This simply wasn't so. It is not surprising, then, that the perception of the increase in crimes committed by girls is similar in the two countries. While the overall trends in youth court processing of girls and boys are different in the two countries, in neither country is there evidence of substantial increases for girls relative to boys, increases that would lead to a convergence of rates. To the extent that there is any evidence of convergence in rates (see, for example, fig. 2.16), the convergence is driven by changes in the rates for boys. Girls, it would seem, are being blamed for changes in the behavior of boys.

Summary

Whether one looks at all delinquency or minor assaults, both girls and boys saw increases in the rate at which they were adjudicated delinquent in the United States from 1985 to 2004. The rate of index violent crimes committed by boys saw substantial increases, followed by decreases, while the rate for such offenses by girls saw slight increases until the late 1990s, followed by stability or a slight decline. This stands in contrast to Canada, where there have been declines in the rates of "all offenses," "serious violence," and "minor assaults" for boys and stability for girls. Moreover, in Canada the absolute values of the differences in the rates between boys and girls were less in 2005–6 than they were in 1991. This was due to the declines seen with boys, as opposed to any changes with respect to trends with girls. The United States, on the other hand, saw larger differences in total delinquency and simple assaults between boys and girls in 2004 than in 1985. This appeared to be because boys exhibited larger rate increases than girls did during this time. For index violent crimes, because of the decline seen with boys, there was almost no difference between boys and girls in 2004 compared to 1985.

For index property offenses, burglary, and thefts, trends in the United States and Canada were quite similar. Both the United States and Canada saw declines with boys, though the U.S. declines for thefts involving boys started in the latter part of the 1990s, while the Canadian declines ran throughout the decade. With respect to girls, the United States saw stability in index property offenses and burglary but increases in the rate of adjudicating girls delinquent in cases of theft. Canada also saw relative stability (or perhaps small declines) in the rate of finding girls guilty of all property and burglary offenses but, in contrast to the United States, saw declines in the rate of finding girls guilty of thefts. In both the United States and Canada, the differences between boys and girls in the rate of their being adjudicated delinquent for these property offenses were smaller in 2004 (for the United States) or 2005–6 (for Canada) than they were in 1985 (for the United States) and 1991 (for Canada). This tended to be due to declines in the rates for boys and stability in the rates for girls—except for thefts, where the narrowing of the absolute rate differences between boys and girls in the United States was due not only to a decline for boys, but also to increases seen with girls. Drug offenses in both countries increased during this period. However, Canada saw an enormous one-year decrease with the implementation of the new youth justice legislation, which emphasized dealing with minor offenses (e.g., possession of marijuana) outside of the court system.

The different patterns seen in the use of the courts in Canada and the United States likely reflect the differing roles each country sees its youth justice system as playing. In Canada, it was the official policy of the federal government from the mid-1990s onward to decrease the use of youth court (especially for minor offenses). Canada, it seems, more than governments in the United States, has been trying to reserve the use of youth court for the more serious offenses, though it has had relatively limited success in doing so. Nevertheless, a clear downward trend in the use of youth court—especially for boys—appeared to develop during the 1990s, culminating in 2003–4 with the implementation of the YCJA. It would, therefore, be a mistake to think that the Canadian youth justice system changed only after the YCJA was implemented. While the YCJA clearly had an impact, declines were seen throughout the 1990s (especially the late 1990s), which almost certainly reflected the view generally held by policy makers at the time that the youth justice system was overused for minor offenses. The data from the United States suggests that no such mood has prevailed there. It may be that the youth justice system's goal of treatment or intervention is more strongly adhered to in the United States, and thus, using the system for minor cases, especially for girls, does not raise serious concerns, as it does in Canada.

But the perception of an ever-increasing number of girls being involved in the youth justice systems of both countries can now be easily explained as an artifact of the relative rates at which boys and girls were being brought into the courts in both countries.

Conclusion

Although the youth justice systems in both countries appear to be used differently, they are similar in that girls are much less likely to be in court than boys, and in that, when girls are in court, they are more likely to have been involved in the least serious forms of offending. This finding, as mentioned earlier, is common to many other countries. Whether looking at self-reported, arrest, or court data, girls are simply less involved in offending than boys. What is notable, however, is that each of the quite different trends in the two countries can, in its own way, be seen as providing evidence to support the perception that crime—including violent crime—was increasing for girls. We have shown that a casual observer would see a higher proportion of girls in court on any given day than they had seen in earlier times. In other words, someone who walked into court in the early years of this century and counted the numbers of boys and girls adjudicated delinquent (in the United States) or found guilty (in Canada) in a sample of 100 youths would find more girls than this same observer would find in the late 1980s or early 1990s. It is hardly surprising, then, that people believed girls were catching up to boys in their involvement in crime. The only problem with that conclusion is that it doesn't describe the data.

One needs to remember that if one's interest is in actual crime committed by youths, youth court data or police arrest data are inevitably going to be inadequate. One would be better off looking at self-reported offending or victimization. Those data suggest that girls' involvement in crime and violence has not changed substantially over the past 20 years. However, for those interested in how society chooses to use youth court and what types of cases are brought into youth court and adjudicated delinquent, figures 2.9 through 2.22 illustrate the trends. Alternately, if one wants to understand why youth justice officials and other observers of youth court could, understandably, mistake the indicators of offending in girls, one needs to look at figures 2.23 and 2.24.

Chapter 3

Paternalism and the Social Control of Adolescent Girls: Juvenile Justice Reform in the United States

In order to understand the controversies involving girls in the juvenile justice system, one must first understand the controversies involving the youth justice system itself. Historically, girls have not been high-rate offenders. This is still true. However, in more recent years there has been concern about the treatment of girls in the youth justice systems of both the United States and Canada. What is the history behind this concern?

The history of youth justice—and the separation of the youth justice system from the adult justice system—appears to have occurred largely in the absence of any discussion of girls. This does not mean that there was no focus on girls. Indeed, some authors have focused on the dedicated courts, probation workers, and custodial institutions for girls (Chesney-Lind and Shelden, 2004; and Knupfer, 2001). Girls, even more than boys, were seen as needing "treatment" or "rehabilitation" for such offenses as sexual immorality and incorrigibility. What was largely absent was any discussion about the differences between the treatment of girls and that of boys. The treatment of girls, if even noted, was generally dismissed, perhaps in large part because of the widely held belief that they needed moral rehabilitation. Early policy debates and discussions about the youth justice system generally tended to focus exclusively on boys.

Some may wonder why we have chosen to cover this topic if girls were largely absent from the debates. However, we believe that one needs to understand this history in part to emphasize that girls were *not* part of policy makers' theorizing about youth justice. The dog in the Sherlock Holmes story "Silver Blaze" is important because it *didn't* bark on the night of the crime. The absence of any discussion of girls at the end of the 19th century in Canada and in the United States is perhaps just as significant as the silent dog. We would suggest that the absence of consideration of girls in the various approaches that were debated, implemented, and modified were—by the latter part of the 20th century—responsible, at least in part, for the different impact that youth justice systems had on girls compared to boys.

The history of the development of the juvenile justice system in the United States is sometimes presented as if it were a relatively simple, straightforward story of a child-saving era beginning in the mid to late 19th century, followed by concerns about due process beginning in the 1960s and then by a "retributive" or "punishment" era beginning in the 1980s or 1990s. The history, however, is actually much more nuanced. When the first juvenile court in North America opened in Toronto, Ontario, in 1894, followed closely by one in Chicago, Illinois, in 1899, the youth justice systems of these two countries bore little resemblance to what they became over the following few decades. Indeed, many of the features that came to be seen as hallmarks of the early juvenile courts—private hearings, probation officers, and special detention facilities, for example—took many years to develop. When the Chicago juvenile court first opened on July 3, 1899, hearings were open, records were public, and there were no public funds to pay the salaries of probation officers or maintain detention facilities (Tanenhaus, 2002). In fact, it took some time for private hearings to be put in place. In the early years of the juvenile court, people actually used the publicity to educate the public about the goals of the court (Tanenhaus, 2002). It was not until the 1920s that private hearings started to become the norm; however, as late as 1927 one can find concerns about limiting public access to juvenile hearings (see, for example, Lou, 1927).

Thus, the features that eventually came to be seen as defining the juvenile court were actually not originally part of it. They were added over time, and only after considerable struggle (see Tanenhaus, 2002, for a complete review of this history). As Tanenhaus (2002) notes, "Scholars must be careful not to describe early juvenile courts in anachronistic terms that obscure how the actual process of state building played out in the early twentieth century. . . . Juvenile courts, including Chicago's model court, were not immaculate constructions; they were built over time" (p. 43).

The opening of the first juvenile courts in the late 1890s also did not mark the first attempt to treat youths differently from adults. For example, in Massachusetts, a law was passed in 1870 that required separate hearings for children.[1] New York followed with a similar law in 1877 and also prohibited youths from associating with adult offenders in courts and institutions. In 1892 New York went further and passed legislation requiring juvenile trials to be held separately from those of adults, and that dockets and records in cases of children younger than 16 be separated from those of adults. Philadelphia passed a similar law in 1893. Edward Lindsey, then a county judge in Pennsylvania, noted in his 1914 article on the history of the youth court movement that "most of the [youth justice] statutes referred to have been passed within the last fifteen years but, as has already been indicated, it would be a mistake to suppose that they originated spontaneously within this period; indeed there is much less that is entirely new about them than is generally supposed" (Lindsey, 1914: p. 143).

Tappan (1949) noted that "Chicago, where the first juvenile court was ultimately established, had foreshadowed its development as early as 1861, when its mayor was given the power to appoint a commissioner to hear and determine petty cases of boys from six to seventeen; he had the power to place these boys under probationary supervision or in reform schools. This function passed to judges in 1867" (p. 12). These were the diverse roots from which the juvenile court at the end of the 19th century evolved. Consequently, small but cumulative steps towards separating youths from adults were being taken before the first juvenile courts were enacted, and those steps continued to be taken well after these courts were officially established.

For the most part, the early history of the juvenile court is ungendered. Where girls did enter into the discussion it was often in relation to behaviors that were not normally considered to be criminal—offenses that came to be known as status offenses. As one might expect, the history of status offenses also predates the formal establishment of the juvenile courts. Child savers were out there plucking girls out of the sea of sin before there was a specialized court in which to place them. Hence, prior to the last decade of the 19th century, there were procedures whereby girls were brought into court and committed to custody for noncriminal behaviors, especially sexual behaviors. Statutes had been enacted that created "certain substantive offenses under which young girls might be treated by commitment to any of a series of sectarian reformatory institutions" (Tappan, 1949: p. 176). Tappan argued, for example, that legislation from 1886 in New York could "be seen as early formulations of the general and loose concept of incorrigibility that later marked delinquency statutes" (1949: p. 176). The law stated:

Whenever any female over the age of 12 years shall be brought by the police or shall voluntarily come before a committing magistrate in the city of New York, and it shall be proved to the satisfaction of such magistrate by the confession of such female, or by competent testimony, that such female (first) is found in a reputed house of prostitution or assignation; or is morally depraved; or (second) is a prostitute, or is of intemperate habits and who professes a desire to reform and has not been an inmate of the penitentiary, such magistrate may judge that it is for the welfare of such female that she be placed in a reformatory. (Quoted in Tappan, 1949: p. 176)

More generally, the notion of "status offenses" did not originate with the juvenile court. As Teitelbaum (2002) has argued, punishments for status offenses such as disobeying one's parent have been around since before biblical times. Early American statutes in some jurisdictions also provided for punishments for youths who were "stubborn and rebellious" (see Sutton, 1988, for a complete review). For the Massachusetts Bay Colony in 1646, however, the punishment for a youth older than 16 who was "stubborn and rebellious" was not indefinite detention, but death, a treatment that would almost certainly would have reduced recidivism to zero. Although "it does not appear that any youth was actually put to death under this statute, the norm was well settled" (Teitelbaum, 2002: p. 160).

By the 19th and 20th centuries, however, views started to become more forgiving and optimistic, and "misconduct by children came to be understood as reflecting a wide variety of modern circumstance: parental failure . . . industrialization, and urbanization" (Teitelbaum, 2002: p. 160). More people started to believe that manipulation of the environments in which children found themselves could change their behaviors. This led to the growth of various programs and "houses of refuge" for children (see Chesney-Lind and Shelden, 2004, or Knupfer, 2001, for a review). By some accounts, in the 1870s up to 18 states institutionalized youths for "wayward behaviour" either by constituting it as a criminal offense or by broadening the committal grounds for noncriminal conduct (see Sweet, 1991). Though the creation of the juvenile court, with its broad jurisdiction, arguably cast the net even wider and took interventions for noncriminal behaviors to new heights, clearly it was not the first attempt to address, and at times incarcerate youths, for status offenses.

Early Justifications for the Youth Justice System: Unrecognized Tensions

Just as the development of the juvenile courts has been oversimplified in many accounts, so too have the justifications for a separate juvenile justice system. While many have discussed the early child-saving era and the ideals of rehabilitation for juveniles in the juvenile court, in fact, tensions were evident from the beginning about the purpose of a separate system for juveniles (Zimring, 2005). Clearly there was considerable agreement that the court's primary purpose was to divert youth from the harmful effects of the adult justice system (Tanenhaus, 2002). However, experts disagreed over the extent to which the justice system should intervene in the lives of children. Advocacy of a positive role for a court in the lives of young children automatically raises the question of the proper scope of the youth justice (or juvenile court) system. For example, John McManaman, a chief youth probation officer in Chicago, raised concerns in 1905 that "public officials [were] peeping into the home and attempting to establish a standard of living—a standard of conduct and morals—and then measuring all people by that standard" (McManaman, 1905: p. 377).

Others were concerned about the longer-term consequences of delinquency adjudications and the fact that delinquency adjudications were made without the benefit of legal advice. For example, J. Pretence Murphy, executive secretary of the Children's Bureau of Philadelphia, cautioned that

> one should here keep in mind the increasing tendency of the adult courts to give weight to the conduct records of children appearing in the juvenile courts. Record after record of adult prisoners include as part of their "criminal record" their history of truancy and the commission of misdemeanors. Being without wise legal advice at the time of appearance before a bad judge might result in grave injury to a child. (Murphy, 1929: p. 92)

There were also early criticisms of committals to secure institutions for rehabilitative purposes. For example, the Honorable Edward Lindsey argued that "there is often a very real deprivation of liberty, nor is that fact changed by refusing to call it punishment or because the good of the child is stated to be the object" (Lindsey, 1914: p. 145). Similarly, Edward Waite, a district court judge in Minneapolis, gave a talk during a 1921 conference on the Standards for Juvenile Courts (held jointly by the Children's Bureau and the National Probation Association) in which he argued that

> no judge on any bench has need to be more thoroughly grounded in the principles of evidence and more constantly mindful of them than the judge of a juvenile court. The boy against whom it is proposed to make an official record of misconduct involving possible curtailment of his freedom at the behest of strangers has a right to be

found delinquent only according to law. . . . Surely, those substantial
rules of evidence which would protect the boy if the State called its
interference "punishment" instead of "protection," . . . should apply
to issues which may involve the right of the boy to liberty. (Waite,
1921: p. 343)

Interestingly, however, Waite did not discuss in much detail the issue of
bringing girls into court for behaviors that were not criminal, or of girls being dealt with "in their best interests" whether or not they, or their parents,
agreed. His main suggestion in this area was to have "referees" for "noncriminal" matters such as "sexual delinquency" (p. 346).

Waite's concerns, however, appeared not to be recognized in the publication *Juvenile Court Standards,* which grew out of that initial conference
in 1921. These "standards" explicitly chose not to endorse due-process elements. The final report, approved in 1923 and reprinted in 1934, advocated,
for example, that hearings "should be conducted with as little formality
as possible, and the formal adherence to the practice and rules of procedure that characterized the criminal court should be avoided" (Perkins and
Lenroot, 1934: p. 5).

Katharine Lenroot, assistant to the chief and later acting chief of the
Children's Bureau, and a key player behind the 1934 edition of *Juvenile Court
Standards,* clearly endorsed broad jurisdiction and informal adjudications
for juvenile courts. She also apparently felt that all due-process concerns
had been dealt with by the courts by the early 1920s, arguing that

> within ten years after the enactment of the first juvenile court law,
> the constitutionality of such statutes had been well established. A
> number of cases had been brought, in which juvenile court acts and
> similar statutes had been attacked on constitutional grounds, and it
> had been held by the overwhelming weight of authority that juvenile
> courts were not criminal in nature, and hence that they were not
> unconstitutional because of the informality of procedure or because
> of the deprivation of the right to trial by jury, the right of appeal or
> similar protection afforded persons charged with crime under the
> constitutions of the United States and the various states. (Lenroot,
> 1923: pp. 214–15)

Lenroot's suggestion that due process had been settled might have been
slightly premature. Others, such as Lindsey (1914), Murphy (1929), and
Waite (1921), disagreed that the constitutionality of such laws had been well

established and questioned whether the statutes really could be challenged, given that most youths in the justice system were poor and unable to secure help in developing a case. They continued to criticize the court, and although they were upset with court decisions that upheld these statutes in many jurisdictions, they also noted that there were some decisions against such laws.

> It would seem that constitutional safeguards as far as minors and the relation of parent and child is concerned have completely broken down. Many of the provisions of the juvenile court acts are clearly in conflict with constitutional provisions and this conclusion can only be escaped by evasions. . . . Perhaps it may be premature to regard the constitutional questions as settled. . . . It may be that a period of criticism will succeed the period of encomium as to these statutes and that then the features really out of harmony with our existing legal system will be eliminated. There are some indications of the development of a critical attitude [through some recent court decisions]. (Lindsey, 1914: p. 145)

There were also some concerns about the expansive range of cases brought into juvenile courts. Many such cases—dependency, neglect, pensions, and adoptions—were seen by some as beyond the scope of juvenile courts, for two reasons. First, it was argued by some that regardless of the rhetoric, juvenile courts did maintain some of the punitive practices from adult criminal courts, and second, those sorts of cases took time and energy away from delinquency cases. Murphy (1929), for example, noted that

> the committee in charge of the Survey of Criminal Justice in Cleveland (1922) held that dependency and widows' pensions are not proper subjects for juvenile court administration which carries over too many traditional practices from courts for adults. It is significant that the scope of the juvenile courts in New England is much more limited than it is in the rest of the country. The Boston Court—one of the best in the country—because it is not concerned with dependency, mother's aid and adoptions—does have time to do thorough work with cases of delinquency and waywardness. (p. 87)

Interestingly, at this time there appeared to be no discussions of limiting the juvenile courts' jurisdiction over status offenses and, once again, no special focus on girls.

Clearly, though, there were tensions from the beginning about the over-all goals of the youth justice system and concerns about whether what was going on was really rehabilitation. Although many have presented the early development of juvenile court as a simple process where all involved agreed to the nature and jurisdiction of the court, clearly there were some dissenting voices throughout this period.

As we have pointed out, Zimring (2005) has argued that there were, in fact, two differing justifications for a separate juvenile justice system. There was the "diversionary" approach, which argued that the purpose of juvenile court was to divert youths from adult court processing in order to shield them from the harms associated with criminal court. But in addition—and to some extent in contrast—there was the "interventionist" approach, which argued that the juvenile court was created in order to provide help and support for any children "in need." Here the broad jurisdiction of the court was seen as beneficial, as was the elimination of the formal adjudicatory procedures found in adult court. Those formal procedures were seen as impediments to helping the children who stood before the judge. Moreover, because the overall goal was to help a child, it made sense to expand the court's jurisdiction to broader familial issues. In order to get a complete picture of the child and his or her problems, one would want to incorporate all aspects of the family. Thus, a logical extension of the interventionist justification for the juvenile court would be to incorporate dependency, neglect, pensions, adoptions, and the like. The end result, obviously, would be that the distinctions among some of those cases, on the one hand, and "delinquency" cases, on the other, would be blurry at best. Of course, that would not matter, because the goal was to intervene and provide help.

The diversionary approach, on the other hand, would not be opposed to due-process protections. Indeed, they might be seen as necessary to reduce any potential harms associated with youth court processing. Moreover, if the goal was to divert youth from adult court processing, then adding in a broad range of cases (dependency, neglect, pensions, etc.) was not necessarily a logical extension. Rather, one would likely be inclined to want only delinquency cases.

As Zimring (2005) notes, those justifications can, at times, be opposed to one another. However, although these two aims are conceptually distinct, there appears to be little awareness during the development of the juvenile court that they could come into conflict with one another. Zimring argues that some of "the same people who believed in the diversionary virtues of a new court affirmed its interventionist potential as well. Because there was no contemporary awareness of potential conflict, the courts' supporters did not have to choose between these separate but attractive rationales for the new institution" (2005: p. 36). Perhaps that was why there was little objection to bringing status offenses into youth court. Even those who advocated diversion simultaneously endorsed some degree of intervention.

So why did the diversionary approach not receive more attention in historical accounts of the development of the juvenile justice system? Zimring argues that it was because the interventionist theory was new and somewhat controversial, whereas the diversionary approach had been consistently endorsed throughout the last century: "The diversionary sentiments of 1899 do not set that era far off from 1940 or 1980. The claims of interventionist prowess are considered by contrast a striking historical artifact by the 1960s and 1970s, if not before" (Zimring, 2005: p. 37). As will be discussed, these tensions between the ultimate goal of the juvenile court—diversion from the adult system or intervention—appear to still exist today, especially with respect to adolescent girls.

Due-Process Concerns and the Beginning of the End of Status Offenses

Although many commentators on the history of the juvenile court in the United States highlight the Supreme Court decisions in the 1960s (e.g., Kent and Gault) as a time when due-process concerns were first expressed, like most things in history, it is neither that clear nor that straightforward. As already argued, due-process concerns were actually expressed as early as the inception of the juvenile court. Lindsey (1914) and Waite (1921), as quoted earlier, advocated for more due-process procedures, especially when there was a potential for secure confinement. Murphy (1929) was also concerned about the power the courts had to incarcerate youths and the lack of due-process procedures that could help to limit abuses of power: "There is a check on the authority which the judge wields in adult courts, but there is very little, if any, control now being exercised over juvenile court judges; yet these same judges are responsible for the separation of great numbers of children from their parents for long and short periods" (p. 88).

These concerns did not disappear. In the 1940s one still sees concerns about a lack of due process. For example, Tappan (1949) argued that the rhetoric around the juvenile court did not match the reality of what happened in it.

> The motives and objectives in the juvenile court are far from homogenous or consolidated. In some respects the movement appears to

be struggling in opposed directions; often it pays lip service to one set of theoretical norms but in the actual procedures employed it reveals drives that are in utter contrast to its avowed ideals . . . And the disparity between belief and practice is usually ignored in self-appraisal: it is the ideal that is presented complacently to the community as accomplished fact. The result upon the child who is exposed to realities rather than theory is unfortunate. (Tappan, 1949: p. 219)

Because Tappan felt that the reality of the juvenile court was far from the theory that surrounded it, he believed that due-process protections were essential.

The presumption is commonly adopted that since the state has determined to protect and save its wards, it will do no injury to them through its diverse official, so that these children need no due process protections against injury. Several exposures to court; a jail remand of days, weeks, or even months; and a long period in a correctional school with young thieves, muggers, and murders—these can do no conceivable harm if the state's purpose be beneficent and the procedure be "chancery"! Children are adjudicated in this way every day, without visible manifestations of due process. They are incarcerated. They become adult criminals, too, in thankless disregard of the state's good intentions as *parens patriae*. (Tappan, 1949: p. 205)

However, with the exception of Tappan's work (1947 and 1949), there appeared to be little discussion with respect either to status offenses generally or to girls specifically. Although some data from the early 1900s showed that girls were more likely than boys to be in court and sentenced to custody for status offenses and sexual promiscuity,[2] this information appeared to generate little discussion (see Knupfer, 2001: chapter 5, for a more detailed discussion of the data).[3] Moreover, there was some evidence that during the early 1900s, because of racial segregation, African American girls (and boys) were less likely than their white counterparts to be placed in custody (Knupfer, 2001). Custody, it seemed, was initially reserved for white youths; African Americans were sent back to the family.

Following the trend of "noting and then dismissing," Tappan (1949) noted that girls were more likely to be brought into court for status offenses and more likely to be committed to custody than were boys. Beyond that, however, girls warranted little mention. This is somewhat curious, given that two years earlier Tappan published one of the first books on girls in juvenile court. Specifically, he looked at the adjudication of girls in New York's Wayward Minor Court. The Wayward Minor Court was an experimental court for girls whereby those who were brought into the system and adjudicated were, at the end, adjudicated to the status of a "wayward minor." Girls could be referred to this court through a variety of mechanisms and for a variety of behaviors—typically sexual promiscuity.[4]

Tappan (1947) noted in his analysis that there was a relatively high use of court and custody given the supposed emphasis on diversion and probation. Moreover, when he examined the juvenile boys' courts in Brooklyn and Queens, he noted the relatively few cases involving "mild conduct or personality problems" compared to the vast number of cases in the New York Wayward Minor girls' court (p. 177). By the 1940s, therefore, the broad child-saving provisions of the juvenile court, combined with the creation of status offenses, provided an efficient means of intervening in the lives of girls, at least in New York. By ignoring the fact that girls could be (and apparently were) more likely to be brought under the control of the state for behavior that tested the limits of morality and compliance with authorities rather than for criminal behavior, the youth justice systems of the two countries drifted, without much thought, into an area in which girls were singled out for special control by the state.

Tappan was unusual in that he was also clearly concerned with the lack of due process for girls, particularly pre-hearing adjudications that were based on informal social data. He also noted that a girl's demeanor had a great effect on the type of disposition she would receive. More generally, however, he questioned whether the law should be used to deal with these kinds of concerns. He asked, presumably rhetorically, "What is sexual behavior—in the legal sense—of the nonprostitute of sixteen, of eighteen, or of twenty when fornication is no offense under the criminal law?" (Tappan, 1947: p. 34). He also wondered, "In an era of increasing emancipation of youth, to what standard of obedience should the daughter be held?" (p. 36).

At the same time, however, he seemed hesitant to suggest that these types of cases be removed from the jurisdiction of the court. On the one hand, Tappan argued that "it is clear . . . that the function of protecting the adolescent girl is not efficiently served under the statutes and their administration either by this court or by other courts of the city. The courts neither reach an adequate proportion of the girls who need treatment, nor [do they] accomplish adequate treatment [for] those who[m] . . . they do reach" (Tappan, 1947: p. 185). On the other hand, however, he seemed reluctant to give up court jurisdiction for girls under the age of 18 (p. 185).

Later he appeared to suggest that a narrowing of the court jurisdiction to only criminal acts, coupled with increased treatment provisions, could be a useful option.

> Perhaps the most that may be hoped for, then, is that the court may come to shift its emphasis toward two more definite objectives: (1) to adjudicate to an adolescent offender status those who have committed acts which if committed by an adult would be a crime . . . and (2) to adjudicate and treat therapeutically those girls whose conduct had been promiscuous, commercial, and indicative of moral depravity, and who have failed to respond to the efforts of other social agencies. Under a statute thus designed the purpose would be neither retributive nor preventive, but reformative and rehabilitative. (Tappan, 1947: p. 187)

Here again, one can see tensions between the desire to "divert" criminal acts committed by youths from adult court processing and the desire to "intervene" in the lives of girls who displayed a range of noncriminal behaviors. Thus, a narrowing of the courts' jurisdiction (to criminal offenses only) and concern over limiting the harm that might be done by official court processing were simultaneously endorsed alongside a desire to provide intensive interventions for noncriminal behaviors. This could be a classic example of what Zimring (2005) described: the lack of awareness of the conflicting goals and people simultaneously endorsing both. But what is particularly notable about Tappan's view is that the first category of cases that were seen as appropriate raw material for the juvenile court—what might be called "ordinary criminal offenses"—was ungendered. The second category involved girls. This is not the last time these tensions between diversion from the adult system and intervention with respect to girls would appear.

A few years later, Wattenberg and Saunders (1954) investigated police department complaint cases in the Detroit area. They found that girls were significantly more likely than boys to come to the attention of police for general conduct problems, especially sexual behavior: "The girls showed disproportionately high percentages charged with incorrigibility, sex offenses, and being truants from home. The boys were high in burglary, assaults, and malicious destruction of property" (p. 26). They also noted that the offenses with which the youngest girls (12 and younger) were charged were similar to what boys of all ages were charged with—predominantly larceny. However, in the 13- and 14-year-old category for girls the most frequent charge was "incorrigibility," and among the 15- and 16-year-olds the most frequent charge was "sex violations." They concluded that

> the major differences in the development of misconduct among girls as contrasted with boys can be traced to cultural differences in the way the sexes are treated. Outstanding in this respect is the fact that sex activity is regarded as more serious for girls than boys, and that although available evidence indicates that, if anything, boys are actually more active sexually, charges are mainly made against girls. (p. 31)

A few years later, in an attempt to examine whether those results were specific to Detroit, Gibbons and Griswold (1957) conducted a similar study, this time looking at court referrals and dispositions in Washington state. They too noted the larger proportion of girls compared to boys referred for status offenses (running away, ungovernable conduct, and sex offenses). Roughly 46 percent of the cases involving girls were for running away and being ungovernable. Another 10 percent of the girls' cases were for sex offenses, while only 5 percent of boys' cases were for sex offenses. They also noted that the youngest girls had cases that were most similar to boys—typically property offenses—while the older girls had cases that were predominantly for running away and being ungovernable. Finally, they found that although girls' cases were slightly more likely to be dismissed, when they were adjudicated they were significantly more likely to receive custody compared to boys. Figure 3.1 shows the results: while only 11 percent of the nondismissed boys' cases were sentenced to an institution, a little more than 25 percent of the girls' cases received such a sentence. The relatively high

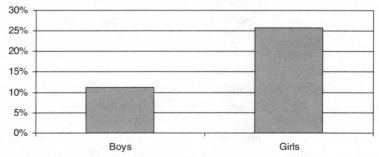

Figure 3.1. Percentage of nondismissed cases in youth court that were sentenced to an institution in Washington State, 1953–55
Source: Gibbons, D., and Griswold, M. J. (1957). Sex differences among juvenile court referrals. *Sociology and Social Research*, 42, 106–10.

use of custody for girls was interesting, given the less serious offenses they tended to be referred to court for.

These early findings, however, seemed not to receive much response from the juvenile court community, in large part because the interventionist function of the court was almost certainly seen by most observers as especially appropriate for girls. What might be considered to be the criminalization of girls' (but not boys') sexual behavior might have been noticed, but it was not a source of concern. Overall, the topic of the appropriateness of adjudicating status offenses generally, and specifically the use of sexual behaviors to bring girls into juvenile court, did not appear to raise concerns. Using the court to stop girls from having consensual sex was apparently not a due-process problem, but was simply seen as a legitimate function of the court.

In contrast, the official and academic concerns appeared primarily to be concentrated on general ungendered due-process issues, and in that domain some interesting changes were occurring. For example, the *Standards for Specialized Courts Dealing with Children* was still being published in the 1950s, though by then the National Council of Juvenile Court Judges was also involved in their design, along with the Children's Bureau and the National Probation and Parole Association. In 1954, however, it began to endorse some principles that were different from those described in the 1934 publication. In 1954 a desire to keep the juvenile court informal was still clearly evident. However, the *Standards* argued that

> rules of evidence calculated to assure proceedings in accordance with due process of law should be applicable to children's cases. However, it is essential that these rules of evidence be especially designed. They should protect the informality of the hearing and avoid the needless legalisms of the rules of evidence customarily applicable to other judicial hearings. But at the same time they must assure that there will be an orderly presentation of credible facts in a manner calculated to protect the rights of all concerned . . . This principle also entails written findings, some form of record of hearing, and the right to appeal. (Children's Bureau and U.S. Department of Health, Education and Welfare, 1954: p. 7)

Other writers have suggested that throughout the 1950s the criticisms regarding the lack of due-process procedures grew louder (Ketcham, 1965). Although there had been consistent criticisms since the juvenile court's inception, it now appeared that the laws in some jurisdictions were beginning to change. Citing a number of legal decisions in various jurisdictions against the *parens patriae* model, Ketcham argued that juvenile justice was beginning to change—to become more "legalistic." He also noted a number of published criticisms:

> By the decade of the fifties, a chorus of voices was challenging both the constitutional right and the social wisdom of operating juvenile courts largely outside the ordinary legal process. In 1950, the University of Pittsburgh Law Review published an attack under the caption *Juvenile Justice: Treatment of Travesty.* In 1956, under the title *We Need Not Deny Justice to Our Children,* the Civil Liberties Record of the Philadelphia ACLU criticized juvenile court procedure, and Harper's magazine printed, in 1958, an exposé of the juvenile courts, under the title *What Nobody Knows about Juvenile Delinquency.* (Ketcham, 1965: p. 587)

What is important about these due-process concerns, however, is that they did not challenge the interventionist purpose of the juvenile court. Essentially the argument, were it to be made, was that it was acceptable for the court to be interventionist, but some attention should be paid to due process, rules of evidence, and so on. In other words, it was fine to focus a special part of the interventionist approach on girls by targeting them with status offenses. Quite simply, it was part of the ideology of the youth court to intervene, and the fact that certain kinds of interventions happened to be gendered was apparently hardly noticed, and certainly was not a concern.

In 1967 the 19-member President's Commission on Law Enforcement and Administration of Justice, appointed by President Lyndon Johnson, published a 17-volume report. The commission carried out what was almost certainly the most comprehensive study of crime and delinquency ever undertaken by the United States. Due-process concerns were raised throughout the report. In an expanded report on juvenile justice,[5] the commission highlighted the fact that some states had already started addressing some of the due-process concerns (President's Commission on Law Enforcement and Administration of Justice [President's Commission], 1967a). In 1961, for example, New York and California required legal counsel for youths in court. Youths in New York had always been free to hire legal counsel, but few did. However, with court-appointed legal counsel, many more were engaging the process (Isaacs, 1963). California also commissioned a report on the administration of juvenile justice in 1960 and documented numerous problems with respect to providing youths with due-process protections from the policing stage through to adjudication and dispositions (Shain and Burkhart, 1960).

The commission took these reports from, and legal developments in, other jurisdictions seriously and also advocated for more due-process procedures.

The commission also advocated reserving court for serious offenses: "The undesirably of putting a youngster through an essentially criminal process for an unimportant misdeed [vandalism] should be dealt with not by diluting procedures for serious offenders but by improving pre-adjudication screening, expanding services that offer alternatives to court referral and limiting adjudication to cases of grave or repeated misconduct" (President's Commission, 1967a: p. 23). New York had perhaps attempted something similar with the Family Court Act four years earlier. Under the New York Family Court Act (1963), an adjudication of delinquency could be granted only if the act was criminal in nature and the youth required "supervision, treatment or confinement" (President's Commission, 1967a: p. 23).

With respect to status offenses specifically, the commission appeared to want simultaneously to restrict and to expand court intervention for status offenders. The members were, for example, concerned about the potential for abuse:

> The provisions on which intervention in this category of cases [status offenses] is based are typically vague and all-encompassing: Growing up in idleness and crime, engaging in immoral conduct, in danger of leading an immoral life. Especially when administered with the informality characteristic of the court's procedures, they establish the judge as arbiter not only of the behavior but also of the morals of every child . . . appearing before him. The situation is ripe for over-reaching, for imposition of the judge's own code of youthful conduct. One frequent consequence has been the use of general protective statutes about leading an immoral life and engaging in endangering conduct as a means of enforcing conformity—eliminating long hair, levis, and other transitory adolescent foibles so unsettling to adults. (President's Commission, 1967a: p. 25)

At the same time, however, they appeared to want to retain control over youths who seem to be on the road to delinquency.

> On the other hand, the need that led to the creation of that broad and general jurisdiction was and remains a real one. It is not a favor to children to have no authoritative way of attempting to protect them from themselves and, often, from their environments. (President's Commission, 1967a: p. 25)

The compromise, then, led to a suggestion that perhaps a new label for status offenses be created: "A firm, objective way is needed to apply the truancy laws, fortify flagging parents, and encourage substitution of healthful for self-destructive pursuits before it is too late. Two recently adopted juvenile court acts attempt to solve the problem by retaining juvenile court jurisdiction over the conduct in question but naming it something other than delinquency." The commission then highlighted Illinois and New York as examples of how this might be done. Both states relabeled these types of cases, Illinois as "minors otherwise in need of supervision" and New York as "persons in need of supervision," and then attempted to curtail police and court powers such that detention could not be used for such cases (President's Commission, 1967a: p. 26).

Then the commission went a little further and contemplated the wisdom of bringing these kinds of cases in the youth court under any label. Given "the serious stigma and the uncertain gain accompanying official action, serious consideration should be given [to] complete elimination from the court's jurisdiction of conduct illegal only for a child" (President's Commission, 1967a: p. 27). The commission further acknowledged that although relinquishing the power of court over status offenses would necessarily mean the possibility of losing an opportunity to potentially help some youths, they questioned whether, at present, anything could realistically be done to help youths given the state of the system generally (1967a: p. 27).

Interestingly, up until this point there was no mention of girls even though it had been acknowledged two decades earlier by Tappan, and within the commission's own report, that girls were disproportionately affected by status offenses. The commission noted in its second report that "boys and girls commit quite different kinds of offences . . . more than half of the girls referred to juvenile court in 1965 were referred for conduct that would not be criminal if committed by adults; only one fifth of such boys were referred for such conduct" (President's Commission, 1967b: p. 56). Other than stating that as fact, however, little was commented on. Only in the expanded report on juvenile justice did they refer to girls and status offenses—in this case to create the scenario of the sad possibility of losing an opportunity to help a youth:

It is hard to contemplate having no way of preventing a teenage girl from damaging her life with an illegitimate child when a sufficiently strong hand might have gotten her though the belligerent years without so permanent a blight. But in declining to relinquish power over her, we must bluntly ask what our present power achieves and must acknowledge in answer that at most we do not really know and in at least some cases we suspect it may do as much harm as good. (President's Commission, 1967a: p. 27)

Other than the worst-case scenario of being unable to prevent a girl from becoming pregnant by means of a status offense–based intervention instead of birth control pills, there was no mention of the disproportionate effect status offenses had on girls. This scenario, which, however, was presented only in the longer publication on juvenile justice, may help to explain the final recommendation that the commission made with respect to status offenders:

> The conduct of illegal-only-for-children category of the court's jurisdiction should be substantially circumscribed so that it ceases to include such acts as smoking, swearing, and disobedience to parents and comprehends only actions that entail a real risk of long-range harm to the child, such as experimenting with drugs, repeatedly becoming pregnant out of wedlock, and being habitually truant from school. Serious consideration, at the least, should be given to complete elimination of the court's power over children for noncriminal conduct. (President's Commission, 1967b: p. 85)

It would appear that the commission could tolerate losing youths to smoking, swearing and disobedience, but losing the power—however remote the likelihood of success might be—to prevent a girl from becoming *repeatedly* pregnant was too much to ask. No consideration appeared to have been focused on the possibility that boys might *repeatedly* impregnate girls and could, therefore, be in need of court intervention. Similarly, the question about whether prevention of, among other things, multiple pregnancies was best addressed through a court intervention did not appear to be a central one in this context. Regardless, it was clear from the academic publications in the 1940s and 1950s and the commission report in 1967 that due-process concerns and the elimination of status offenses were being considered. Indeed, some jurisdictions had actually revised or enacted new legislation during the early 1960s to address the due-process concerns. The fact that girls appeared to have been disproportionately charged with status offenses was noted and then ignored. Reform of the youth courts' treatment of adolescent girls was, therefore, somewhat slower.

Clearly though, the Supreme Court decisions during the second half of the 1960s pushed due-process concerns to center stage. The first case, in 1966, involved due-process issues around transferring juveniles to the adult system. Morris Kent, who was 16 at the time, was charged with rape and robbery. Kent's attorney, anticipating a transfer to the adult system, filed a motion requesting that the case be kept in the youth justice system. The judge did not rule on the motion and instead simply waived jurisdiction. Kent's lawyer argued that the waiver was invalid, and although lower courts disagreed, the Supreme Court ruled that youths should have transfer hearings that measured up to "the essentials of due process and fair treatment." In this case the Supreme Court said that Kent's counsel should have had "access to all records involved in the waiver, and that the judge should have provided a *written* statement of the reasons for the waiver" (Snyder and Sickmund, 2006: p. 100).

Although that ruling was important, what mattered even more was the criticism of, and potential constitutional challenge to, the underlying *parens patriae* foundation of the youth justice system. In the past, the courts had argued that certain classes of people (e.g., juveniles) could be afforded fewer due-process protections if some benefit followed (e.g., "rehabilitation"; Snyder and Sickmund, 2006). However, in this case the Supreme Court suggested that no such benefit may exist for juveniles. Specifically, Justice Abe Fortas argued that juveniles received the "worst of both worlds," because they receive "neither the protection accorded to adults nor the solicitous care and regenerative treatment postulated for children" (*Kent v. United States,* 383 U.S. 541, 86 S.Ct. 1045). Interestingly, the concern expressed here was strikingly similar to the concerns expressed by Tappan 17 years earlier.

One year later another ruling came from the Supreme Court, this time focused on due-process issues around committing youths to custody. Gerald Gault, who was 15 and on probation for a minor property offense, allegedly made a prank phone call with a friend to a neighbor. Although the victim did not appear in court and the court never determined whether Gault or his friend actually made the call, Gault was committed to a training school until the age of 21. The Supreme Court ruled that in hearings that could result in a commitment to custody, juveniles have four constitutional rights: the right to notice, the right to counsel, the right to question witnesses, and the right to be protected against self-incrimination. The Court based its ruling on the fact that Gault was not helped or rehabilitated during his custodial stay. The Court rejected *parens patriae* as a principle of juvenile justice, arguing that youths were being punished rather than helped.

With these two Supreme Court rulings, due-process concerns were no longer expressed only by certain legal actors in various jurisdictions. And reforms could no longer simply be considered, discussed, and then ignored. Instead, all states had to address concerns about due process and, perhaps more important, to address the fact that there was a large gap between the theory of benevolent treatment and reality of what actually happened to youths. Although the Supreme Court cases were concerned with due-process issues such as the right to be given notice of charges and the right to appeal, the concern, by the highest court in the country, that rehabilitation was more illusory than real likely set in motion some important changes. Specifically, if the system was not rehabilitative and was in fact quite possibly doing more harm than good, then one had to seriously question the wisdom of bringing noncriminal behaviors into the court. Finally, the emperor, officially, had no clothes.

The Juvenile Justice and Delinquency Prevention Act, 1974

In 1974 the United States Congress passed the Juvenile Justice and Delinquency Prevention Act (JJDPA). This was the first piece of federal legislation directed at the youth justice system. The JJDPA had two broad mandates, one of which was to deinstitutionalize status offenders and nonoffenders (DSO).[6] To that end, the act required states that wished to receive funding to provide a plan to show how status offenders would be dealt with, since they should no longer be placed in custody.[7] The act also required states to develop adequate monitoring systems of their jails, detention facilities, and correctional institutions in order to show that they were meeting the requirements and no longer placing status offenders in custody. Thus, the first piece of federal legislation on the youth justice system only went so far as to suggest that states no longer incarcerate youths for status offenses, though they could still, obviously, bring such cases in youth court. Because each state was ultimately responsible for youth justice legislation, the federal act could only encourage compliance with the deinstitutionalization mandate through monetary incentives. Specifically, those states which could demonstrate that they were reducing the use of custody for noncriminal offenses would receive federal funding.

While the JJDPA ultimately took a "deinstitutionalization" approach, other people and other reports were arguing that status offenses should not even be under the jurisdiction of the juvenile court. In a 1974 policy statement, the National Council on Crime and Delinquency (NCCD) advocated that status offenders be removed from the jurisdiction of the court. The council briefly noted that girls were more likely than boys to be in court and committed to custody for status offenses but argued for the removal of these offenses from jurisdiction primarily because of how juvenile courts and corrections actually operated: "We believe that, however sincere the effort of the juvenile court to correct a juvenile's noncriminal behavior, it has frequently resulted in a misapplication of the courts' power, has sometimes done more harm than good, and, as said in Kent, generally gives him 'the worst of both worlds' " (NCCD, 1975).

Other national organizations were also developing guidelines and standards and, interestingly, also recommending the removal of status offenses from the jurisdiction of the court. For example, the National Advisory Committee on Criminal Justice Standards and Goals created a task force on Juvenile Justice and presented suggestions for national standards in 1976. The task force also recommended removing status offenses from the jurisdiction of the court, for reasons similar to those offered by the NCCD in 1974. However, they made no mention of the disproportionate effect these offenses had on girls (Breed, 1976).

The Institute of Judicial Administration and the American Bar Association (IJA-ABA) also suggested removing status offenses from juvenile court. In 1979 they produced a 23-volume report on juvenile justice standards, to which more volumes were added over the years. However, one volume, *Noncriminal Misbehavior,* was never approved by the American Bar Association (Flicker, 1982). In it the IJA-ABA advocated removing status offenses from the jurisdiction in the court for the same reasons given by other organizations—namely, that more harm than good resulted from bringing these cases in court. In addition, however, they noted some of the problems with respect to status offenses and girls:

> As American society has traditionally been more concerned over the preservation of the sexual virtue of girls than of boys, so this concern is reflected in the invocation of the ungovernability jurisdiction. . . . For these reasons, the juvenile courts' status offense jurisdiction had been under increasing scrutiny for some time, with consequent and amounting pressure for its abridgement. (IJA-ABA, 1982: pp. 13–14)

Evidently the ABA found the recommendations in *Noncriminal Misbehavior* to be too controversial and would not approve it without major revisions (Flicker, 1982). The IJA-ABA committee mentioned that they received widespread criticism of their *Noncriminal Misbehavior* volume:

> It was inevitable that protests would be heard when practitioners in the field recognized that the IJA-ABA Joint Commission had adopted the basic assumption that intervention, however benevolently intended, could be harmful and must be limited strictly to actions

warranting official state coercion. The dismay of professionals accustomed to exercising broad discretionary power was not restricted to juvenile court judges, but was expressed by police and probation officers, educators, correctional administrators, psychiatrists, and others. (IJA-ABA, 1982: p. 53)

Although all three of these national organizations recommended removing status offenses from the jurisdiction of the court, the JJDPA was not so amended. The JJDPA called for the development of national standards for the administration of juvenile justice, and even though some national organizations were indeed creating suggested standards, the committee put together specifically for the JJDPA chose not to argue for the removal of status offenses from the jurisdiction of the youth court (U.S. Department of Justice and Office of Juvenile Justice and Delinquency Prevention [USDOJ-OJJDP], 1980). Instead, the committee argued that youth courts should deal with status offenses, though they should only use custody as a last resort. Yet the committee was clearly divided on this issue:

Although its [the National Advisory Committee's] goal was to obviate the need for court jurisdiction over noncriminal misbehavior by assuring the availability of sufficient services for all families and children, current programs were neither numerous nor effective enough to warrant a recommendation that the family court be stripped of its power . . . it [the committee] concluded further that although abuses had occurred, the juvenile courts had been able to assist juveniles and their families and to increase the services available in the community. Although agreeing with that goal, a substantial number of National Advisory Committee members disagreed with the means chosen to achieve it, favoring instead a recommendation for immediate elimination of jurisdiction over noncriminal misbehavior. In support of this position, it was argued that schools, social services departments, and other agencies will not take the initiative for developing alternative means of handling noncriminal misbehavior cases as long as the family court retains jurisdiction; that traditionally girls have been subject to harsher penalties for running away or incorrigibility than boys; and that in practical terms little distinction has been drawn between status offenders and delinquents (USDOJ-OJJDP, 1980: p. 250)

After reviewing the problems with status offenses, the committee ultimately advocated that the juvenile court retain jurisdiction because its members believed that other agencies would not provide services. They did, however, say that court intervention should be a last resort, as should the use of custody, and that federal funds should be made available to "assist any jurisdiction wishing to abolish court jurisdiction over noncriminal misbehavior" (USDOJ-OJJDP, 1980: p. 250). However, they wanted such changes evaluated in order to explore their impact. In other words, even though it had been acknowledged that girls were being treated, from their perspectives, more harshly than boys, and even though it was understood in other areas of life that women should not be disadvantaged because they were women, it was all right—perhaps, harking back to the specter of multiple unwanted pregnancies—to punish girls more harshly than boys.

Although the other national organizations that produced suggested standards for juvenile court may not have been pleased to have the federal government advocate retaining youth court jurisdiction over status offenses, others were clearly pleased. For example, Hunter Hurst, then director of the National Center for Juvenile Justice, the research division of the National Council of Juvenile and Family Court Judges, argued in a 1975 address to the Council on Crime and Delinquency that

> status offenses are offenses against our values . . . [girls are] seemingly over represented as status offenders because we have a strong heritage of being protective towards females in this country. . . . [It offends] our sensibility and values to have a fourteen year old girl engage in sexually promiscuous activity. . . . [One cannot] be sure that the police, the church or vigilante groups [will do something]. . . . I would rather that something occur in the court where the rights of the parties be protected. (Hurst, 1975, quoted in Chesney-Lind and Shelden, 2004: p. 175)

Hurst seemed to want the court to retain control of status offenses in part to "help" youths generally and girls specifically, and in part to respect due process. That the desire to intervene was gendered—apparently there was no need to intervene in the life of the boy who was presumably "engaging in sexually promiscuous activity" with this same 14-year-old girl—was ignored.

A few years later, in 1980, the National Council of Juvenile and Family Court Judges (NCJFCJ) published "evaluation standards" for juvenile courts. The council took an interventionist approach, saying that courts should strive for "individualized justice, looking less to the offense done in the past and more to the needs of this particular child" (NCJFCJ, 1980:

p. 4). Given that approach, they said, not surprisingly, that "there are no conspicuous areas of Court non-use in cases of child abuse, status offenses, neglect, parental payment towards costs of care, delinquency, contributing to neglect or delinquency" (NCJFCJ, 1980: p. 4). They did note that the least restrictive programming should be used for status offenders and that they should not be detained in a secure facility "unless they have previously run from an appropriate insecure facility" (p. 5).

Overall, then, there was considerable tension about how to respond to status offenders. While many national organizations were advocating the removal of status offenses from youth court jurisdiction, others clearly wanted to retain control of them. Interestingly, the effect on girls charged with these offenses was not consistently mentioned. Although it was well-known that in many jurisdictions girls were more likely than boys to be brought into court and placed in custody for these offenses, that was evidently not always seen as a serious problem. The reason was quite simple: girls needed protection. On the other hand, the main justification offered for removing status offenses from youth court jurisdiction was that youth courts could be doing more harm than good.

Although the JJDPA maintained that status offenders should not be placed in custody, an amendment was introduced in 1980 by Congressman John Ashbrook (Republican from Ohio) that would permit states to create legislation allowing status offenders who violated a court order to be placed in custody, without the state's losing federal funding. Thus, the youth would have to come into court for a status offense, receive an order from the judge, and then violate that order. Upon violation of that order, custody could then be used, and the state would still be in compliance with the JJDPA (assuming the state had passed such a law). Interestingly, during the discussion of this amendment in the House of Representatives—similar to other debates about how to respond to status offenders—when a speaker wanted to talk about the ability to "help" a youth, the typical example involved a girl, not a boy. If, however, a speaker wanted to show how the use of status offenses encroached on due process or civil liberties, an example using a boy was provided.

On November 19, 1980, Ashbrook described his amendment and, in justifying it, used an example of a girl who was abandoned at birth and had therefore been placed in various children's aid homes throughout her life. As a teenager, however, she experienced problems in the various homes and continually ran away. Her problems in the homes were described as being "related to her inability to accept responsibility and her inability to interact with her peers beyond a superficial level" (Congressional Record,

1980: p. H10932). At age 17 she had left another home, and currently the courts did not know her whereabouts. After describing this scenario—the court placing this girl somewhere, only to have her run away—Ashbrook stated that "obviously there is a need to give the courts some authority to deal with a situation such as this. My amendment provides this discretion by . . . enabl[ing] juvenile courts to place status and nonoffenders in secure detention and correctional facilities if they are found to be violation of a valid court order" (Congressional Record, 1980: p. H10932). Only "sugar and spice" needed protection, it seems. Furthermore, the different impact on girls was avoided by removing the initial offense from the ultimate reason that the court order had been placed on a youth. Thus, all offenses for violating valid court orders were seen as similar, and the justification of the use of custody was that the youth had not done what the court had ordered him or her to do. But the original behavior—in effect, the status offense—was untouched and technically unpunished.

There was, however, some opposition to this "valid court order" (VCO) amendment. For example, Congressman Dale Kildee (Democrat from Michigan) argued that "this amendment is not directed at youth who have committed criminal acts, rather it is intended to permit the incarceration of children known as status offenders. . . . If adopted, this amendment would permit us to lapse back to the lazy method of confinement rather than trying to deal with a child's problems in a positive manner" (Congressional Record, 1980: p. H10933). Congressman George Miller (Democrat from California) also questioned, "Why do we not require the courts to become more creative . . . this is really a very good amendment for a lazy judge. All he has to do is lock the child up and somehow that threat is going to turn around years of problems these young people have" (Congressional Record, 1980: pp. H10934–35). Congressman Tom Railsback (Republican from Illinois) also said that "what really disturbs me more than anything is that we are talking really about young people who are runaways. They are truants. They have not committed a serious criminal offense" (Congressional Record, 1980: p. H10937).

The debates continued for close to an hour. Those in favor of the amendment used examples of wanting to hold a runaway until parents came, or of wanting to "strengthen" the power of the court. Sometimes the amendment was portrayed as "helping" youths; other times it was described as a punishment for those who would not accept the authority of the court. Those against the amendment used examples of youths running away from intolerable home situations where they were beaten and ultimately being ordered back by a judge who was unaware of the "logical" reasons the youth had for leaving in the first place. Some were against the amendment whether it was described as a means to help or punish a youth: "Incarceration is difficult to justify as either a treatment or a punishment. Status offenders rarely receive counseling that meets their specific emotional and mental health needs while institutionalized. . . . If status offenders are incarcerated for punishment purposes, institutionalization punishes the less serious offender more than the criminal offender" (Mr. Kildee, Congressional Record, 1980: p. H10933). None, however, said anything about the well-known gender disparity with respect to status offenses or to the potential effect this current amendment could have on girls.

Ultimately the amendment was accepted—55 percent voting for it and 28 percent against it, with 17 percent abstaining (Congressional Record, 1980: p. H10937). After the VCO amendment was passed, some argued that it "effectively gutted . . . [the Juvenile Justice and Delinquency Prevention Act] by permitting judges to reclassify a status offender who violated a court order as a delinquent. This meant that a young woman who ran away from a court-ordered placement (halfway house, foster home, or the like) could be relabeled a delinquent and locked up" (Chesney-Lind and Shelden, 2004: p. 176).

Interestingly, although the VCO amendment was passed in 1980, the debate over how to respond to status offenders—in particular runaways—did not disappear. Concern was again raised in the mid-1980s that the courts had no ability to "help" youths—especially girls—who had run away from home. The Office of Juvenile Justice and Delinquency Prevention produced two reports in the 1980s on "runaway" and "exploited" children and ultimately argued that the courts had no power to take runaway children into custody in order to control and help them (OJJDP, 1985; and OJJDP, 1986). In one report in particular, case studies of girls were presented along with interviews with police and youth court workers who expressed frustration over their inability to incarcerate these girls in order to help get them off the streets (OJJDP, 1985). In the introduction of this report, Al Regnery, then the administrator of the OJJDP, wrote that deinstitutionalization had "darker consequences" because "running away is legal. The question which needs to be asked is whether or not it is in the best interest of children to afford them such a right" (OJJDP, 1985: p. 2).

More recently, the state of Washington in 1995 created "Becca's Law" in response to the case of a 13-year-old runaway girl who was murdered. The law attempts to address a number of issues (truancy and running away in particular), but, most important, it authorizes the creation and use of Secure Crisis Residential Centers to hold runaway youth (for up to five days). That provision of the law puts the state in conflict with the deinstitutionalization requirement of the JJDPA, and since that makes the state not in compliance with the federal act, it has not received full federal funding. Throughout the 1980s and 1990s, then, status offenders, specifically runaway girls, appeared to be a lightning rod for interventionist efforts (see also Chesney-Lind and Shelden, 2004).

Implementation of the JJDPA was, not surprisingly, quite difficult, and there was considerable resistance to its guiding principles. The General Accounting Office (GAO) examined the implementation in 1978 and noted that few states were monitoring their compliance with the federal law. Moreover, they felt that the agency implementing the legislation (the Law Enforcement Assistance Administration [LEAA]) had actually "downplayed its [the act's] importance and to some extent discouraged states from carrying out the Federal requirement" (GAO, 1978, p. 10; cited in Chesney-Lind and Shelden, 2004: p. 175). However, over time changes were seen, and greater compliance was eventually noted. Later GAO reports began finding some evidence of decreases in the numbers of incarcerated status offenders in case studies of selected states, though there were always calls for greater monitoring in order to know whether various jurisdictions were complying (see, for example, GAO, 1983; GAO, 1984; and GAO, 1991). See Appendix C for more details on the 1981 and 1991 reports.

The 1991 GAO report also examined VCOs. They noted that "since the VCO provision took effect, most states have reported to OJJDP that their judges detained juveniles for violating a VCO. According to OJJDP data through December 1988, the most recent year on which OJJDP has complete statistics for all states, 38 states have used VCO exclusions at least once" (GAO, 1991: p. 22). A "VCO exclusion" meant that the state could incarcerate a status offender without jeopardizing its federal funding if the offender did not follow the orders of the court. Unfortunately, there were very few observations or data related to gender—only one figure in an appendix showing the numbers of girls and boys who were detained as status offenders in three facilities in three different states. These data showed that one facility had more girls, one had more boys, and one had equal numbers of the two. It was rather curious, given the known issues with gender and status offenders and the concerns about the use of VCOs, that so little was mentioned about girls in this report.

As the deinstitutionalization effort continued, girls finally became the focus of the 1992 hearings on the reauthorization of the JJDPA. In his opening statement to the hearings, the chairman, Congressman Matthew Martínez (Democrat from California), said:

In today's hearing we are going to address female delinquency and the provision of services to girls under this Act. There are many of us that believe that we have not committed enough resources to that particular issue. There are many of us who realize that problems for young ladies are increasing, ever increasing, in our society and they are becoming more prone to end up in gangs, in crime, and with other problems that they have always suffered. Girls committing the juvenile crimes and offenses are often ignored, even though they account today for a significant percentage of the juvenile delinquent population. However, generally, they commit different kinds of crimes than boys, crimes where the girls are more a threat to themselves than they are to the community. A high percentage of girls committing delinquency offenses are committing status offenses such as running away, anti-social behavior and cutting school. In fact, studies show that one-fifth of the girls arrested are arrested simply for running away, and even though there are four times more arrests of boys than girls every year, girls account for 56 percent of the arrests for running way and 33 percent of the arrests for curfew violations. Even though there is a difference in types of offenses committed between boys and girls, on the whole we are not providing specialized services for girls in the juvenile justice system. Therefore, they are receiving less and unequal treatment than boys when they are arrested. . . . We treat our female delinquents differently than we treat our boys. We try to protect them. If a young woman has run away and the authorities think she is sexually or physically abused at home, they will not return her to the home. But they do not want to turn her out on the streets where she can be exploited. Without any program especially for girls, there is only one alterative. The authorities put her into juvenile detention with a valid court order to protect her, and hold her there longer than they would any boys. I wonder why, why are there no alternatives than youth jail for her? (U.S. House of Representatives, 1992: p. 2)

A substantial portion of the report focused on the programming and treatment needs of girls. In the end, additional money was set aside for the JJDPA grant programs for states wishing to prohibit gender bias in placements and treatments and for states to develop needed gender-specific services. In addition, from these hearings grew the first GAO report on gender discrimination in youth court processing (GAO, 1995). This 1995 report did not find consistent evidence of gender bias when examining how status offenses were adjudicated. Once factors such as age, race, prior contact with police, prior offense history, pretrial detention, and so on were controlled for, there were inconsistent findings across states and across types of status offenses with respect to how these cases were handled. Sometimes boys seemed to be treated more harshly at various decision points, in some jurisdictions, and for some offenses, while other times girls were. Given the inconsistencies, the report concluded that overall there were minimal gender biases. It should be noted, of course, that the focus was on the *court* processing of these cases. Potentially discriminatory practices at earlier stages—such as apprehending girls but not boys for engaging in sex—were not investigated.

More recently, policy concerns about girls in the juvenile justice system have focused more on treatment needs. For example, in 2001 the American Bar Association and National Bar Association reported that there was a serious lack of prevention, diversion, and treatment alternatives for girls in the justice system (ABA-NBA, 2001). In addition, the reauthorization of the JJDPA in 2003 still provided money to states to develop plans for providing gender-specific programs. Also in 2003 the OJJDP awarded funding to the Research Triangle Institute to establish the Girls Study Group. This large, multidisciplinary project will explore causes of delinquency, treatment effectiveness, treatment options, and juvenile justice processing of girls.

Overall, then, since the JJDPA was enacted, there have clearly been gains made to deinstitutionalize status offenders—and girls have undoubtedly benefited from such efforts. Current efforts now appear to be focused on understanding the specific needs and treatment of girls. Interestingly, though, over the past few decades, when there has been interest in status offenses at the federal or national level, girls have been inconsistently highlighted. Some reports and discussions mention the disproportionate effect these offenses have on girls, while other times nothing is mentioned. And although the number of status offenders incarcerated in correctional facilities appears to have decreased since the 1974 JJDPA, there are still concerns, in particular about the use of VCOs, the use of private facilities (see Chesney-Lind and Irwin, 2008), and simply moving those accused of status offenses such as incorrigibility from one system to another, to be ultimately incarcerated. Each of these concerns is especially pronounced when focused on girls.

What we are left with, however, is profound ambivalence about the use of juvenile justice law to intervene in the lives of apparently troubled girls. The idea in the United States that juvenile justice interventions in the lives of youths should be limited to instances in which normal criminal acts have apparently been committed was not a widely held position during the latter half of the 20th century. Hence, it would not be surprising to find that girls, more than boys, would be disproportionately targeted for interventions, whether these offenses are justified as status offenses or as violations of valid court orders.

As we will see, however, north of the border, the arguments and the law played out somewhat differently. Whether these differences made much of a difference to the girls with whom interventionists were concerned is, of course, a different matter that will be dealt with in a later chapter.

Chapter 4

Paternalism and the Social Control of Adolescent Girls: Juvenile Justice Reform in Canada

Canada's history of the development of the juvenile justice system is, like that of the United States, more complex than it is often described as being. Steps had been taken to treat youths differently from adults long before the first juvenile courts appeared. Though it took until 1894 for the first juvenile court in Canada to receive formal legislative recognition, legislation had been passed almost 40 years earlier that emphasized the necessity of providing different treatment for juveniles.[1]

The Canadian federation was established in 1867. Legislative powers were shared thereafter between the federal and provincial governments: legislation involving the criminal law became the exclusive jurisdiction of the federal government, while the provinces were in charge of administering those laws. As part of their responsibility for health and welfare, the provinces assumed jurisdiction over children in need of care or protection, as well as over various court services, police, prisons, and institutions for juveniles. Some provinces used their jurisdiction over juvenile institutions to establish institutions for abandoned children (typically called "industrial schools") and for juvenile offenders ("reform schools").[2]

In 1894 the federal government legislated its first separate juvenile court, indicating, among other things, that "the trials for young persons apparently under the age of sixteen years shall take place without publicity and separately and apart from the trials of other accused persons." The legislation also stated that youths "shall be kept in custody separate from other persons" (An Act Respecting Arrest, Trial and Imprisonment of Youthful Offenders, 1894: sec. 1, p. 337). Ontario also created more sentencing options for juveniles. For example, instead of only the two options of a fine or imprisonment, youths under the age of 14 could be committed to "any home for destitute and neglected children . . . or . . . any children's aid society" (An Act Respecting Arrest, Trial and Imprisonment of Youthful Offenders, 1894: sec. 3, p. 337). Interestingly, in Ontario the local Children's Aid Society was to be notified of any charge against a boy younger than 12 or a girl younger than 13. Children's Aid could then advise the court on the case, and, instead of having a trial and sentencing the youth, the judge could order Children's Aid to take the child or commit the child to a foster home. The judge could also impose a fine, impose a suspended sentence, or, if the child was "willfully wayward and unmanageable," commit the child to a reformatory (if a boy) or house of refuge (if a girl). This could be seen as an early instance of treating a child as a status offender.

Thus, during the late 1800s there were developments across Canada that established separate proceedings and institutions for juveniles. And in the latter part of the 19th century, separate courts were beginning to be developed. There was also a focus on reforming youths who committed criminal offenses and perhaps an early articulation of status offenders, though this was applicable only to girls under 13 and to boys under 12 in Ontario. However, the most well-known and comprehensive legislation—which aimed to bring youths in youth court not only for federal (criminal) offenses, but also for violation of provincial and municipal by-laws—was passed in 1908.

The Juvenile Delinquents Act, 1908–84

The Act Respecting Juvenile Delinquents (Juvenile Delinquents Act, or JDA) was passed in 1908. Like juvenile legislation in the United States, it defined "delinquency" quite broadly and was based on the improvement of children's welfare. When the act was first passed, a juvenile delinquent was any boy or girl under the age of 16

> who violates any provision of *The Criminal Code,* chapter 146 of the Revised Statutes, 1906, or any Dominion or provincial statute, or of any by-law or ordinance of any municipality, for which violation punishment by fine or imprisonment may be awarded; or, who is liable by reason of any other act to be committed to an industrial school or juvenile reformatory under the provisions of any Dominion or provincial statute. (JDA, 1908: sec. 2(c), p. 303)

Section 31 of the act also emphasized to the provinces that this federal legislation was to be implemented with a focus on rehabilitation and treatment as opposed to punishment:

This Act shall be liberally construed to the end that its purpose may be carried out, to wit: That the care and custody and discipline of a juvenile delinquent shall approximate as nearly as may be that which should by given by its parents, and that as far as practicable every juvenile delinquent shall be treated, not as a criminal, but as a misdirected and misguided child, and one needing aid, encouragement, help and assistance. (JDA, 1908: sec. 31, p. 401)

This broad definition of delinquency and the welfare focus of the act created an interesting situation. Canada's constitutional mandate making the provincial governments responsible for welfare legislation and the federal government responsible for criminal legislation meant that the federal government could not create civil legislation applicable to all of the provinces. Thus, in order for the federal government to claim jurisdiction over offending by youths, it had to pass criminal legislation, but with an emphasis on welfare-based responses to youths who were adjudicated delinquent under the act. Creating an offense of delinquency for those who violated any law at any level of government or who were, in effect, troublesome accomplished the legislative goal of being welfare oriented while remaining under the criminal-law jurisdiction of the federal government.

When the act was initially passed, it was clear that the intent was focused in large part on diverting youths from the adult justice system. However, over time additional sections were added that aimed to further encourage the provinces to treat the child not as a criminal but as a misguided and misdirected child. Thus one sees, as the welfare-based sections of the legislation grew, repeated tensions between criminal-law principles and child welfare.

The parliamentary debates around the passage of this act in 1908 suggest that in Canada, as in the United States, there were simultaneous endorsements of both diversion and intervention, though the overwhelming majority of the discussion focused on the act's diversionary benefit. The minister of justice, Sir A. B. Ayelsworth, said when introducing the bill that "where this Act is not in force, if any one under the age of 16 years commits an offence, the only recourse under the present law is prosecution leading to fine and imprisonment. This statute will confer upon the court a much wider discretion so as to avoid going the length of imprisonment where it is a young offender" (Canadian Parliament, 1908: p. 12403).

There were, however, some concerns about the informal nature of the process. In particular, a Conservative member of Parliament—Edward Lancaster—was troubled by the lack of a guarantee of legal representation for youths. When Lancaster questioned the minister of justice about the lack of legal representation and jury trials, the minister replied that the "Bill would prevent the advantage of trial by jury, but possibly there are countervailing advantages to the person accused which would be of even greater value. The provision is distinctly made that a child is not to be sent to a common gaol before or after sentence" (Canadian Parliament, 1908: p. 12404). Lancaster then countered, "You could provide for a less severe penalty without depriving the child of the advantage of trial by jury" (Canadian Parliament, 1908: p. 12404). However, the minster of justice justified his objection to jury trials by citing the publicity that attached to them: "The whole idea is to avoid that [publicity]. There is even a provision to prohibit the publication of offenses of young people in the newspaper" (Canadian Parliament, 1908: p. 12404).

While the minister of justice was focused primarily on the diversionary benefits of the act, one member of Parliament did appear to hold hopes for interventions. George Perry Graham—a Liberal member of Parliament—cited Judge Benjamin B. Lindsey's Denver, Colorado, court as a model for what the JDA might be able to accomplish—"trying to reclaim rather than to condemn the child" (Canadian Parliament, 1908: p. 12404). In these debates, however, Graham appeared to be in the minority. Most members of Parliament focused on diversion. The interventionist ideals became enshrined more clearly in later amendments to the act by both broadening the definition of delinquency and creating another statement on how juvenile delinquents should be treated.

In 1924 an amendment was introduced to broaden the definition of delinquency to include "sexual immorality or any other form of vice." The "sexual immorality" part of this phrase engendered little debate. Instead, the concerns centered on the addition of "any other form of vice" as an offense. For example, Arthur Meighen—a Conservative member of parliament, who was prime minister for a few months in 1921 and 1926—noted that this addition

virtually constitutes, as respects a juvenile, a new offence. I am not saying that, if it does so, it is wrong, but the effect of it should be clearly understood. The Criminal Code clearly defines immorality of this character, but heretofore no juvenile guilty of it was a juvenile delinquent within the meaning of the act. If this goes through it virtually makes the judge the arbiter of what constitutes a vice on the part of a juvenile delinquent. Are we not going to get into a condition where we will have a rather variegated system of jurisprudence under which we will have a Nova Scotia magistrate deciding a thing that is all right, and a Manitoba magistrate deciding that it is all wrong? (Canadian Parliament, 1924: p. 3508)

However, the Liberal minister of justice, Ernest Lapointe, argued for the addition of "any other form of vice," saying that "the object is to have young boys and girls under the supervision of probation officers with the object of trying to reform them. A discretion will be given to the magistrates which they did not formally possess. I do not think the provision is likely to be abused. In any case, the amendment is in the interest of the children themselves, and for the proper administration of the act" (Canadian Parliament, 1924: p. 3508). However, after more criticisms about the broad scope of this phrase, the ultimate power given magistrates to define what was criminal, and the variation across provinces that could result, the minister of justice began to back away from his proposed amendment, saying, "I have taken the responsibility of presenting this bill to the House. But I did not originate the clause myself" (p. 3509). He then proposed removing the words "or any other form of vice," to which everyone agreed. However, one of main opponents, Meighen, changed his mind later and became concerned that he was "disarming the organizations that have to deal with these matters." He suggested adding "who is guilty of sexually immorality or any *similar* form of vice." All agreed, and the new definition was accepted. It was in effect until 1984, when the JDA was replaced.

What is interesting about the debates at this time was that although the addition of the phrase "sexual immorality" would undoubtedly disproportionately impact girls, nothing was said about girls specifically. Instead, the debates centered on the power magistrates would have to decide what was criminal if the phrase "any other form of vice" was added. Moreover, in all the examples of the dangers of this amendment, members of Parliament described boys engaging in minor behaviors that could, under the proposed change, be considered a "vice" and therefore "delinquent." The fact that girls would be brought in for similarly insignificant behaviors under "sexual immorality" was irrelevant—or, perhaps, desirable.

Interestingly, in the late 1970s—what turned out to be the dying days of the JDA—there were a few cases across the provinces that addressed "sexual immorality." These involved issues of whether a boy had "contributed to the delinquency" of a girl by having sexual intercourse with her. However, in order to answer that question, the courts had to first address whether sexual intercourse constituted "delinquency" for girls. The cases tended to categorize sexual intercourse as "delinquency" if the boy was considerably older than a girl. However, if the youths were of the same age, then the courts tended to argue that "sexual activity resulting from the high spirits, exuberance, curiosity or healthy affection of the young are a concern only of the young and their parents—not of the Courts" (*R. v. Frost,* 1977: p. 73). At the same time, however, distinctions were made between sexual activity between a girl and her boyfriend and sexual activity generally: "Sexual immorality within the meaning of the Juvenile Delinquents Act connotes sexual behavior which is not publicly acceptable because it is wrong, bad, vicious or promiscuous" (Garson, in *R. v. Frost,* 1977: p. 71; see also *R. v. Tomlin,* 1977).

The final change to the JDA, which clearly cemented—at least symbolically—its welfare orientation, was a clarification in 1929 of how juveniles should be treated under the act. A section was added to it that said, "Where a child is adjudged to have committed delinquency he shall be dealt with, not as an offender, but as one in a condition of delinquency and therefore requiring help and guidance and proper supervision" (JDA, 1929: sec. 3(2), p. 3). There was not much debate around adding this section. Instead, the debates focused on other aspects of the act—namely the broad definition of delinquency and the variation across provinces in the maximum age of juvenile court jurisdiction.

Both Liberals and Conservatives questioned whether bringing youths into the justice system for violating a provincial or municipal by-law was appropriate.[3] None, however, questioned whether "sexual immorality" should be included in the definition of delinquency. The Liberal minister of justice Lapointe defended both the broad definition and bringing youths in for violating provincial or municipal by-laws because "such a child would be treated with benevolence and care" (Canadian Parliament, 1929: p. 2569). Even the Conservative Party leader who was in opposition at the time agreed with Lapointe, and thus members from both their parties questioned them about the wisdom of including provincial and municipal by-laws in the definition of delinquency. Most of the questions were met with a simple answer: "It has always been that way" (Canadian Parliament, 1929: p. 2569).

Also at this time an amendment was introduced to clarify the maximum age at which a child could still fall under juvenile court jurisdiction. The presumption was that the maximum age would be 16, but provinces could raise it to 18. Although there were concerns about the lack of uniformity this created, no one questioned the presumption that the increase to 18 could "apply either to boys only or to girls only or to both boys and girls" (JDA, 1929: sec. 2(a), p. 203). In fact, in later years one province—Alberta—had different maximum ages for boys and girls.

Interestingly, one Conservative member of Parliament, Peter McGibbon, foreshadowing concerns that followed over subsequent decades, questioned whether the juvenile justice system was as benevolent and caring as the minister of justice suggested: "It must be remembered that punishment is a means to an end, and I am rather afraid that much of the legislation we pass here has not that object in view, but rather that punishment is really punishment, instead of reform" (Canadian Parliament, 1929: p. 2570). An amendment was also introduced, which was not even discussed but was simply agreed to by everyone, that allowed youths to appeal youth court decisions. However, permission to appeal was to be granted only at the discretion of a judge, and only in extraordinary circumstances (Gagnon, 1984).

There were minor amendments to the JDA over the next 50 years, but nothing that rivaled the importance of the broad definition of a juvenile delinquent. However, in 1938 a significant governmental report on the correctional system of Canada was published. The *Report of the Royal Commission to Investigate the Penal System of Canada* (the Archambault Commission) included a chapter on the operation of juvenile courts and endorsed both the diversionary and the interventionist goals of a separate youth justice system. For example, the commissioners noted that "during the present century, there has been a constantly increasing recognition by public opinion of the fact that, in a wise administration of justice, children should not be dealt with in the same manner, or according to the same standards of trial and punishment, as adults" (Canada, *Report,* 1938: p. 182). Clearly, then, diversion from the adult criminal justice process was seen as a worthy goal of the JDA. The commissioners also noted that, despite the legal requirements that youths be kept separate from adults, in many jurisdictions this was not happening. This was an early acknowledgment that the true effects of the act could be very different from its original intent.

The commission also highlighted some of the recommendations made in a report by the Departmental Committee on the Treatment of Young Offenders that had been presented by the secretary of state for home affairs to the British Parliament in 1927. Specifically, they highlighted the recommendation from that report that young people should have a right to a trial based on principles of English law. Given that the JDA was developed by the federal government and was therefore *criminal* legislation, the Canadian commission recommended that youth be represented by counsel. At the same time, however, they said that representation by counsel should only apply to a "portion of the cases"—presumably those that involved more serious criminal offenses or perhaps those involving a formal trial.

And although they wanted legal representation for those cases, they also suggested rules that would tend to lead the proceedings to be seen as other than a court. In this context, for example, it was suggested that "gowns are unnecessary and ought not to be worn. . . . He [the judge] should preserve a dignified informality to gain, and maintain, the confidence of the child who comes before him" (Canada, 1938: p. 187).

Thus, as in the United States, concerns about the lack of due process and the broad definition of delinquency were voiced long before the 1960s. In addition, there appeared to be a simultaneous endorsement of both diversion and intervention. Also as in the United States, almost nothing was mentioned about girls specifically. In the 1938 report on the penal system, for example, the 418-page report only had two chapters—totaling 11 pages—devoted to women. Although the report at times referred to "girls," the authors were clearly talking only about adult women prisoners—and said little more than that their crimes were not as serious as men's and they should not be incarcerated.

Reforms in the 1960s and 1970s

Youth justice reforms were more seriously entertained by the government of Canada during the 1960s and 1970s. It is perhaps here that the Canadian history begins to diverge from the American. Although the recommendations and concerns were similar in both countries during this time, the fact that Canada's youth justice legislation was criminal may have given added weight to the arguments in favor of due-process concerns and the removal of status offenses. People could not, for example, argue as they did in the United States that the lack of due process was justified because the cases were civil procedures.

In 1961 the Canadian Department of Justice started a process of examining the need for change by setting up for the first time a committee whose sole task was to examine the youth justice system. The committee produced a report in 1965 that included about 100 recommendations, some of them focused on narrowing the definition of delinquency and introducing more due-process elements (MacLeod, 1965). This was the first step on a path toward removing the welfare justifications.

Because the JDA was criminal legislation, the committee was quite concerned with the broad definition of delinquency, and for the first time it was officially acknowledged that including "sexual immorality" in the definition of delinquency had a disproportionate effect on girls (although no data were provided):

A statute, especially a quasi-criminal one, should not be any more vague or ambiguous than is absolutely necessary. . . . it has been urged that there is an element of discrimination inherent in the operation of the "sexual immorality" clause. Studies of the juvenile court show that, for one reason or another, it is usually persons from a lower economic level who are charged with this offence. More importantly, perhaps, the great majority of children adjudged delinquent because of sexual misconduct are girls. Indeed, some jurisdictions have set the juvenile age for girls higher than for boys in order that teen-age girls can be "protected" for a longer period of time from the consequences of their own waywardness. . . . It is our view that broad offence provisions of the kind that are now contained in the Act are justified only if there is no other reasonable means available to ensure that children are protected from moral or other danger. This is not, in our opinion, the case. . . . We do not deny the importance of dealing with behavioural problems early. What we question is the means adopted to achieve this result. . . . We think it a sound proposition to assert, therefore, that as a matter of public policy quasi-criminal legislation should not be used to achieve welfare purposes if those purposes can be achieved by non-criminal legislation. To this end we recommend that children be charged only with specific offences as is the case in proceedings against adults, and that any provisions in the law that are inconsistent with this principle be repealed. (MacLeod, 1965: pp. 66–67)

The committee ultimately recommended that the federal legislation governing delinquency be concerned only with specific criminal offenses and provincial and municipal by-laws. They recommended the removal of those behaviors that might cause a child to be described as "incorrigible," "unmanageable," or "in moral danger" from the jurisdiction of the JDA. Instead, they believed, provincial statutes could best respond to these types of behaviors, given that the provinces were responsible for welfare legislation. They also wanted to drop the terminology of "incorrigible" or "in moral danger" and instead, as in the United States, call these youths "persons in need of supervision" or "in need of protection and discipline." Although youths would not be convicted of a crime if they were adjudged to be "in need of supervision," the committee still recommended that the provinces have the authority to commit them to a training school. "Neglected" or "dependent" children were seen to be different from those "in need of supervision," and thus the committee argued that the former could not be committed to training schools, while the latter could be. Clearly, then, at this time the committee was still comfortable with girls being placed in custody for "morally inappropriate" behavior; they simply did not want that to happen under federal criminal legislation.

The committee also recommended that there be a uniform maximum age for juvenile court jurisdiction across Canada. At the time, the act allowed the age to range from 16 to 18, and the committee discussed the provincial variation, in Alberta most notably, where the maximum age was 16 for boys and 18 for girls (see MacLeod, 1965: p. 54). In arguing for uniformity, however, they did not address the gender disparity specifically, instead arguing more broadly that disparity generally could be problematic because a "federal statute, especially one concerned with matters of criminal law, should not be open to the charge of discrimination" (MacLeod, 1965: p. 61).[4] Because the law was criminal, there was a need to make it apply equally to everyone, and the varying age ranges were therefore seen as problematic. The committee members were clearly concerned with equality across provinces, as opposed to gender equality, but girls would nonetheless benefit. Finally, like many U.S. states at this time, the committee recommended more due-process procedures, such as the right to retain counsel and appeal decisions.

Based on the committee's recommendations, the government of Canada produced draft legislation entitled An Act Respecting Children and Young Persons in 1967. After considerable discussion with the provinces it was introduced into Parliament in 1970 as the Young Offenders Act (Fox, 1977). The bill received harsh criticism from various groups because it incorporated principles of criminal law and was thus seen as overly legalistic and simply a "criminal code for children" (Fox, 1977; Fox and Spencer, 1971; and Gagnon, 1984). And although some academics applauded the due-process elements, they criticized the bill for being overly complex (Grygier, 1968). Interestingly, although the bill did incorporate due-process elements such as the right to be informed of legal representation (though it did not guarantee such representation) and making the process much more formal, it still retained some of the welfare terminology. One provision in particular stated that youths "shall be dealt with not in a punitive manner, but as a child or young person requiring help, guidance and proper supervision" (Department of the Solicitor General, 1967: sec. 4, p. 14). Clearly, however, the greater formality of the proceedings, coupled with ability to convict youths of specific offenses instead of "delinquency," was seen as a significant step away from the JDA.

The bill never passed. However, during the period in which it was being debated, a case was proceeding through the court system that challenged the broad definition of delinquency. In effect, the case concerned whether the (federal criminal) JDA had authority over provincial statutes (such as the highway traffic laws). Though this could be seen as a narrow issue, in addressing it the courts had to look carefully at the definition of delinquency. This case ultimately ended up in the Supreme Court in the 1960s.

In 1960 a British Columbia youth, identified as "Smith," was charged with speeding and was tried as an adult under the provincial motor vehicle act. The magistrate was aware that Smith was a juvenile but decided that it was in the best interest of the child that the case proceed through regular (traffic) court instead of youth court. The youth was subsequently found guilty and ordered to pay a fine of $400. Smith appealed the case to the Supreme Court of British Columbia (a trial court, which, as a minor part of its responsibilities, dealt with appeals from juvenile courts), arguing that he should have been tried under the JDA. On appeal, the conviction was quashed, and the judge agreed that the youth should have been treated not as an adult, but as a youth, and therefore been subject to the JDA. The case was appealed again to the British Columbia Court of Appeal, where the judges again decided in favor of the youth. The final appeal—to the Supreme Court of Canada—resulted in yet another decision in favor of the youth. In 1969 the Supreme Court agreed with the two lower (appeals) courts and said that the youth should have been tried under the JDA. In defending the broad definition, the court argued that

> consistent with the declared purpose of the Act and obviously designed for its attainment, these operative provisions [treating the youth not as a criminal, etc] are . . . illustrative of the true nature and character of this legislation. They are directed to juveniles who violate the law or indulge in sexual immorality or any other similar form of vice or who, by reason of any other act, are liable to be committed to an industrial school or juvenile reformatory. They are meant—in the words of Parliament itself—"to check their evil tendencies and to strengthen their better instincts." They are primarily prospective in nature. And in essence, they are intended to prevent these juveniles from becoming prospective criminals and to assist them to be law-abiding citizens. Such objectives are clearly within the judicially defined field of criminal law. For the effective pursuit of these objectives, Parliament . . . deemed it necessary to create the offence of "delinquency," an offence embracing, *inter alia,* all punishable breaches of the public law, whether defined by Parliament or the Legislatures and to adopt, for the prosecution of this offence, an enforcement process specially

adapted to the age and impressibility of juveniles and fundamentally different, in pattern and purpose, from the one governing the case of adults. (*Attorney-General of British Columbia v. Smith*, 1969: pp. 250–51)

Thus, the broad definition of delinquency was upheld. In their judgment, the justices of the Supreme Court of Canada even addressed the issue of disparity, noting that "it matters not . . . that there be a lack of uniformity in the application or operation of the Act . . . in the proscribed conduct—the holding of which constitutes, under the Act, the offence of delinquency—may vary, throughout Canada" (*Attorney-General of British Columbia v. Smith*, 1967: p. 251). Although this case was not focused on the different impact the JDA had on girls compared to boys, it is noteworthy that the Supreme Court defended the broad definition, including "sexual immorality," and also defended provincial disparities in what constituted delinquency. Clearly, both of those issues affected girls: if the courts were willing to tolerate provincial disparity in the administration of a federal statute, they would likely tolerate gender disparity as well. Moreover, this 1969 decision came after the Department of Justice's Committee on Delinquency (1965) report, which noted gender disparity in who was being brought into court for "sexual immorality" and thus argued to remove it from the jurisdiction of the JDA. Interestingly, this decision appeared to raise concerns among those who wanted the act to contain strong welfare principles, because the judges in the Supreme Court referred to it as "criminal legislation." Some were concerned that "if the appeal courts fail to understand the social welfare philosophy of the juvenile court, in the *Smith* case, then the children's court may well suffer other incursions on its powers" (Parker, 1970: p. 174).

In 1973 the Solicitor General of Canada appointed another committee to reassess youth justice. A report, including draft legislation, was published in 1975, and this one went further than the previous one. Although the commissioners did not recognize the existence of gender disparity, they recommended removing not only "sexual immorality" from the jurisdiction of the youth courts, but also provincial statutes and municipal by-laws:

> We are concerned that provisions of the Juvenile Delinquents Act make non-criminal behaviour including truancy, and sexual immorality, offences which have come to be referred to as "status offences." Thus, young persons are being unnecessarily criminalized for behaviour which would not be an offense in the case of an adult.

We believe that the only reasonable solution to this discrimination is the elimination of "status offences." . . . We further believe that the legislation should confine itself to offences against federal statutes and regulations and should leave it to the provinces to deal with offences against provincial statues and municipal by-laws. (Solicitor General of Canada, 1975: pp. 17–18)

They also noted the varying age ranges—again commenting that Alberta had different maximum ages for boys and girls—and, while not addressing the gender disparity, suggested a uniform maximum age of 18 and a minimum age of 14. Those under 14 would be dealt with by way of provincial welfare legislation (Solicitor General of Canada, 1975).

In the end, then, this report and draft legislation incorporated more criminal-law principles than did its predecessor. However, the preamble to the bill stated its overall goals, and the commissioners attempted to blend welfare aspects with criminal-law principles. In particular, the preamble stated that young people "should be considered as persons who, because of their state of dependency and level of development and maturity, have special needs and require aid, encouragement and guidance and, where appropriate, supervision, discipline and control. . . . Young people have basic rights and fundamental freedoms no less than those of adults."

Ultimately, this set of proposals never made it into the formal legislative process. However, in anticipation of legislation to come, the Canadian government in 1977 published some highlights for "new youth justice legislation." The highlights from the policy document were quite similar to the previous bill—indeed, they were based on many of the same recommendations from the 1975 report (Solicitor General of Canada, 1977). There were some changes with respect to the maximum and minimum age ranges—in particular, this policy document suggested that provinces be allowed to keep the varying age ranges, and thus Alberta could still have two different ages for girls and boys. This paper, however, like the 1975 draft bill, restricted youth court jurisdiction to federal criminal offenses, and in the preamble there was still some suggestion of a welfare approach: "young persons require supervision, discipline and control, but also, because of their state of dependency and level of development and maturity, young persons have special needs and require guidance and assistance" (Solicitor General of Canada, 1977: p. 3).

There was an election as this policy document was being discussed, and the Conservatives, who were in opposition, formed the new government in 1979. Although their government only lasted about nine months before another election was called, they managed to outline some youth justice legislation during that time (Solicitor General of Canada, 1979). It was, for the most part, identical to the outline of the Young Offenders Act that had been proposed by the Liberals in 1977.

The (minority) Conservative government fell in late 1979, and after the ensuing election the Liberals regained power (as a majority government). The Liberals introduced new youth justice legislation entitled the Young Offenders Act. However, as the bill was going through the legislative process, Canada acquired a Charter of Rights and Freedoms, which, among other things, guaranteed "equal protection and equal benefit of the law without discrimination and, in particular, without discrimination based on race, national or ethnic origin, colour, religion, sex, age or mental or physical disability" (Canadian Charter of Rights and Freedoms, 1982: sec. 15(1)). The youth justice legislation was therefore amended during the legislative process to set a uniform maximum age of 18 for the whole country. The bill passed in 1982 and went into effect in 1984. That age range—the 12th to the 18th birthday, which went into effect in 1985—still stands. It was set as a result of a combination of political necessity (the perception or assumption of a newly established constitutional requirement) and political compromise. There is, however, still pressure to lower both ages, though no serious discussion has occurred since 1982 about having different age ranges for girls and boys.

The Young Offenders Act, 1984–2003

As already mentioned, the Young Offenders Act (YOA) eliminated status offenses and created uniform maximum and minimum age ranges. The jurisdiction of the act was limited to federal offenses, and youths were to be charged with specific criminal or other federal offenses. Due-process rights (e.g., the right to a lawyer, rights of appeal, definite sentences, and a hint of proportional sentencing) were all now part of the youth justice system in Canada. Nevertheless, legislators were reluctant to remove some of the welfare language. This resulted in some inconsistency and tension: young persons might require "supervision, discipline and control," but they might also have "special needs" that "require guidance and assistance" (YOA, sec. 3(1)(c)). The YOA was unambiguously, however, criminal law. Though carefully referred to throughout the act as "dispositions," sentences under the YOA were now definite sentences (with maximum custody terms of two or three years, depending on statutory maxima in the adult Criminal Code).

Symbolically, one important change brought about by the proclamation of the YOA was that it put an end to the court's ability to turn a criminal matter into a child welfare matter. Under the JDA the court, after finding a young person delinquent, could "commit the child to the charge of any children's aid society" (JDA, sec. 20(1)(h)). This was no longer possible after the YOA became law. At least in theory, there were two separate approaches: proceedings under the provincial child welfare laws, or charges under the federal (criminal) young offender laws. The YOA made no reference to the provincial child welfare laws.

There were, however, continued conflicts between criminal-law and welfare principles. One case that ended up in the Supreme Court in the 1990s exemplified the classic tension between criminal law and welfare. A boy, one of nine children and with a "depressing" family history (according to the court), was sentenced to two years in open custody for three counts of break, enter, and theft, and one count of breach of probation. It is worth noting that a two-year sentence was the maximum available under the law. The child had an extensive prior record. His parents appeared to the court to be "prone to alcohol abuse" and violent with each other and with the children. Eight of the nine children had histories of youth (criminal) court involvement. The Supreme Court of Canada decided that "the home situation is a factor that should always be taken into account in fashioning the appropriate disposition. . . . Intolerable conditions in the home indicate both a special need for care and the absence of any guidance within the home." The Court further decided that "proportionality has greater significance in the sentencing of adults than the sentencing of young offenders. For the young, a proper disposition must take into account not only the seriousness of the offence but also all other relevant factors" (*R. v. M. (J. J.)*, 1993: p. 423).

In that case, then, the Supreme Court of Canada essentially noted that child saving was alive and well under the YOA. Interestingly, however, three years later the government introduced an amendment stating that custody could not be used for welfare purposes. Specifically, judges were told that "an order of custody shall not be used as a substitute for appropriate child protection, health or other social measures" (YOA: sec. 24(1.1)(a), p. 43). Thus, in 1996, the federal government essentially tried to "undo" the 1993 Supreme Court decision that justified long custodial sentences based on the needs of the young person.

There were other amendments to the YOA during the late 1980s and 1990s. The majority of these, however, either focused on responding to the public perception of leniency and thus increased the length of custodial dispositions (for those found guilty of murder in youth court), or aimed to appear to facilitate the transfer of youths to adult court. These changes ended up being more symbolic than anything else, for the operation of the justice system did not change (Doob and Sprott, 2004). For example, on two separate occasions the government amended the YOA in order to make it apparently easier for judges to transfer cases to youth court. Neither amendment appears to have affected the number of youths transferred to adult court: that figure stayed relatively stable, at an average of about 82 cases per year (of approximately 80,000–100,000 cases per year) for the entire time the YOA was in place (Doob and Sprott, 2004).[5]

An amendment introduced in 1986, however, created a new offense when a youth breached a condition of probation. When the YOA took effect in 1984, a young person who breached a condition of a probation order could be brought back into court and resentenced for the original offense. However, in 1986 a new offense under the YOA was created: failure to comply with a disposition. This new offense was described as being justified because it would streamline the procedure, allowing the police to respond quickly to violations rather than to wait for a judge to review the initial disposition. Moreover, it was seen by some as problematic that adults could be charged with breaches of probation whereas youths apparently could not. This amendment was seen as rectifying that problem, or at least clarifying the options that were available. Thus, from 1987 on, when a youth breached a condition of probation, the youth could clearly be charged with a new offense—"failing to comply with a disposition"—and sentenced for that offense.

Interestingly, there was no debate in Parliament about this amendment. The overall amendment was revised as it went through the legislative process such that noncompliance with treatment orders were exempted from the offense. The view, at the time, was that consent to treatment should be voluntary, so charging a youth criminally for noncompliance was problematic. There were, however, no discussions about how this provision might be implemented with respect to girls and whether it was, in effect, allowing status offenses back into the jurisdiction of the court.

Concerns over bringing youths into youth court for this new offense were soon expressed. Although youth court data for all of Canada were not available until 1991–92, evidence began to come almost immediately from various jurisdictions of increasing numbers of charges for administration of justice offenses, including failing to comply with a disposition (Reitsma-Street, 1993). There was also some early evidence from various jurisdictions of a relatively high use of custody for administration of justice offenses (e.g., Doob and Meen, 1993). This was perplexing to some, because many of the conditions—violating a curfew or failing to reside where ordered—were not in themselves criminal offenses. Thus, a few years after the amendment, some began to argue that these failure-to-comply offenses were really status offenses in disguise (see, for example, Reitsma-Street, 1993).

Reitsma-Street (1993) examined trends in charging youth and noted larger percentage increases in the rates of administration of justice offenses—in particular, failure to comply—for girls than for boys. Others also noted a higher use of custody for girls for these types of noncompliance charges (Conway, 1992). These early studies, however, were based on incomplete data, including, it would appear, somewhat different jurisdictions. It was not until 1991–92 that data were available from all Canadian provinces and territories.

Later studies using national data saw substantial increases in the rates, for both boys and girls, in bringing failure-to-comply cases into court, finding the accused guilty, and sentencing them to custody (Sprott and Doob, 2003). However, there were no data on the types of conditions that led to failure-to-comply charges, so this important dimension of the prosecution of this offense has not been investigated. Early in 2000, however, it was found that youths found guilty of these types of failure-to-comply cases were as likely to receive custody as those found guilty of serious violence——and at times more likely—even when criminal record was controlled for (Sprott, 2006). We discuss these trends in more detail in chapter 6.

Pressure for Change

By 1996 the YOA had been in place for only slightly over a decade, yet it had been amended three times. The two sets of amendments in the 1990s focused on trying to make the act tougher (or at least to make it appear tougher) and focused primarily on increasing the maximum sentences for murder and facilitating transfers to youth court. Since the YOA dealt with only an average of 46 cases of homicide (murder, manslaughter, and infanticide) a year between 1991–92 and 1995–96 (out of an average of over 62,000 yearly cases),[6] this change could not have affected very many youths. Indeed, as we have noted, there did not appear to be any important change in the likelihood that a case would be transferred to adult court. To the extent that this was predictable—and it probably was—it appears likely that changes were made more to placate public opinion than to bring about any change in youth courts.

However, the minister of justice in the mid-1990s, Allan Rock, had another problem. He had promised a full review of the YOA. In fact, two parallel reviews took place *after* the government had passed the last set of amendments in 1995. These two reviews—one by a Federal-Provincial-Territorial Task Force (of government officials from both levels of government) and the other by the Standing Committee on Justice and Legal Affairs of the House of Commons—reported in 1996 and 1997, respectively. The necessity for the federal-provincial-territorial review derived from the fact that the provinces and territories administered the law and would have been left out of the review by the House of Commons committee, except as witnesses before the committee.

The report of the Federal-Provincial-Territorial Task Force (1996) contained one chapter specific to girls. In particular, the report noted that

> one feature of youth justice common to all jurisdictions in Canada is the relatively large number of female offenders re-entering the system as a result of a breach of a community disposition . . . [and] especially [being sent] to custody. . . . The conventional view of the apparent gender differential in the proportions of males versus females committed to custody for breach charges is that this may reflect vestiges of the former use of "immorality and similar forms of vice" provision under the *Juvenile Delinquents Act*. . . . This situation is not unique to Canada. In the United States, status offenders . . . are disproportionately female. (p. 617)

At the same time, however, the report noted that the higher use of custody for girls who breach conditions of probation "is due to the less frequent committals to custody for other types of offences (probably because of the less frequent and serious offending)" (p. 618). In the end, however, the committee noted that a provision in the 1995 amendments stating that custody could not be used as a substitute for child protection, health, or other social measures "may have an impact on the disposition of breach charges" (p. 618). The committee also recommended more alternatives to custody "that apply equally to males and females and should benefit both sexes" (p. 619). Finally, there was concern about the lack of gender-specific programming, but the committee noted that the small numbers of girls made it difficult, fiscally, to provide comprehensive and specialized programming.

The second report—that of the House of Commons' Standing Committee on Justice and Legal Affairs (1997)—said nothing specific about girls nor did it mention the offense of failure to comply with a disposition (breach of probation). The committee acknowledged in the beginning the report does not deal in detail with the situations of aboriginal youth, young women and visible minority young people. This does not mean that the Committee does not appreciate or is unaware of the fact that one's ancestry, gender or race may be important in their contact with the youth justice system. The Committee's mandate called for a general review of youth crime, the youth justice system and the Young Offenders Act. (p. 3)

Thus, out of their 14 recommendations, nothing specifically dealt with girls or the issue of failure to comply with dispositions or breaches of probation. They did, however, note high levels of incarceration and recommended trying to decrease the use of custody for young offenders generally.

In 1997, soon after these bodies reported, a federal election was held, and a new minister of justice was appointed, Anne McLellan. Again, the government had promised to respond to the House of Commons committee reports and to change the YOA. In its response, in May 1998 the minister released a white paper entitled "A Strategy for the Renewal of Youth Justice," which contained broadly written outlines for new legislation that was to replace the YOA.

The Youth Criminal Justice Act, 2002

he two main problems with the administration of the YOA that had been
ntified by the end of the century were that the youth justice system was
g overused for minor offenses, and that too many youths were going to
ly, especially for relatively minor offenses. The Youth Criminal Justice
CJA) aims to create more direct guidance in the use of court and cus-
hat were admonitions under the YOA are now more formal tests or
is not that these hurdles—or guidelines, to use a more common
not be surmounted or avoided. But it became clear with the new
hat Parliament's intent was in many cases.
aneous endorsement of welfare and criminal-law principles
t even under the YOA no longer exists under the YCJA. The
Canada made a clear statement about the act by including
al" in the act's formal name. Although youth justice law
n formally criminal (originally by creating an "offense"
y), the government of Canada chose to emphasize this
w nature.
criminal orientation, an important theme of the act
court, and especially out of custody. The pream-

ble to the act noted, among other things, that "Canadian society should have a justice system . . . that reserves its most serious intervention for the most serious crimes and reduces the over-reliance on incarceration for non-violent young persons." Moreover, judges who hand down sentences are told that the sentence must be proportionate to the seriousness of the offense and the offender's degree of responsibility. Other goals (e.g., rehabilitation of the offender) must be accomplished within the constraints set out by the proportionality principle.

Other than using gender-neutral language and lots of "his and her" constructions, there was nothing specific with respect to girls in this legislation other than a statement in the Declaration of Principle endorsing diversity. This section stated that "within the limits of fair and proportionate accountability, the measures taken against young persons who commit offences should . . . reflect gender, ethnic, cultural and linguistic differences and respond to the needs of aboriginal young persons and of young persons with special requirements" (sec. 3(1)(c)). What is notable, however, and a recurrent theme of the act, is that the principle of proportionality is designed to limit the intrusiveness of any measure imposed on a youth under the act.

As mentioned, the previous legislation had been amended in 1996 to restrict the use of custody for welfare purposes, among other things. Nevertheless, more than a third of youth court judges who were surveyed in early 2001 indicated that in at least half of the cases in which they sentenced an offender to custody, a "poor home or living conditions" was one of the reasons for imposing a custodial sentence (Doob, 2001: p. 39). Even when asked specifically about their reasons for giving *short* custodial sentences, 23 percent of the judges indicated that the social conditions in the youth's life were important factors.

It would appear that Canadian youth court judges wanted to "do good" for youths. Though a similar prohibition against imposing custody for social welfare reasons was written into the YCJA, the act also gave judges one way of dealing with child welfare concerns when they arose in their (criminal) court hearings. Judges were allowed, "at any stage of proceedings against a young person, [to] refer the young person to a child welfare agency for assessment to determine whether the young person is in need of child welfare services" (YCJA, sec. 35). Clearly this was put in as an attempt to allow judges some way to respond to welfare issues but at the same time maintain the distinction between criminal and child welfare concerns. That distinction, however, is still a difficult one for judges to make. As recently as 2007 a 13-year-old girl who was arrested for prostitution was placed in custody for three months for her own protection. In sentencing her, the judge claimed that "she's 13 and she's going to be dead by the time she's 16 if she goes down this road. . . . It's her choice, but it's not going to happen on my watch" (Canadaeast News Service, August 14, 2007). In this case it would appear that the judge saw his child-saving role as trumping the principles that had been approved by Parliament. As in the United States, then, young girls appear to bring the tension between criminal-law and welfare principles to the forefront.

Failing to comply with a sentence is still a criminal offense under the YCJA. However, the act makes it more difficult for a judge to place a youth in custody for this offense. Section 39(1) of the act states that "a youth justice court shall not commit a young person to custody . . . unless" one of four conditions is met: it is a violent offense, the young person has failed to comply with noncustodial sentences, the young person has committed a relatively serious offense and has a history of findings of guilt, or when a noncustodial sentence cannot be found that is proportionate to the seriousness of the offense (this last condition involves exceptional cases). The critical letter in the restriction related to failure to comply is the "s" appended to the end of the word "sentence." In other words, a youth is not automatically eligible for a custodial sentence the first time he or she fails to comply with a sentence. For a youth to be sent to custody for failing to comply with a sentence, there must be at least two instances of failure to comply.

It could be argued, therefore, that the drafters of the YCJA were attempting to remove the last vestiges of the unstable marriage of welfare principles and criminal-law principles that had been contentious for almost a century. Given the history of the use of administration of justice offenses as a means of indirectly creating status offenses, changes that limited the breadth of such offenses as failure to comply with a disposition would, of course, have a different impact on girls than on boys.

Youth Justice in Canada and the United States: Continuities and Discontinuities

Comparing legislative developments in both the United States and Canada reveals some interesting similarities as well as differences. In both countries the youth justice system exposed mixed motives. People simultaneously endorsed both diversionary and interventionist aims when talking about the "benefits" of a separate system for juveniles. People also failed to recognize the tensions or conflicts between the two aims. Those who highlighted the benefits of not treating youths the same as adults (diversion) also extolled the possibility of providing services and rehabilitation, even in the form of incarceration (intervention).

Canada and the United States also periodically recognized the problems with respect to the youth court processing of girls—in particular the larger proportions of girls brought in for status offenses generally and sexual behavior specifically. Yet they did not always respond to the problems and at times seemed to forget the problems altogether. Most recently, for example, the legislative discussions around the VCO strategy in federal law in the United States and failure-to-comply offenses in Canada did not raise concerns with respect to girls in either country, notwithstanding the long history of the problems with girls and status offenses. Both countries also had the tendency to use examples involving girls to create images of how legislative initiatives could provide help or rehabilitation, whereas they used examples of boys when they wanted to create imagines of how various initiatives could infringe on civil liberties.

With respect to differences, though, Canadian youth justice legislation has experienced only two major changes since 1908, when (federal) youth justice legislation first came into force. The legislation has been substantively amended only rarely in its century-long history, and the amendments seem not to have had much impact. The United States, in contrast, not only has the federal JJDPA—which itself has an impact on state legislation—but, in addition, each state produces its own youth justice legislation. Recent decades have seen enormous changes in the way many if not most states deal with almost all aspects of the operation of the juvenile justice system.

It appears, then, that the more dominant role the federal government plays in Canada, as compared to the United States, has resulted in fewer pieces of legislation. The Canadian federal government typically consults extensively with the provincial and territorial governments before developing new legislation. Doob and Webster (2006) and Roberts (1998) have noted that the federal government tends to be reluctant to legislate criminal justice policy without consensus, at least from the larger jurisdictions. The most obvious reason for this is fiscal: as pointed out earlier, the Canadian federal government has the responsibility for making criminal law and has chosen to deal with delinquency matters under criminal law. But because all criminal law (including youth justice law) is administered by the provinces, federal governments are loath to do very much if large numbers of provinces, particularly the large provinces, oppose their actions. This inevitably leads to a rather time-consuming process and thus relatively few pieces of youth justice legislation in comparison with the United States.

In recent years, even after legislation is introduced into Parliament (usually after a substantial amount of consultation), the legislative process is quite long. In the case of the YOA, for example, the law was first introduced into (federal) Parliament in 1981 and was not fully implemented until 1985. In the case of the YCJA, the bill was first introduced into Parliament in March 1999, but it did not complete its legislative history until February 2002. It finally became law on April 1, 2003, slightly more than four years after it was first introduced into Parliament and almost five years after its general principles were made public.

Although Canada has produced less youth justice legislation than has the United States, the direction of legislative reforms throughout the twentieth century were the same in the two counties. Both Canada and the United States moved to eliminate status offenders from the jurisdiction of the youth court and/or from custody. Ultimately however, the United States only succeeded in encouraging the removal of status offenders from custody, whereas Canada removed them (at least in law) from the jurisdiction of the youth court in the early 1980s by the simple act of saying that juvenile justice (criminal) law dealt only with federal offenses. In this way, without having to say so, the federal government precluded the provinces from creating criminal status offenses. Though the provinces could, and did, create status offenses (such as curfew laws) in their own provincial statutes, these could not, in any formal way, be criminal, just as highway traffic offenses are not criminal. Indeed, after 1984, the provinces had to modify their laws and/or procedures in order to be able to deal with youths who had violated municipal or provincial laws.

Although the reforms were similar in nature, Canada's legislative changes dealing with status offenses occurred some number of years after the U.S. (federal) legislation. The United States passed the JJDPA in 1974, but it took Canada until 1984 to pass new legislation that addressed due-process issues and removed status offenders from the jurisdiction of the youth court. But when the Canadian bill became law, status offenses such as sexual immorality were gone completely. The lower levels of government did not need to act. The two countries also created similar amendments to deal with a perception that the courts could not respond to youths who were violating orders of the court—the VCO in the United States and "failing to comply with a disposition" in Canada. Once again, however, Canada was slower in passing its legislation: the VCO amendment was passed in 1980 in the United States, but Canada's failure-to-comply legislation was not passed until 1986.

The next three chapters shift the focus of this book to the actual use of youth court. Though it is tempting—and analytically simple—to assume that changes in the operation of the youth justice system are the consequence of new laws being enacted, in matters such as the manner in which the law responds to misbehavior by young people there is reason to believe that the effect (the change in practice) may precede the cause (the change in law).

For example, the ability of the police to exercise discretion with youths who are apprehended for offending is well established in both countries, and the decision as to whether to use the youth courts to respond to criminal or status offenses is, at least initially, in the hands of the police. To the extent that attitudes have been changing—with respect either to status offenses specifically or to the use of youth court more generally—one might expect that change in the administration of the law would precede, rather than follow, formal legal changes in the countries.

We will begin our investigation of the changes that actually took place by first looking at trends in the use of youth court for criminal offenses from the 1980s until the early 2000s in the United States and from the 1990s until the early 2000s in Canada. (National data appear to be available only for these time periods in both countries.) Thus, in chapter 5 we hope to show how youth courts in both countries have been used for "regular" criminal offenses. With Canada's focus during the 1990s shifting toward developing youth justice policy that incorporates more criminal-law principles, and a desire to reduce the use of court for minor offenses, one tends to see different trends occurring in the two countries. Chapters 5 and 6 explore in detail the trends in adjudicating status offenses, and, more generally, in incarcerating girls, in the United States and Canada.

Chapter 5

The Impact of Law Reform: Deinstitutionalization in Law and Practice in the United States

The last four decades of the twentieth century were turbulent ones for youth justice in both the United States and Canada. As we have discussed, the 1960s brought dramatic changes in the principles that governed offending youths in the United States. The imposition of due-process requirements in the manner in which the state intervened into the lives of youths meant, at least in theory, that there would be controls on the type of behavior that warranted intervention. More obviously, the Supreme Court decisions of the 1960s required different standards to be used when dealing with youths. Nevertheless, it cannot be argued that there was a clear move toward a criminal standard for interventions. The perceived need to intervene in the lives of apparently troubled youths was an issue that did not disappear with the beginning of the concerns over due process that were expressed by the Supreme Court.

In fact, the youth justice systems of the two countries can be seen as struggling with the classic youth justice conflict: the desire to deal fairly with youths who committed criminal offenses, and the desire to intervene in youths' lives in positive ways. Nowhere does this conflict become more salient than in the issue of how the courts deal with behavior that disturbs adults not because it constitutes a criminal offense, but rather because it is more general misbehaving: behavior that generally falls into the category of status offenses. But even though the treatment of girls may have been the site on which this conflict played out, the arguments—at least in the early days—did not predominantly focus on it as a gendered issue.

As mentioned in chapter 3, the 1974 Juvenile Justice and Delinquency Prevention Act was the first substantial piece of federal juvenile justice legislation that affected juvenile justice in the individual states. One of the main goals of this act was to separate youths from adults in custodial facilities. Another central goal was to deinstitutionalize status offenders. The former goal was hardly controversial; it simply acknowledged one of the original purposes of the juvenile justice system—to keep youths and adults separate from one another. The deinstitutionalization goal, however, could be seen as conflicting with what some people might characterize as a central aspect of the youth justice system—intervention. As discussed in chapter 3, there were tensions from the beginning about the main purpose of the youth justice system. Clearly, however, many saw the youth justice system's ability to intervene in the lives of youths prior to them having committed an offense as a means by which the state could, at least theoretically, help or rehabilitate them. Therefore, encouraging the removal of status offenders from custody could be seen as dealing a devastating blow to a central assumption of the youth justice system. This chapter will explore how the tension between wanting to intervene and wanting not to incarcerate youths for noncriminal behaviors played out.

More important, in the context of our interests, any shift away from the use of status offenses could be seen as a shift that would have a much more dramatic impact on girls than boys. The abolition of status offenses could easily be seen as a direct attack on one of the fundamental purposes of having a separate youth justice system, *especially* with respect to girls. The treatment of status offenses by the youth justice system can be seen, then, as a lens through which we can examine not only how girls were seen and responded to by the youth justice system, but also how the system itself changed (or stayed the same) in response to outside pressures.

Unfortunately, the collectors and keepers of youth justice statistics did not always feel that it was worthwhile to separate out what was happening to boys and girls, just as they often did not keep different categories of behavior as separate as we might have liked. The picture that we give is, therefore, necessarily incomplete. What we will be presenting are snapshots of how the youth justice system in the United States (and in Canada, in the following chapter) dealt with minor offending by boys and girls during the latter part of the 20th century.[1] Though incomplete, the story is, we think, worth telling.

A variety of sources of data can be used to explore how the youth justice system in the United States changed its responses to status-type offenses over time. One can, for example, explore trends in arrests, in bringing cases to youth court, and in adjudicating cases delinquent, as well as custodial populations. All of these measures must be interpreted for what they are: records created by those working within the youth justice system of certain types of contacts between youths and the youth justice system. For obvious reasons, as pointed out earlier, youth justice statistics tell us little about the extent or distribution of youth crime. Given the rates of offending by youths in their mid-adolescence, the economists would probably suggest that it is best to think of there being an infinite supply of offending behavior in the community that could come to the attention of youth justice officials. In other words, because most detailed assessments of offending by youths suggest that large portions of or even almost all young people do things that could be considered to be offenses, the rate at which youths are brought into the youth justice system is best thought of as an indication of how the youth justice system operates and what we, as a society, are deciding to bring into it.

Given that we are dependent on administrative data when trying to understand the operation of the youth justice system across time, one has to be careful in interpreting what these data might signify. The most conservative way of looking at the data presented in this chapter would be to suggest that we are looking at the manner in which the youth justice system responds to boys and girls at different points in time. Other things also change over time; hence, we would suggest that comparisons of the figures are especially problematic, since they may reflect differences in definitions or differences in the sample of jurisdictions covered.

Our primary focus in this chapter is on the youth court processing (e.g., bringing the juvenile into court, adjudicating the delinquent, and sentencing the offender to custody) of status offenses. However, we will also look briefly at arrest data and custodial populations. We begin with arrest data, followed by youth court processing data, and end with a look at custodial populations. For the youth court processing section, we examine two types of relatively minor offending—obstructing justice and disorderly conduct—in order to see if there are any consistencies in how these status-type offenses are handled for boys and girls. We examine the rate at which these cases are brought to court, the rate at which the accused are found guilty, and the rate at which offenders are sentenced to custody, as well as the proportion of the court population at each stage that these cases constitute. Although both may seem relatively minor offenses, leading one to expect to see smaller proportions of these cases as one moves deeper into the system, this is not necessarily the case.

Our custody section explores two separate issues. First, we examine the proportion of the youth custodial population made up of girls and contrast that to the proportion of the adult custodial population made up of women. Because girls and women are less likely than boys and men to commit serious offenses, there might be expected to be similar proportions of girls and women in custody. However, if there is more of an interventionist aim with respect to juveniles than adults, girls may account for a larger proportion of the custodial population than do women. The second issue we explore is the types of offenses girls are in custody for versus the types for which boys are in custody. We focus exclusively on the proportion of girls and boys in custody for status offenses.

Arrest Data

FBI arrest data reveal that no matter which jurisdictions were reporting in any given year, from 1970 to 2006 girls accounted for anywhere from 20 percent to 30 percent of all juvenile arrests. However, it is important to remember that this does not mean that the distribution of offenses that brought girls and boys into the youth justice systems was the same for boys and girls. For example, whereas the offense of running away accounted for anywhere from 4 percent to 7 percent of boys' arrests, this justification for involvement in the youth justice system accounted for 11 percent to 28 percent of girls' arrests. Moreover, when looking at all arrests made for running away, the majority—53 percent to 59 percent—involved girls. There was less variation in curfew violations: they accounted for anywhere from 4 percent to 6 percent of both boys' and girls' arrests.

Youth Court Processing

Our primary interest is in the changes in youth court processing of status-type offenses. We use the same court data described in chapter 2, which were collected and maintained by the National Center for Juvenile Justice (see chapter 2 for a detailed description of the data). For our purposes, we were interested in youth court processing of status-type offenses. We therefore examined obstructing-justice and disorderly-conduct cases and contrasted them with one another.

Obstructing Justice

The rather broad category of behavior classified as obstructing justice includes, among other things, failing to abide by a VCO,[2] a category created in 1980 as an exception to federal custody prohibitions. Specifically, this category of offenses includes intentionally obstructing a court (or law enforcement) in the administration of justice, acting in a way calculated to lessen the authority or dignity of the court, failing to obey the lawful order of a court [VCO offense, introduced in 1980], and violations of probation or parole other than technical violations, which do not consist of the commission of a crime or are not prosecuted as such. It also includes contempt, perjury, obstructing justice, bribing witnesses, failure to report a crime, nonviolent resisting arrest, etc." (http://ojjdp.ncjrs .gov/ojstatbb/jcsdb/asp/glossary.asp)

At the time of the writing of this book, court data were available from 1985 to 2004 (Puzzanchera and Kang, 2007).

Looking first at the rate at which these cases of obstructing justice were brought in youth court, we see increases during the early 1990s for both boys and girls, followed by a leveling off in the later 1990s (see fig. 5.1). Girls are consistently brought into court for obstructing-justice offenses at a lower rate than boys. Moreover, although both boys and girls saw a rather dramatic increase in the rate of court referrals for this category of offense during the 1990s, the increases appear to have been larger among boys than among girls. The rate increase between 1985 and 2004 for boys was 56.4 (90.4 in 2004 minus 34.0 in 1985), whereas the rate increase for girls was 24.8 (37.2 in 2004 minus 12.4 in 1985). Moreover, the difference between the boys' and girls' rates was larger in 2004 than it was in 1985 (see Appendix E for the numbers).

Looking next at the rate of cases in which those accused of obstructing justice were adjudicated delinquent, one again sees increases starting in

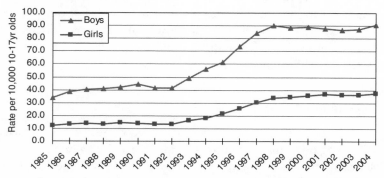

Figure 5.1. Rate at which obstructing-justice cases (petitioned and nonpetitioned) were brought to youth court

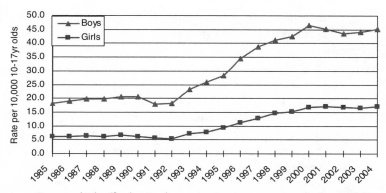

Figure 5.2. Rate at which offenders in obstructing-justice cases were adjudicated delinquent in youth court

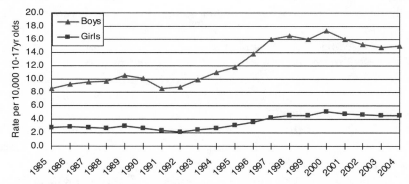

Figure 5.3. Rate at which offenders in obstructing-justice cases were sentenced to custody

the early 1990s, but the leveling off does not appear until early 2000 (see fig. 5.2). Once again, boys have seen larger increases than girls. Boys saw a rate increase of 27.0 (from 18.2 in 1985 to 45.2 in 2004), while girls saw a rate increase of 10.8 (from 6.3 in 1985 to 17.1 in 2004). In addition, the difference between the rates at which boys and girls were adjudicated delinquent increased between 1985 and 2004 (see Appendix E for the numbers).

Finally, one also sees increases, from the mid-1990s until 2000, in the rate of cases in which those convicted of obstructing justice were sentenced to custody (see fig. 5.3). Once again, the rate for boys increased (from a rate of 8.5 in 1985 to 15.0 in 2004) more than that for girls (from a rate of 2.8 to 4.6), and the differences between boys and girls were larger in 2004 than they were in 1985 (see Appendix E for the numbers).

Overall, then, for both boys and girls, there have been increases in the rate at which obstructing-justice cases were brought to court and the rates at which the accused were found guilty and sentenced to custody. At all stages, boys saw larger rate increases than girls. Moreover, the rate differences between boys and girls grew larger, indicating a greater difference in the early part of this century than in 1985 between the rates at which girls and boys were brought to court and the rates at which they were found guilty and sentenced to custody for obstructing justice.

Though we might suggest that boys have seen larger increases than girls in these obstructing-justice cases, there is another dimension that must be considered: the proportion of the youth court caseload that these obstructing-justice cases account for. Examining over time the proportion of the total youth court caseload (petitioned and nonpetitioned cases) that these cases account for, one sees two things. First, the caseload for girls includes a slightly larger proportion of these cases than for boys. Second, after relative stability in the late 1980s and early 1990s, these cases started accounting for an increasing proportion of the overall youth court caseload, for both boys and girls (see fig. 5.4). For girls, these cases accounted for approximately 8 percent of the youth court caseload in 1985, and by 2004 they were accounting for close to 14 percent. Boys increased from having these cases account for 5 percent of their youth court caseload in 1985 to having them account for 13 percent in 2004.

Looking next at the proportion of the youth court caseload in which the accused were adjudicated delinquent that these obstructing-justice cases account for, one again sees that girls have a larger proportion of these cases than do boys (see fig. 5.5). Interestingly, at this adjudicated-delinquent stage, these cases account for an even larger proportion of both the boys' and

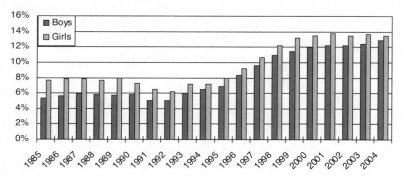

Figure 5.4. Percentage of all boy/girl cases (petitioned and nonpetitioned) in which obstructing justice was the most serious charge

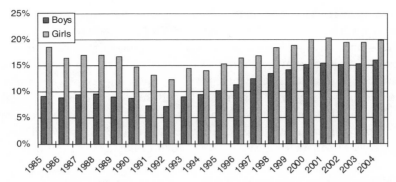

Figure 5.5. Percentage of all boy/girl cases (adjudicated delinquent) in which obstructing justice was the most serious conviction

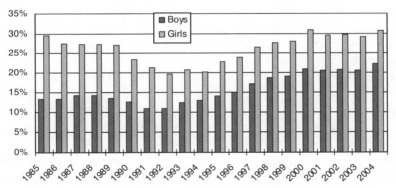

Figure 5.6. Percentage of all boy/girl cases (sentenced to custody) in which obstructing justice was the most serious conviction

girls' youth court caseload. For example, in 2004 these cases accounted for close to 14 percent of the girls' total youth court caseload (petitioned and nonpetitioned), while they accounted for close to 20 percent of the girls' adjudicated-delinquent youth court caseload. And, while these cases accounted for 13 percent of the boys' total youth court caseload, they accounted for 16 percent of their adjudicated-delinquent youth court caseload. Putting figures 5.4 and 5.5 together demonstrates that those accused in obstructing-justice cases were more likely to be adjudicated delinquent than were those accused in traditional "criminal" cases brought to the attention of the juvenile court.

Finally, looking at the proportion of obstructing-justice cases in which offenders were sentenced to custody, one again sees that these cases account for a larger proportion for girls than for boys (see fig. 5.6). Moreover, the

gender gap is the largest at this stage. Obstructing-justice cases constitute a larger proportion of the cases resulting in custody for girls than for
boys—anywhere from 9 percent to 14 percent more custody cases involved
obstructing justice for girls than for boys. That difference stands in contrast to the preceding stage, where girls saw 4 percent to 9 percent more of
these cases than boys did in their adjudicated-delinquent caseload. And the
findings for those adjudicated delinquent stand in contrast to the first stage
(petitioned and nonpetitioned court caseload), where girls only had about
0.5 percent to 2.5 percent more cases in their caseload than did boys.

The absolute size of these findings is important. At this stage of the proceedings these cases are accounting not only for a larger proportion of the
caseload for both boys and girls, but for a substantial portion of the custodial
sentences. At the sentencing stage, these cases account for anywhere from
20 percent to 30 percent of the girls' caseload, whereas in early stages they
account for only 12 percent to 20 percent (adjudicated-delinquent caseload) or 6 percent to 14 percent (total youth court caseload, petitioned and
nonpetitioned). The same is true for boys. At the sentencing stage, these
obstructing-justice cases account for anywhere from 12 percent to 22 percent
of the boys' cases in which the offender is sentenced to custody, whereas in
earlier stages these cases account for 7 percent to 16 percent (adjudicated-
delinquent caseload) or 5 percent to 13 percent (total youth court caseload,
petitioned and nonpetitioned).

The obstructing-justice cases are clearly important for two reasons. First,
girls are more likely to be involved (at all stages in the court process) in
this rather marginal category of offense than are boys. In other words, even
though the behavior of girls is generally less problematic than the behavior of boys, it would appear that for these offenses, which largely involve
behavior other than normal criminal activity, girls are being targeted at a
disproportionately high rate. Second, the deeper one goes into the youth
justice system (from the case being brought to court, to the offender being
adjudicated delinquent, to the offender being sentenced to custody), the
more likely it is that the case will involve obstructing justice.

These cases by definition involve youths who have had some sort of prior
involvement in the juvenile justice system. Hence, there is an increased
likelihood that they will be sentenced to custody. However, according to
the self-reported data available, girls tend to be more compliant and law
abiding than boys. It is therefore curious that girls are more likely than boys
to be in court and sent to custody in these sorts of cases. The most plausible explanation may be the most simple. Allowing them to be sentenced
to custody for violating a valid court order resolves the tension between

authorities' wanting to intervene in youths' lives yet not to incarcerate them for noncriminal behavior: the noncriminal behaviors are redefined in this instance as the equivalent of criminal behavior, so states are not financially penalized for using custody. And for girls—who are less likely to be involved in "normal" criminal activity (e.g., property or violent crime), these "noncriminal" offenses are available as opportunities for interventions. The states are able to intervene and place the youth—disproportionately girls—in custody, but because violating a VCO is an offense, the states do not lose federal funding.

Disorderly Conduct

It is important to note that obstructing-justice cases are different in important ways from another rather minor offense: behavior that might be categorized as disorderly conduct. Disorderly conduct is characterized as "unlawful interruption of the peace, quiet, or order of a community, including the offenses of disturbing the peace, vagrancy, loitering, unlawful assembly, and riot." These might include status offenses, but the main difference between obstructing justice and disorderly conduct is that the latter can be committed by young people who have had no previous contact with the courts. Moreover, it involves, though perhaps in a relatively minor way, forms of direct social harm to the community. From our perspective, however, the most important distinction between obstructing-justice and disorderly-conduct offenses is that the latter consist of minor forms of offending. Hence, one might plausibly expect them to constitute a higher proportion of the court-bound caseload for girls than for boys, since girls are disproportionately brought to court for less serious offenses.

We first present the rates at which boys and girls are brought into court for disorderly conduct, found guilty, and sentenced to custody. We next look at the proportion of the youth court population at each stage of the proceedings that these cases account for.

The reason we look at these two categories of offenses separately is that if the patterns for cases of obstructing justice and disorderly conduct are the same, it is less likely that obstructing justice could be considered a disguised status offense. If, on the other hand, the data for disorderly conduct are different in a predictable and understandable way, we would have more confidence in considering obstructing-justice charges to be largely status offenses.

When we look at the rate at which these cases are brought in court (petitioned and nonpetitioned), we see that, similar to the trends with obstruct-

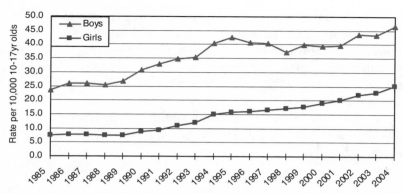

Figure 5.7. Rate at which disorderly-conduct cases (petitioned and nonpetitioned) were brought to youth court

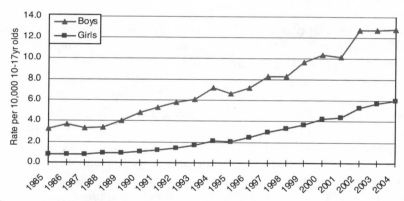

Figure 5.8. Rate at which offenders in disorderly-conduct cases were adjudicated delinquent

ing justice, boys are consistently brought in at a higher rate than girls (see fig. 5.7). In 1985 boys were brought into court a rate of 23.6 per 10,000, while for girls the rate was 7.5 per 10,000. By 2004 the rate for boys had increased by 23.1 to 46.7 per 10,000, whereas the rate for girls had increased by 17.8 to 25.3 per 10,000. Thus, boys saw a larger rate increase than did girls, and in 2004 the difference between boys and girls was larger than it had been in 1985 (see Appendix F for the numbers).

Looking next at the rate at which offenders in these cases are adjudicated delinquent, we see similar trends emerging. Boys are adjudicated delinquent at a higher rate than girls, but both saw increases throughout this period (see fig. 5.8). However, boys saw larger rate increases than girls, and once again the difference between boys and girls was larger in 2004 than in 1985 (see Appendix F for the numbers).

Finally, figure 5.9 shows the rate at which boys and girls in disorderly-conduct cases are sentenced to custody. Here again, both boys and girls have seen increases throughout this period, though boys have consistently been sentenced to custody at a higher rate than girls. Moreover, the rate difference between boys and girls is, once again, larger in 2004 than it was in 1985 (see Appendix F for the numbers).

Generally, then, when looking at the rate at which youths charged in disorderly-conduct cases are brought into court, found guilty, and sentenced to custody, we find the trends were similar to those for obstructing justice. Both boys and girls saw increases across all three stages, with the boys seeing larger rate increases than girls.

However, one must again consider the proportion of girls' and boys' youth court caseload that these cases account for. And it is here that we see that the overall pattern for disorderly-conduct charges looks more like one we would expect for a minor offense. This stands in contrast to what we saw with cases of obstructing justice.

We saw earlier that the deeper an obstructing-justice case was in the court process (the offender is brought to court, adjudicated delinquent, and sent to custody), the *higher* the proportion of the caseload these cases constituted throughout the period for which we have data. This pattern makes no sense if these are merely minor criminal cases. Moreover, those cases were accounting for a larger proportion of the girls' youth court caseload than the boys'. This was especially true at the sentencing stage (compare fig. 5.6 to fig. 5.4).

In contrast, disorderly-conduct cases look more like what one would

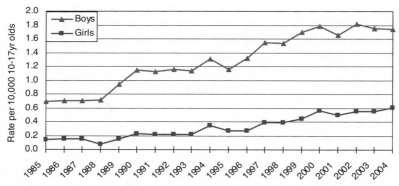

Figure 5.9. Rate at which offenders in disorderly-conduct cases were sentenced to custody

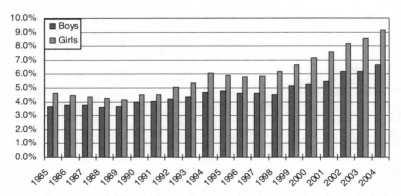

Figure 5.10 Percentage of all boy/girl cases (petitioned and nonpetitioned) in which disorderly conduct was the most serious charge

expect for relatively minor cases: the deeper into the system one goes, the *lower* the proportion of the youth court caseload they constitute. Figure 5.10 shows the proportion of disorderly-conduct cases out of all cases brought to court (petitioned and nonpetitioned). With both boys and girls these cases accounted for an increasing amount of the youth court caseload. In 1985 they accounted for close to 5 percent of the girls' caseload and close to 4 percent of the boys' youth court caseload. In 2004 they accounted for a little over 9 percent of the girls' caseload and close to 7 percent of the boys' caseload. This difference is similar to the initial difference between boys and girls in the proportion of obstructing-justice cases. However, whereas the difference between boys and girls grew with respect to cases of obstructing justice, the same did not happen with cases of disorderly conduct.

When looking at the "adjudicated delinquent" stage of proceedings, we see that there is now a smaller proportion of disorderly-conduct cases (see fig. 5.11). These cases accounted for 2.4 percent of the girls' cases in 1985 and increased to around 7 percent by 2004. They accounted for close to 1.7 percent of the boys' caseload in 1985 and a little over 4 percent in 2004.

Finally, we examine the proportion of disorderly-conduct cases in which the offender was sentenced to custody out of all cases in which the offender was sentenced to custody (see fig. 5.12). The proportion of these cases at this final stage of proceedings is even smaller. They accounted for roughly 1.6 percent of the caseload for girls in 1985 and 4.1 percent in 2004, and about 1 percent of the caseload for boys in 1985 and 2.6 percent in 2004.

Overall, then, there are some important differences between boys and girls in youth court processing in these two relatively minor and potentially status-type offense categories. For both offense categories boys are brought in to court, adjudicated delinquent, and sentenced to custody at higher rates than girls. Moreover, for both boys and girls, in both offense categories and across all three stages of youth court processing, the rates have been generally increasing. The similarities between these two offenses end there, however. When looking at the proportion of the youth court caseload for which these offenses account, we see interestingly different patterns emerge.

First, as one moves deeper into the system, cases of obstructing justice constitute larger and larger proportions of the caseload. These cases appear, almost certainly because they are seen as important juvenile justice cases, to have more staying power than those involving other offenses. Moreover, although the proportion of these cases in the girls' caseload is always larger than in the caseload for boys, the differences become larger as one progresses

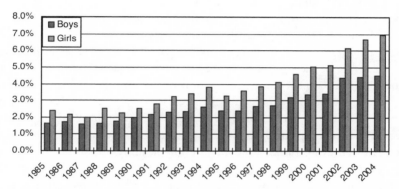

Figure 5.11. Percentage of all boy/girl cases (adjudicated delinquent) in which disorderly conduct was the most serious conviction

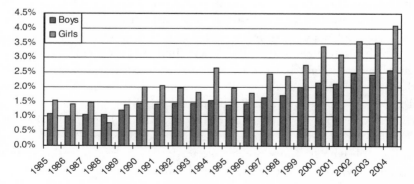

Figure 5.12. Percentage of all boy/girl cases (sentenced to custody) in which disorderly conduct was the most serious conviction

through the system. At the beginning stage (petitioned and nonpetitioned), these cases accounted for roughly 13.5 percent of the girls' caseload and 12.9 percent of the boys' caseload in 2004. By the sentencing-to-custody stage, these cases accounted for 30.7 percent of the girls' cases and 22.2 percent of the boys' cases (in 2004). The same was not found with disorderly conduct. As one moved through the system, these cases accounted for smaller proportions of the caseload for both boys and girls. Moreover, although these disorderly-conduct cases accounted for a larger proportion of the girls' caseload than the boys' (because boys, in general, are more likely than girls to commit more serious offenses), the difference was never more than about 1 or 2 percent. The broad differences between these two types of cases could have resulted from the nature of the offense: obstructing justice could be seen as offenses against—or disagreements between—the court or judge while disorderly conduct could be seen as offenses against the police or perhaps the community more generally. Thus, an obstructing-justice case might have more staying power than a disorderly-conduct case in part because of the presence of a criminal record and in part because of whom (the judge vs. the police or the community) the behavior offended. However, this still would not explain the increased use of obstructing-justice cases with girls.

To the extent that obstructing-justice cases are, in effect, "constructed cases"—that the youth is being sanctioned for behavior that normally would not have merited punishment—one can see the youth court processing trends as reflecting a *relatively* controlling—or, more important, a *relatively* "interventionist"—approach to girls compared to boys. That this offense accounted for an increasing portion of the caseload as one went deeper into the system demonstrates either that it was seen as more serious than most cases or, more likely, that these cases involved youths who were more deserving of, or more in need of, serious intervention. This supports our contention that these obstructing-justice cases—primarily consisting of youths who have violated a court order—are status offenses in disguise. One way in which to reconcile the somewhat conflicting approaches of providing intervention yet not incarcerating status offenders would be to redefine those status offenses as criminal offenses such as violating a court order. That would explain why a higher proportion of girls relative to boys are in court and custody for these types of offenses when all other data indicate that they are, if anything, more law abiding than boys generally.

If people who are young and female are deserving of intervention simply because of who they are, one might expect females to constitute a larger proportion of those placed in custody or prison among juveniles as compared to adults. The next section, on custodial populations, explores that issue.

Custodial Populations

The data for youths in custody come from the Children in Custody survey, which began in 1971 and obtained information on youths who were in publicly operated detention centers, training schools, shelters, halfway houses, and group homes. Some later data also came from private institutions. Serious limitations on the use of these data are described in more detail in Appendix D, but we have chosen to use them because they are the best we could find. We have no reason to suspect that the limitations have any effect on our interpretation of these data.

Differences across years may reflect sampling changes rather than changes within jurisdictions. Thus, in the first section we show comparisons *within* each sampled year of the proportion of adults and youths who are female. The second section explores the proportion of boys and girls in custody for status offenses.

Adults and Juveniles in Custody

As we pointed out earlier, it is one of the most well-established facts of criminology that women and girls have offending rates that are lower than those of men and boys, respectively. In addition, the severity of the offenses in which women are involved is generally less than that of men, just as the severity of the offenses that girls commit is less than that of boys.

But if the difference in offending rates were the only factor determining the proportion of the prison population that is female, then one might expect that the proportion of the adult prison population that is female to be roughly the same as the proportion of the youth custody population that is female. On the other hand, if youth custody is being used, in part, to control young girls, one would expect that the proportion of youths in custody who are girls to be higher than the proportion of adults in custody who are women. In other words, a very rough index of the use of custody for status offenses for girls might result in a higher rate of incarceration of girls than women, especially if this surplus incarceration of youth did not occur for boys. This is, not surprisingly, exactly what one finds (see Zimring, 2005).

Beginning in 1971, one sees that the proportion of the imprisoned population made up of women in either sentenced (state or federal) populations or in local jails was relatively low—5 percent or less (see fig. 5.13). In the juvenile populations however, girls account for a dramatically larger proportion of the custodial population—slightly over 30 percent of the detained population of juveniles and slightly over 20 percent of the juveniles com-

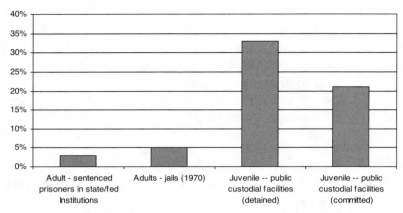

Figure 5.13. Proportion of females and girls in various correctional populations (1971)
Note: The adult state and federal incarceration population includes only those people who are physically in state or federal custodial institutions. Later definitions (post-1977) were broadened to include those "under jurisdiction." See source for more details.
Source for sentenced adult prisoners: Sourcebook, 2003: table 6.28, p. 500, http://www.albany.edu/sourcebook/pdf/t6282005.pdf/.
Source for adults in jails: Sourcebook, 1974: table 6.11, p. 426.
Source for youths in custody: Sourcebook, 1974: table 6.5, p. 419.

mitted to custody. We would suggest that the most plausible reason for this surplus incarceration of girls is the desire on the part of the state to place girls in custody for what are in effect status offenses.

The Juvenile Justice and Delinquency Prevention Act, passed in 1974, included provisions designed to reduce the use of status offenses for controlling youths. One might expect, then, that a few years later the surplus of incarcerated girls would disappear. For 1977 we were able to examine data on a range of incarcerated populations—youths and adults in jails, sentenced adult prisoners, and incarcerated youths (detained and committed combined) in public and private facilities. Looking at the imprisonment data that are available for adults and youths in 1977, one sees the same relationship that was evident prior to the implementation of this act: the proportion of girls in the incarcerated juvenile population was larger than the proportion of women in the incarcerated adult population. Regardless of what population one examines, girls always accounted for a larger proportion of the incarcerated population than did women (see fig. 5.14). The same trends hold for 1987 (see fig. 5.15) and 1997 (see fig. 5.16).

The disproportional use of custodial sentences for girls persisted for more than 30 years after the first data were released. Given the evidence provided earlier in this chapter for the *non*disappearance of status-type offenses, the persistence of this difference should not be a surprise. Girls accounted for a larger proportion of the juvenile population than women accounted for in the incarcerated adult population as recently as 2006 (see fig. 5.17).

But what happens when we go behind these figures and look at actual rates of incarceration (per 10,000 people in the population)? The advantage

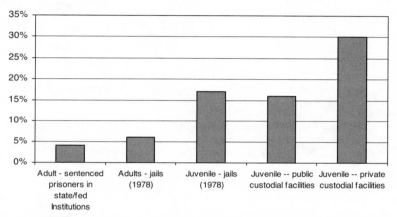

Figure 5.14. Proportion of females/girls in various correctional populations (1977)
Note: It is not clear whether youth custody data (public and private) include only sentenced youths. Adult state and federal incarceration includes only those people who are physically in state or federal custodial institutions. Later definitions (post-1977) were broadened to include those "under jurisdiction." See Sourcebook for more details.
Source for sentenced adult prisoners: Sourcebook, 2003: table 6.28, p. 500, http://www.albany.edu/sourcebook/pdf/t6282005.pdf.
Source for youths and adults in jails: Sourcebook, 1980: table 6.8, p. 482.
Source for youths in custody: Sourcebook, 1980: table 6.6, p. 481.

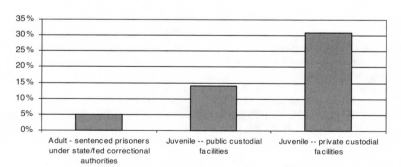

Figure 5.15. Proportion of females and girls in various correctional populations (1987)
Note: Youth custody data (public and private) include all youths in custody (sentenced and detained).
Source for adults under state/federal correctional authorities: Sourcebook, 2003: table 6.28, p. 500, http://www.albany.edu/sourcebook/pdf/t6282005.pdf.
Source for youths in custody: Sourcebook, 1988: table 6.8, p. 595.

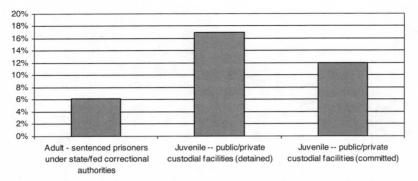

Figure 5.16. Proportion of females/girls in various correctional populations (1997)
Source for adults under state/federal correctional authorities: Sourcebook, 2003: table 6.28, p. 500, http://www.albany.edu/sourcebook/pdf/t6282005.pdf.
Source for youths in custody (committed and detained): Authors' analysis of OJJDP's Census of Juveniles in Residential Placement 1997 and 2003 (machine-readable data files).
Reference: Sickmund, M., Sladky, T. J., and Kang, W. (2005). *Census of Juveniles in Residential Placement Databook*. http://www.ojjdp.ncjrs.org/ojstatbb/cjrp/.

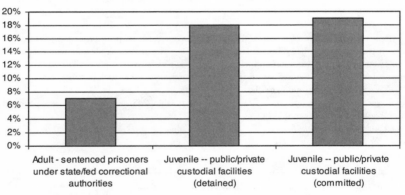

Figure 5.17. Proportion of females/girls in various correctional populations (2006)
Source for adults under state/federal correctional authorities: Sourcebook, 2006: table 6.28, http://www.albany.edu/sourcebook/pdf/t6282006.pdf.
Source for youths in custody (committed and detained): Authors' analysis of OJJDP's Census of Juveniles in Residential Placement 1997 and 2006 (machine-readable data files).
Reference: Sickmund, M., Sladky, T. J., and Kang, W. (2008). *Census of Juveniles in Residential Placement Databook*. http://www.ojjdp.ncjrs.gov/ojstatbb/cjrp/.

of looking at actual rates rather than ratios is that it is easier to see where the effects we have just examined come from.

When we look at the rates, we find that the imprisonment rate for girls in juvenile facilities is higher than that for women in adult facilities. Table 5.1 shows the rates (per 10,000) of girls, boys, women, and men in public custodial facilities in 1971 and 1977. The ratios of the rates of girls to women and boys to men are also shown. In 1971, roughly 20.8 percent of the youth custodial population were girls, while only 3.2 percent of the sentenced adult population were women. Girls were sentenced to custody at a higher rate than women, resulting in a ratio of 6.97 girls to women in prison. The advantage of presenting the data in this way is that we can see that this same pattern does not hold for boys. The ratio of boys to men shows just the opposite trend: the rate for boys was lower than that for men in 1971 (ratio = 0.78). If the surplus of girls (in comparison to women) in prison was a result of the use of custody for status offenses, it would appear that this was not an issue for boys.

By 1977 the rate of imprisonment of girls decreased slightly and the rate of imprisonment of women increased slightly, resulting in a ratio of 3.30

Table 5.1. Rates (per 10,000 girls/women or boys/men in the population) of boys and girls in public custodial institutions (and percentage of custodial population)

1971	Girls or women	Boys or men	Ratio of rates (girls/women)	Ratio of rates (boys/men)
Youths (committed) in public facilities	6.13	22.53	6.97	0.78
(Proportion of population)	(20.8%)	(79.2%)		
Adults sentenced to state/federal institutions	0.88	29.06		
(Proportion of population)	(3.2%)	(96.8%)		

1977	Girls or women	Boys or men	Ratio (girls/women)	Ratio (boys/men)
Youths ("residents")* in public facilities	4.52	22.36	3.30	0.62
(Proportion of population)	(16.3%)	(83.7%)		
Adults sentenced to state/federal institutions	1.37	36.13		
(Proportion of population)	(4.0%)	(96.0%)		

* It is not clear whether the 1977 definition of "residents" includes detained youths. However, even if it does, the population is larger (including both those detained and those committed) than the population in 1971 (committed only), yet the ratio of girls to women is still smaller for 1977.

Note: "Youths" = age 10–17; "adults" = age 18+.

Table 5.2. Rates (per 10,000 girls/women and boys/men in the population) of girls or women and boys or men in public and private custodial institutions (and percentage of custodial population)

1977	Girls or women	Boys or men	Ratio (girls/women)	Ratio (boys/men)
Youths ("residents"*) in public and private facilities	10.00	34.71	7.30	.96
(Proportion of population)	(21.7%)	(78.3%)		
Adults sentenced to state/federal institutions	1.37	36.13		
(Proportion of population)	(4.0%)	(96.0%)		

1987	Girls or women	Boys or men	Ratio (girls/women)	Ratio (boys/men)
Youths ("in"**) in public and private facilities	14.17	51.36	4.94	0.82
(Proportion of population)	(20.8%)	(79.2%)		
Adult sentenced prisoners under state or federal jurisdiction	2.87	62.33		
(Proportion of population)	(4.8%)	(95.2%)		

1997	Girls or women	Boys or men	Ratio (girls/women)	Ratio (boys/men)
Youths (committed and detained) in public and private facilities	9.00	55.55	1.28	0.48
(Proportion of population)	(13.3%)	(86.7%)		
Adult sentenced prisoners under state or federal jurisdiction	7.05	115.41		
(Proportion of population)	(6.2%)	(93.8%)		

2006	Girls or women	Boys or men	Ratio (girls/women)	Ratio (boys/men)
Youths (committed and detained) in public and private facilities	8.28	44.92	0.93	0.35
(Proportion of population)	(14.9%)	(85.1%)		

Table 5.2. (*continued*)

2006	Girls or women	Boys or men	Ratio (girls/women)	Ratio (boys/men)
Adult sentenced prisoners under state or federal jurisdiction	8.90	127.45		
(Proportion of population)	(6.9%)	(93.1%)		

* It is not clear whether the 1977 definition ("residents") includes detained youths.

** It is not clear whether the 1987 definition ("in") includes detained youths.

Note: "Youths" = age 10–17; "adults" = age 18+.

(see table 5.1). With respect to males, the rate for men increased slightly but remained stable for boys between 1971 and 1977. Regardless, in 1977 the rate for men was still higher than for boys (ratio = 0.62). (Appendix G contains the raw number of custodial counts and population estimates.)

Table 5.2 shows the rate (per 10,000) of girls, boys, women, and men in public and private custodial facilities in 1977, 1987, 1997, and 2006. Again, the ratio of girls to women and boys to men is also shown. Although slightly different populations have been sampled over time (committed only or detained and committed), one sees a trend toward a decreasing proportion of girls in public and private facilities—from 21.7 percent in 1977 to 14.9 percent in 2006. The ratio of the rates (per 10,000) for girls to women also decreases over time—from 7.30 girls per woman in 1977 to 0.93 girl per woman in 2006. Thus, in 2006, for the first time ever, there were slightly fewer girls in prison for every woman. The decreasing ratio of girls to women is due both to slight decreases in the rates of girls in prison and to rather substantial increases in the rates of women in prison. For the ratio of boys to men, the ratios also decreased (from 0.96 in 1977 to 0.35 in 2006), but this decline was due to an explosion in the imprisonment rate for men over this time period (from a rate of 36.13 in 1997 to 127.45 in 2006).

While the ratio of girls to women appears to have decreased over time, it is interesting to note that the ratio is still quite different when compared to that of boys to men. On a per capita basis, there are always fewer boys in prison than men—the opposite of what is found with respect to girls, for until 2006 there was always a higher proportion of girls in prison than of women. However, given the nature of girls' delinquency compared to women's criminality (e.g., if nothing else women are likely to have a more extensive criminal record than girls), the fact that ratio of incarcerated girls to women was just under 1 does not necessarily mean "equality" for girls. Indeed, the ratio of incarcerated girls to women should be a fair bit below 1—that is, there should be many fewer incarcerated girls for every woman in prison. The most plausible explanation for why this is not the case is that girls are being placed in custodial facilities for interventionist purposes.[3]

It is important to note, in table 5.2, that although some may argue that girls are still overrepresented in custody (compared to women, men, and boys), the degree to which they are overrepresented has decreased in the three decades that followed the implementation of the Juvenile Justice and Delinquency Prevention Act in 1974. There were declines in the rate of girls in custody over this time period which stands in contrast to women, boys and men, all of whom saw increases. Thus, it appears that the incarceration of girls for welfare purposes still may exist in 2006, but was considerably less severe than in the 1970s.

Status Offenses

There has long been some concern that for comparable nonthreatening behavior, girls are incarcerated "for their own good" more often than are boys. Indeed, researchers have found that in many jurisdictions girls were more likely than boys to be brought to court and incarcerated for status offenses (see, for example, Chesney-Lind, 1973; Chesney-Lind and Shelden, 2004; Datesman and Scarpitti, 1977; Gibbons and Griswold, 1957; Odem, 1995; Pope and Feyerherm, 1982; and Shelden, 1981). In 1971—looking only at youths who were adjudicated delinquent and placed in publicly operated facilities—it is clear that offenses for which girls were likely to be incarcerated were more likely to be status offenses than if the youth were a boy. Although the estimates in 1971 were that a little more than 20 percent of incarcerated boys were imprisoned for status offenses, roughly 70 percent of incarcerated girls were there for status offenses (see fig. 5.18).

In 1987—13 years after the Juvenile Justice and Delinquency Prevention Act was passed—incarcerated girls were still more likely to be in a custodial facility because of a status offense than incarcerated boys were (see fig. 5.19). Whether looking at public or private institutions, a larger proportion of girls than boys who were in custody were in a youth custody facility for status offenses. Status offenders were particularly likely in 1987, it appears, to be incarcerated in privately run facilities. However, there appears to have been a rather substantial reduction in the proportion of status-offense cases for which girls were sentenced to custody. Whereas around 70 percent of girls in custody in 1971 were there for status offenses (see fig. 5.18), in 1987 only a

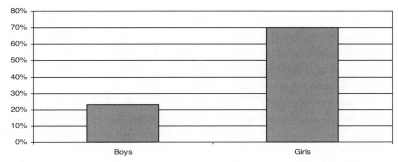

Figure 5.18. Proportion of youths in custody (adjudicated delinquent—public facilities only) who had a status offense as the most serious conviction (1971)
Source: Sourcebook, 1974: table 6.8, p. 422.

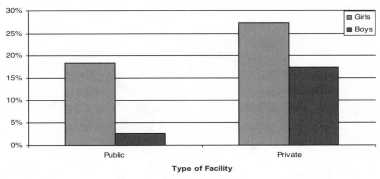

Figure 5.19. Proportion of girl or boy custody population (detained and committed) where the most serious conviction is a status offense (1987)
Source: Sourcebook, 1988: table 6.9, p. 596.

little over a quarter of the girls in private facilities, and just under 20 percent of those in public ones, were there for status offenses (see fig. 5.19).

Estimates in 1997 still showed a larger proportion of girls being incarcerated for status offenses than boys (see fig. 5.20). The largest proportion of girls incarcerated for status offenses were found in the committed (sentenced) population. Estimates at this time placed roughly 25 percent of the (committed) girl population to have status offenses as their most serious conviction, whereas less than 5 percent of the (committed) boy population had such offenses.

The pattern was still evident in 2006: the female custodial population (detained or committed) was more likely to have a status offense as the most serious charge than was the male custodial population (see fig. 5.21). Because

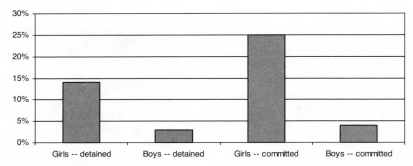

Figure 5.20. Percentage of cases that are status offenses (as most serious charge/conviction) in various populations (public and private facilities, 1997)
Data source: Authors' analysis of OJJDP's Census of Juveniles in Residential Placement 1997 and 2003 (machine-readable data files).
Reference: Sickmund, M., Sladky, T. J., and Kang, W. (2005). *Census of Juveniles in Residential Placement Databook*. http://www.ojjdp.ncjrs.org/ojstatbb/cjrp/.

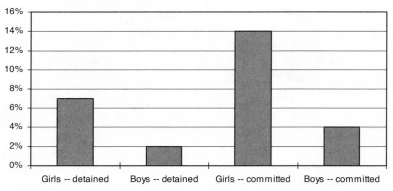

Figure 5.21. Percentage of cases that are status offenses (as the most serious charge/conviction) in various populations (public and private facilities, 2006)
Data source: Authors' analysis of OJJDP's Census of Juveniles in Residential Placement 1997 and 2006 (machine-readable data files).
Reference: Sickmund, M., Sladky, T. J., and Kang, W. (2008). *Census of Juveniles in Residential Placement Databook*. http://www.ojjdp.ncjrs.gov/ojstatbb/cjrp/.

of the lack of continuity of the sampling and measurement of these the data across years, we are reluctant to draw strong inferences about the size of the change from any one year to a subsequent one. Nevertheless, it does appear that over time fewer girls may have been incarcerated for status offenses. When the survey first started, well over half of the incarcerated girls were there for status offenses. Although an exact comparison cannot be made because the available data do not isolate those who have been adjudicated delinquent and placed in a public facility, the data now suggest that the proportion of the incarcerated female population who are there for a status offense was lower in 2006 than it had been in previous years. This conclusion is, of course, consistent with the data presented in table 5.2, in which it was shown that the surplus girls (in relation to women) decreased over time.

As we mentioned in chapter 1, our ability to investigate youth court processing by gender and race or ethnicity was hampered by the lack of comparable data in both counties. In the case of Canada there are, in effect, no data released by gender and race. In the United States, however, there are some data available—by both gender and race—on those who are in custody. Figure 5.22 shows the rate (per ten thousand 10-to-17-year-olds) of boys and girls in custody (detained or committed, public or private institutions, all offenses) in 1997 and 2006, broken down by race.[4] One sees that for both boys and girls, there were reductions in the rate of whites, blacks, and Asians in custody between 1997 and 2006. The rate for boys who were identified as American Indian was stable, while the rate for American Indian girls increased slightly (see fig. 5.22).

Figure 5.23 shows the rate of boys and girls in custody for status offenses in 1997 and 2006, again broken down by race. One notices three things from these data. First, like the trends for all offenses, for both boys and girls the rates of whites, blacks, and Asians in custody for status offenses declined between 1997 and 2006. Second, for both boys and girls, American Indians

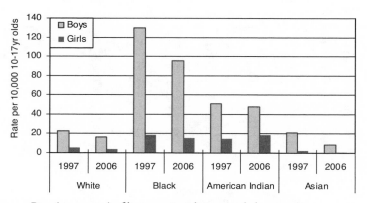

Figure 5.22. Rate (per 10,000) of boys versus girls in custody by race
Custody data source: Sickmund, M., Sladky, T. J., Kang, W., and Puzzanchera, C. (2008). *Easy Access to the Census of Juveniles In Residential Placement*. http://ojjdp.ncjrs.gov/ojstatbb/ezacjrp/.
Population data source: Puzzanchera, C., Finnegan, T. and Kang, W. (2007). *Easy Access to Juvenile Populations*. http://www.ojjdp.ncjrs.gov/ojstatbb/ezapop/.

stand out as the only group to have seen an increase in the rate at which they are in custody for status offenses (see fig. 5.23). Given that the rate of American Indians in custody for status offenses increased, there must have been a reduction in some other category of offenses such that overall the rate of those in custody was relatively stable (see fig. 5.22). Third, although boys were in custody for status offenses at a higher rate than girls (except for American Indians in 2006), the rates were much closer than when looking at custody overall.

Finally, figure 5.24 shows the proportion of those in custody who are there for status offenses (as the most serious conviction in the case). Here one sees, not surprisingly, that status offenses account for a much larger proportion of cases in which girls are in custody than cases in which boys are in custody, among all race and ethnicity categories and in both 1997 and 2006. However, white boys and girls saw reductions between 1997 and 2006 in the proportion of custodial cases for which these status-offense cases accounted (see fig. 5.24). Black, Asian, and Hispanic girls also saw reductions, whereas boys were stable. American Indians saw increases in the proportion of custodial cases in which a status offense was the most serious offense conviction in the case. As figure 5.23 showed, for both boys and girls there was an increase in the rate of American Indians in custody for a status offense. Why this increase is seen for both boy and girl American Indians is unclear.

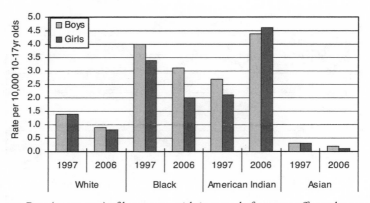

Figure 5.23. Rate (per 10,000) of boys versus girls in custody for status offenses by race
Custody data source: Sickmund, M., Sladky, T. J., Kang, W., & Puzzanchera, C. (2008). Easy Access to the Census of Juveniles in Residential Placement. http://ojjdp.ncjrs.gov/ojstatbb/ezacjrp/.
Population data source: Puzzanchera, C., Finnegan, T. and Kang, W. (2007). *Easy Access to Juvenile Populations.* http://www.ojjdp.ncjrs.gov/ojstatbb/ezapop/.

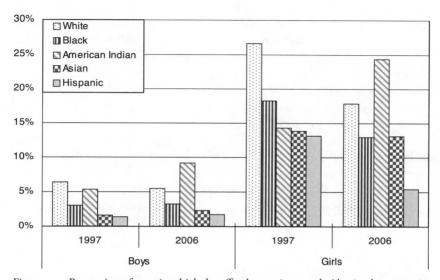

Figure 5.24. Proportion of cases in which the offender was in custody (detained or committed) where the most serious offense was a status offense
Custody data: Sickmund, M., Sladky, T. J., Kang, W., and Puzzanchera, C. (2008). *Easy Access to the Census of Juveniles in Residential Placement.* http://ojjdp.ncjrs.gov/ojstatbb/ezacjrp/.

Conclusion

In 1974 official *federal* policy in the United States was changed such that status offenses were no longer to be mechanisms for placing youths in custody. Though not discussed in terms of gender, this change clearly should have had a greater impact on the manner in which girls were treated than it would have had for boys. Girls, as we have seen, when they are involved in "crime," are much more likely than boys to be involved in less serious forms of it. One would expect that once status offenses were eliminated, the number of girls in custody would be significantly reduced, because they had been disproportionately likely to be in court and in custody for status offenses.

We are not confident that we can meaningfully estimate the size of the decrease in the (relative) overrepresentation of girls, in large part because the estimate depends completely on which measure one uses. However, looking generally at the available data from the early 1970s to the early 2000s, one sees general reductions in the proportions of girls in custody, and the proportion of girls in custody for status offenses specifically. The changes for girls appear to have happened quite slowly, quite some time after the JJDPA was first enacted in 1974. What is unclear, then, is whether the reductions seen for girls were the result of the JJDPA or of more broadly changing sentiments about what types of behaviors warrant a custodial sentence, sentiments that led to the creation of the JJDPA.

Although girls saw decreases, it has to be remembered that women constitute only a small proportion of the (adult) prison population—between about 3 percent and 7 percent of the population, depending on the year and the exact measure one looks at (see tables 5.1 and 5.2). Girls, on the other hand, constitute between about 15 percent and 21 percent of the youth population that is in custody, depending again on the measure that one uses and the year (see tables 5.1 and 5.2). In other words, compared to their male counterparts, it would appear that girls are still more likely to be the recipients of the state's harshest punishments (excluding capital punishment) than are women.

We believe that this extra portion of the custodial proportion for girls (as compared to women) is largely (or at least disproportionately) made up of those convicted of status offenses. Few women are locked up "for their own safety or proper development," but if girls (by way of obstructing-justice charges, for example) are, then at least some portion of the "extra" imprisonment of girls might be the fingerprint left by the use of custody for status offenses. In support of this idea, we found evidence of increasing rates of obstructing-justice cases. In 1985 obstructing-justice offenses—a category of offenses that includes violating a valid court order—constituted only 5–7 percent of the juvenile court load, whereas by 2004 they constituted 12–13 percent. Not surprisingly, they were always a larger portion of the court caseload for girls.

That these obstructing-justice cases were taken seriously—particularly for girls—has already been demonstrated. Though there is little difference in the proportion of cases entering the juvenile court system for girls and boys in which obstructing justice was the most serious charge, these differences become larger when one looks at cases of youths who were adjudicated delinquent and sentenced to custody. Indeed, by 2004, approximately 30 percent of the girls (and about 20 percent of boys) sentenced to custody lost their liberty not for a normal substantive offense, but for a constructed offense—something that offended the court, not society at large. Indeed, one can see how seriously these obstructing-justice cases were taken by comparing the proportion of the court intake load they constituted (for example, 12 percent and 13 percent in 2004 for boys and girls, respectively) to the proportion of custodial sentences that they constituted (20 percent and 30 percent for boys and girls, respectively).

As we have noted, the pattern for another objectively minor offense—disorderly conduct—is quite different. In only a small portion of the disorderly-conduct charges arriving at the door of the juvenile court is disorderly conduct the most serious charge (6–8 percent in 2004; figure 5.10), but these cases constitute an even smaller portion of cases in which the offender was sentenced to custody (3–4 percent in 2004; see fig. 5.12).

For girls, interestingly, these status-like offenses almost always constituted a larger portion of the caseload than they did for boys. But girls, like women, when they offend, tend to commit less serious offenses than do boys. Does it really seem that there is any special attention being paid to girls? Is there any evidence that girls are especially likely to be locked up "for their own good"? We think that there is, though there are indications that during the latter part of the twentieth century the tendency to do so may have decreased. And this decrease must be put into the broader U.S. context of increasing incarceration rates for boys, women, and men. Indeed, with the well-documented explosion in U.S. rates of incarceration, it is remarkable that girls saw any decreases in incarceration, because it is plausible that the policies related to the imprisonment of girls could be influenced by policies related to the imprisonment of boys and adults.[5] One wonders if, without the JJDPA, girls might have seen increases, like everyone else. Indeed, the great success of the JJDPA might have been the slight declines seen with girls, given the increased use of incarceration more generally. One may further wonder how, in a more stable criminal-justice climate—a climate without any such increases in incarceration—trends in incarcerating girls for status offenses or minor criminal offenses would have unfolded throughout the 1960s to 2000s. For this, we look to Canada.

Chapter 6

The Impact of Law Reform: Deinstitutionalization in Law and Practice in Canada

Canada, as pointed out earlier, officially abolished status offenses for youths in 1984 when the Young Offenders Act replaced the Juvenile Delinquents Act. Prior to 1984 two major status offenses were controversial in large part because of their breadth. The first, described in chapter 4, was the offense of sexual immorality (or any similar form of vice). The second was incorrigibility—a description probably given to most adolescents at one time or another by their parents. "Incorrigibility" could result in a court hearing and a custodial disposition, because the definition of delinquency included anything, in provincial legislation, that could result in commitment to a training school. By saying that a youth could be sent to training school (under provincial legislation) for being incorrigible, the provinces effectively created a federal offense under the JDA. This ended in 1984 with the passage of the much more restricted YOA, which defined as an offense only those matters that would be offenses under federal law for adults. However, prior to that time, status offenses were alive and well in Canada.

Although the YOA did not go into effect until 1984, youth justice legislation was on the federal government's political agenda throughout the 1960s and 1970s. As described in chapter 4, during the 1960s issues such as removing status offenses from the jurisdiction of the juvenile court were discussed and debated. And thus Canada, like the United States, was struggling with the conflicting goals of treating youths who committed offenses in a manner consistent with due process concerns and the desire to intervene in positive ways towards youths. Also like the United States, this tension was most pronounced with status offenses and girls. However, it is important to remember that in Canada, unlike in the United States, laws governing offending by youths were unambiguously the responsibility of the federal government (under its constitutional responsibilities for criminal law), while laws governing child welfare or child protection were unambiguously the responsibility of the provinces. Hence, a separation of legal and administrative responsibilities was hardly revolutionary; that separation had been mandated constitutionally in 1867.

With respect to Canada's status offenses, the most obvious—but by no means the only—area in which the youth justice system responded prior to 1984 in a clearly gendered fashion related to sexual immorality. Boys will be boys, and their sexual behavior was to be tolerated for no other reason than that it was to be expected. Girls, on the other hand, were a different matter. As we saw in chapter 4, it was seen as the responsibility of the state to intervene to save girls from the evils of consensual sex. As recently as 2007, however, the minister of justice, Vic Toews, introduced a bill changing the age of consent (for sexual behavior), or, as he preferred to call it, the "age of protection," for youths in Canada from 14 to 16 (Bill C-22, An Act to Amend the Criminal Code (Age of Protection) and to make Consequential Amendments to the Criminal Records Act). In his press release, issued on the day the bill received its first reading in the House of Commons, Toews gave only two specific examples of how this change would affect things—and both examples involved girls as the underage partner. Furthermore, he stated that in cases of "cyberluring," 93 percent of the victims were female. Thus, although the law itself was ungendered,[1] it was clearly seen as a tool that could be used to control girls and (older) boys. In other words, even in 2007 girls needed to be protected by the state, though the mechanism then was to criminalize the behavior of males rather than to find the girl's behavior immoral. In the second session of the 39th Parliament on October 18, 2007, these provisions were reintroduced (as part of Bill C-2, the Tackling Violent Crime Bill). This bill was passed and became law in 2008.

In this chapter we will describe the manner in which two offenses—incorrigibility and sexual immorality—were handled by the courts during the two decades for which we have data, the 1950s and 1960s.[2] Having data from this time allows us to explore the youth court processing of juvenile status offenders during a period well before the law was replaced. Moreover, these data allow us to compare youth court processing trends of an obviously gendered offense (sexual immorality) with those of a less obviously gendered offense (incorrigibility). We specifically contrast trends in bringing these two types of cases into court, adjudicating the offenders delinquent, and sentencing them to custody. Examining these two offenses separately reveals different trends over time and also provides some insight into how the youth justice system was changing—especially with respect to girls—in the decades before the new law went into effect.

More recently, in the 1990s, youth court data for all of Canada became available again, and although the JDA, "sexual immorality," and "incorrigibility" were all long gone, a new status-type offense had taken their place: failing to comply with a disposition. In this chapter we explore how this failing-to-comply offense—remarkably similar to the "valid court order" strategy in federal law in the United States, and sparking similar concerns—has been processed through Canadian youth courts during the 1990s and 2000s. Again, looking at the use of this offense allows us to draw inferences about the differences between the way the youth justice system is used for boys and the way it is used for girls. We also briefly examine custody populations, in particular the ratio of women to girls, to see whether in Canada, as in the United States, more girls are in custody than women.

We have attempted to draw comparisons between the United States and Canada to the best of our ability throughout this chapter. Our ability is, however, hampered by the different time periods from which the available data are drawn in the two countries. Thus, the more detailed comparisons are found in the section that explores more recent trends in failing to comply with a disposition and in custody populations.

Incorrigibility and Sexual Immorality in Canada

During the 1950s and 1960s in Canada, the rates at which girls and boys were brought into court for incorrigibility did not show any consistent trend and were fairly similar for both (see fig. 6.1). If there is any consistency across time, it is that "incorrigibility" was used with relative stability and as a justification for bringing girls into court at a rate slightly higher than that of boys. Given that the rates of "normal" (e.g., property or violent) offending for girls and boys differ dramatically, it is perhaps notable that the rate for "incorrigibility" for girls was as high as or higher than the rate for boys.

This *relatively* high use of incorrigibility for girls is shown most dramatically in figure 6.2. Here we see that when girls were brought into court, it tended—much more than was the case with boys—to be for incorrigibility. The use of incorrigibility for boys was very low and changed very little during the 1950s and 1960s. In effect, then, boys were—throughout this period—largely being brought into court on ordinary kinds of criminal charges. At the beginning of the 1950s, however, about a quarter of the girls in court had as their most serious charge the designation "incorrigible." By the end of the 1960s—after the first carefully conducted overview of

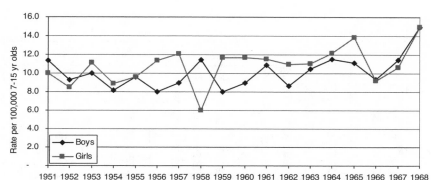

Figure 6.1. Rate at which incorrigibility cases were brought to youth court

Note: The figure for girls for 1958 may be incorrect. We suspect this because, first, it is clearly out of line with the figures for adjacent years, and second, the numbers of cases for girls for this year (and only this year) were, in the printed publication, exactly the same for incorrigibility and sexual immorality. Girls may be cooperative and consistent, but we doubt that they managed to be so organized that these two numbers would exactly match one another.

youth justice had been released and a bill to change the youth justice law was being discussed—the "court caseload" for girls contained only about half that proportion of incorrigibility cases. The fact that the rate at which these cases were brought to court was relatively stable for girls, yet they accounted for a smaller proportion of their youth court caseload, is clearly not a result of a decrease in the use of the "incorrigible" label as a justification for bringing the case to court. Rather, the increase in other types of cases in court accounted for the lower proportion of incorrigibility cases. The rates and proportions (see fig. 6.2) for boys were relatively stable throughout this time period, suggesting little change in how often these cases were brought to court.

For sexual immorality, however, the findings are different in important ways. Here we see clear evidence of a greater use of the youth justice system for girls for this offense throughout these two decades (see fig. 6.3). And, although the rate at which boys and girls were brought to court for sexual immorality or a similar form of vice decreased for both boys and girls, there was a substantially higher rate for girls from the mid-1950s through the latter part of the 1960s.

However, as a proportion of the court caseload (see fig. 6.4), sexual immorality, like incorrigibility, began to decline for girls in the mid-1950s. For boys, the relative decline is less visible, but it is still there. The result was that by the end of the 1960s, sexual immorality cases constituted only about 4 percent of the caseload for girls (compared to about three times that

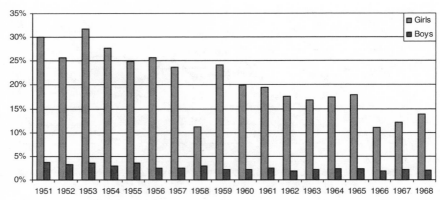

Figure 6.2. Percentage of all girl or boy youth court cases brought to court in which incorrigibility was the most serious charge
See note to figure 6.1 regarding the data for girls for 1958.

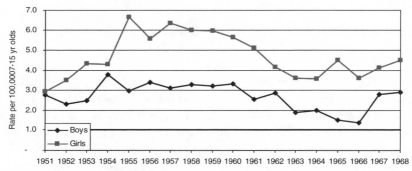

Figure 6.3. Rates at which immorality cases were brought to youth court

15 years earlier) and were a trivial portion (less than 1 percent) of the caseload for boys. Nevertheless, though the decline in both measures (expressed as rates per 100,000 youths and proportion of the court caseload) is clear, it is equally clear that on both measures sexual immorality was, relatively speaking, much more important as a justification for state intervention for girls than for boys. If most cases of sexual immorality involved a girl *and* a boy, it would appear that for boys an active sexual life did not constitute an area of public concern.

Whether looking at rates or at the proportion of the youth court caseload that these two offenses accounted for, the trends at the adjudicated-delinquent stage mirror the trends at the previous stage. Figures 6.5 and 6.7 show the rates at which youths accused in incorrigibility and immorality cases were adjudicated delinquent. One sees remarkable similarity in the rates, for both boys and girls, at this stage compared to the previous brought-to-court stage. Thus, most of the youths who were brought to court for incorrigibility or immorality were, in fact, found to be incorrigible or sexually immoral by the courts. Once again, from the mid-1950s to the mid-1960s we see relative stability in the rate at which boys and girls were adjudicated delinquent for incorrigibility and a decline in the rate at which girls were found to be sexually immoral. The rate at which boys were adjudicated delinquent for immorality also decreased during this period, though there is an inexplicable rise at the end of the 1960s.

Figures 6.6 and 6.8 show the proportion of the youth court caseload for which these offenses accounted for at this stage. Almost exactly as with the previous stage, incorrigibility cases accounted for about 31 percent of the girls' cases in 1951 but by 1968 accounted only for about 14 percent (see fig. 6.6). The cases of boys being adjudicated delinquent for the same reason decreased from around 4 percent to 2 percent (see fig. 6.6).

Once again, because the incorrigibility rates were relatively stable for boys and girls during this time, the decreased proportion of the youth court caseload that these cases were accounting for was not the result of changes in the rates of these types of cases. Instead, there was an increase in other types of cases in which the offender was adjudicated delinquent. Cases of immorality, on the other hand, decreased both in rate and in the proportion of the adjudicated-delinquent youth court caseload they accounted for. In 1951 these adjudicated-delinquent immorality cases accounted for close to 10 percent of the youth court caseload for girls in 1951, but that figure had dropped

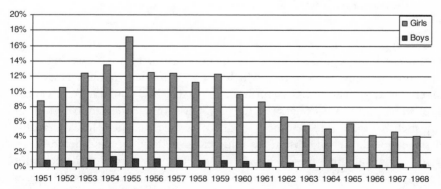

Figure 6.4. Percentage of all girl or boy youth court cases brought to court in which immorality was the most serious charge

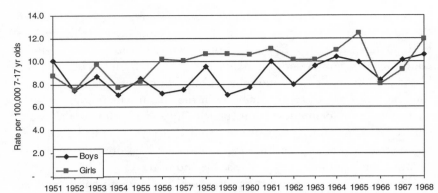

Figure 6.5. Rate of cases in which youths charged with incorrigibility were adjudicated delinquent

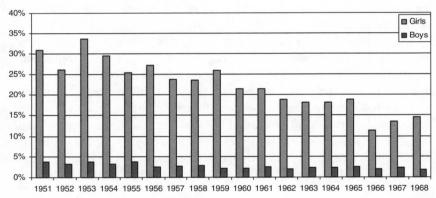

Figure 6.6. Percentage of all girl or boy youth court cases in which the accused was adjudicated delinquent and in which incorrigibility was the most serious charge

to only a little more than 4 percent by 1968 (see fig. 6.8). Such cases were always around 1 percent of the youth court caseload for boys (see fig. 6.8).

Looking next at the rate at which offenders in incorrigibility cases were sentenced to custody, one again sees relative stability, similar to trends at the previous youth court stages (see fig. 6.9). Girls were sentenced to custody at a slightly higher rate than boys during most of this time. The rates at this stage were about half those at the adjudicated-delinquent stage, demonstrating a relatively high use of custody given the minor nature of the behavior typically involved in these cases. However, given that the reasons these cases were brought to court typically did not relate to specific behaviors but rather to the character of the youth, it is certainly not surprising that as many as half would be given custodial sentences. What is notable, of course, is that the rate is as high for girls as it is for boys.

Looking at the proportion of all cases in which youths were sentenced to custody and in which incorrigibility was the most serious charge, one sees that girls and boys were sentenced to custody for different offenses (see fig. 6.10). Because girls were much less likely to be involved in ordinary criminal offenses, the proportion of girls being sent to custody for incorrigibility was dramatically higher than it was for boys. Throughout this period there was relative stability in the proportion of the cases in which the offender was sentenced to custody for which these incorrigibility cases accounted. In 1968 incorrigibility cases accounted for about 45 percent of the cases in which girls were sentenced to custody but only about 7 percent of the boys' cases.

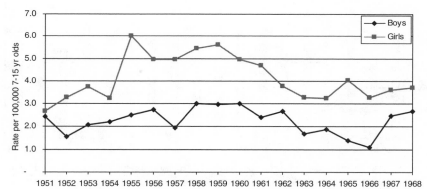

Figure 6.7. Rate of cases in which youths charged with immorality were adjudicated delinquent

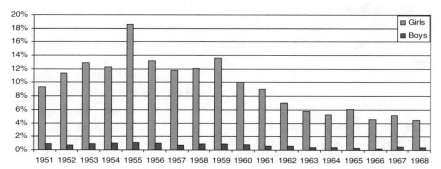

Figure 6.8. Percentage of all girl or boy youth court cases in which the accused was adjudicated delinquent and in which immorality was the most serious charge

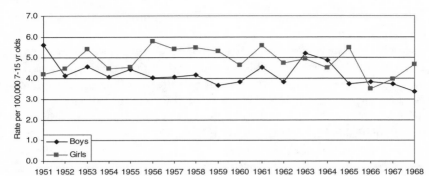

Figure 6.9. Rate at which those found guilty of incorrigibility were sentenced to custody

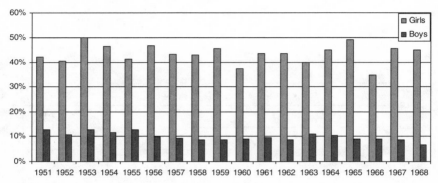

Figure 6.10. Percentage of all girl or boy youth court cases in which the offender was sentenced to custody and in which incorrigibility was the most serious charge

Throughout the 1950s and early 1960s, for both boys and girls, around half or more of the incorrigibility cases in which the youth was adjudicated delinquent resulted in a custodial sentence (see Appendix H). Near the end of the 1960s, however, there were slight reductions in the proportion of these cases in which the youth was sentenced to custody (see Appendix H).

As we said at the outset of this chapter, it is a mistake to think that in Canada these two status offenses were used interchangeably in the middle part of the 20th century. Looking at the rate at which offenders in immorality cases were sentenced to custody, one sees a change during the 1950s and 1960s (see fig. 6.11). For both girls and boys—but most dramatically for girls—youths found guilty of "sexual immorality or any similar form of vice" were much less likely to be sentenced to custody at the end of the 1960s than in the 1950s. Though girls appeared to be somewhat more likely than boys to be sent to custody for these offenses in the mid through late 1960s, the difference between the two groups was much less than it had been 15 years earlier.

The change in sexual immorality policy was wholly a function of official discretion, and it appeared to be incremental, occurring over time rather than as the sudden drop that legislative change might produce. These findings can be seen as highlighting both the potential and the limits of shifts in official sentiment as a mechanism for reform.

Looking also at the proportion of the sentenced-to-custody caseload these immorality cases accounted for, one again sees rather dramatic decreases for girls starting in the late 1950s (see fig. 6.12). These cases always accounted

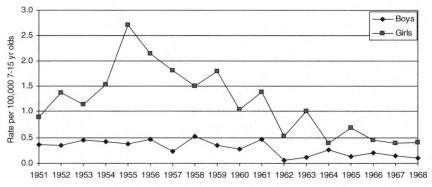

Figure 6.11. Rate at which those found guilty of immorality were sentenced to custody

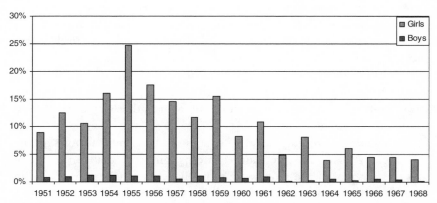

Figure 6.12. Percentage of all girl or boy youth court cases in which the offender was sentenced to custody and in which immorality was the most serious charge

for very few of the custodial sentences for boys, because boys were, in large part, being sentenced to custody for other, more ordinary types of criminal offending. However, because girls were much less likely to be sentenced to custody for criminal offending, these immorality cases accounted for a substantial proportion of the caseload for girls. At its height, in 1955, close to a quarter of the cases in which a girl was sentenced to custody involved immorality. However, from 1955 on one sees substantial declines, so that by 1968 these immorality cases were only accounting for about 4 percent of the cases in which a girl was sentenced to custody (see fig. 6.12). There were also declines in the proportion of adjudicated-delinquent immorality cases in which the girls were sentenced to custody. At its height, in 1955, 45 percent of the cases in which girls were adjudicated delinquent resulted in their being sentenced to custody, but by 1968 only a little more than 10 percent of girls were sentenced to custody in these cases (see Appendix I).

Courts were clearly moving away more rapidly during this period from using the intrusive disposition of custody for sexual immorality cases involving girls than were other parts of the youth justice system. In other words, though the rate at which cases involving "sexually immoral" girls were brought to court (and the rate at which the girls were found delinquent) was decreasing during the 1950s and 1960s, the courts were moving away from using custody for these cases at an even greater rate.

By the end of the 1960s, then, approximately 15 years *before* the law removed "sexual immorality" as a criminal offense for youths, judges in particular, but the youth justice system more generally, had shown a rather dramatic movement away from seeing the youth (criminal) justice system as a way of dealing with sexual immorality. Incorrigibility, on the other hand, looks more stable during this period. It is possible, of course, that incorrigibility was more likely to be linked to other, more traditional offenses than was sexual immorality. It appears that legislative change in the provinces which formally removed "incorrigibility" from their legislation (e.g., in Ontario in 1975; see Grant, 1984) was needed for the use of this status offense to be affected. Cases involving the charge of sexual immorality, on the other hand, seem to have fallen out of favor as the "sexual revolution" of the 1960s took hold.

The focus solely on the treatment of status offenses by the courts during this period tends to obscure another finding: girls in Canada in the 1950s and the first part of the 1960s were more likely than boys to be placed in custody for non–status offenses as well (see fig. 6.13). It could well be that, during this period of optimism about the courts' ability to solve the prob-

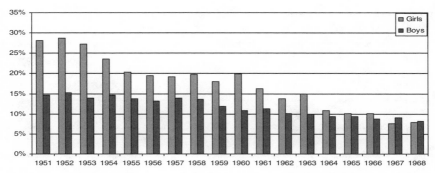

Figure 6.13. Percentage of cases in which the accused was adjudicated delinquent that received custody (excluding immorality and incorrigibility)

lems associated with offending by youth, custody was seen as more "necessary" for girls than for boys. By the end of the 1960s, however, girls and boys were about equally likely to be placed in custody for non–status offenses (see fig. 6.13). (Obviously, when including incorrigibility and immorality in the calculations, girls were more likely to be sentenced to custody than boys, even during the late 1960s; see Appendix J.)

It would be premature, however, to suggest that by the end of the 1960s girls were receiving only slightly more punitive treatment than boys from the youth justice system. To do so would imply that the offenses for which they were being sentenced, their social needs, and their ages and criminal histories (among other things) were similar. We know that this is not the case when we look at the distribution of cases that brought youths into the court system. Figure 6.14 shows a breakdown of the types of cases in which the offender was sentenced to custody in 1968, including the cases involving immorality and incorrigibility. From the bars on the far right, we see that for girls "all other cases, including immorality and incorrigibility," made up a much higher proportion of the cases in which there was a sentence of custody than these cases did for boys. Boys were more likely to be sentenced to custody for more serious property crime in Canada (burglary) and other traditional crimes. Cases involving violence were a small proportion of cases for both boys and girls. Even when the two obvious status offenses (immorality and incorrigibility) are removed (see Appendix K), girls were much more likely to be sentenced to custody for "other" offenses—a broad category that included provincial and municipal by-law offenses (i.e., non-criminal matters).

From self-reported data and detailed analyses of court data from other

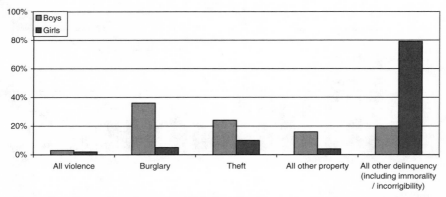

Figure 6.14. Proportion of cases in which the offender was sentenced to custody for girls and boys (including immorality and incorrigibility): Canada, 1968

years, there is every reason to believe that girls were much less likely than boys to be involved in serious crime (see chapter 2). Thus, the relatively equal overall use of custody at the end of the time span in figure 6.13 appears almost certainly to describe more intrusive or harsher treatment for girls than for boys.

Summary

The story told by the preceding analyses of the youth court processing of girls and boys suggests that these two status offenses, incorrigibility and sexual immorality, were used in somewhat different ways. Our findings suggest that the more publicly controversial of the two—"sexual immorality or any similar form of vice" became gradually less important during the later 1950s and 1960s. This justification for labeling a youth "delinquent" was, not surprisingly, used much more often for girls than for boys. By the time the criterion of sexual immorality for delinquency disappeared from the law in 1984, it was likely used relatively rarely, because its use had already declined dramatically as early as the late 1960s. However, the gradual decline in the use of the charge of sexual immorality during the 1950s and 1960s could—we think mistakenly—be seen as a movement away from criminalizing girls "for their own good."

We say that this would be a mistake because the pattern of findings for the other offense—incorrigibility—did not show the same pattern. The use of the charge of incorrigibility as a justification for intervention was roughly the same for girls and boys in the 1950s and 1960s, a finding that is remarkable given that virtually any comparison of males and females in our culture suggests that boys engage in much higher rates of misbehavior than do girls. The demise of the use of incorrigibility as a means by which to bring youths into court came about as a result of two legislative events: the abolition of this offense in some provinces in the 1970s and the eventual decision, in the 1980s, to restrict the use of youth court to federal (criminal) offenses.

Because of the decreased use of status offenses for girls—primarily the decrease in the use of a charge of sexual immorality as a mechanism for taking youths to court—by the end of the 1960s girls were no more likely to be sentenced to prison than were boys. However, given the nature of female delinquency, this equality of outcome would suggest that girls were not being treated equally: girls, it would seem, were being sent into custody for reasons other than their criminal offenses. This, of course, was part of the *purpose* of the JDA, which required judges to consider what they thought were the best interests of the child rather than looking primarily at the offense that had brought the youth before the court.

The Canadian history with respect to status offenses appears to be a somewhat different story from that in the United States. In Canada, the changes in practice preceded the changes in the law for sexual immorality, but not for incorrigibility. The Canadian experience contrasts with that of the United States, where governments struggled for decades after the JJDPA was passed in 1974 to remove status offenders from custody.

Failing to Comply with a Disposition

We have, unfortunately, no meaningful data on the treatment of girls by the youth justice system during the 1970s and early 1980s. Some youth court data were available in the early years of the YOA, but complete data have been available only since 1991. We use these data to explore trends in responding to what is, in effect, a status offense that is quite similar to the valid-court-order strategy in federal law in the United States. This is the Canadian criminal offense of failing to comply with a disposition.

As pointed out earlier, the 1984 YOA drastically limited the offenses that could result in a youth's being brought to court. After 1986, however, the YOA included an important offense of its own: failure to comply with a disposition. This offense could be characterized as a breach of probation, though it is interesting that it was created as a YOA offense (and therefore available only for those sentenced under the YOA). Similar to violating a valid court order in the United States, failing to comply with a disposition could involve a youth who violated a trivial term of a probation order. Such a youth would be brought to court on a new charge of failing to comply. In addition, a youth who was on probation with the mandatory condition of "keep the peace and be of good behaviour" could wind up back in court with two charges related to a minor offense such as shoplifting: theft and the failing-to-comply offense, because shoplifting clearly constituted a failure to be of good behavior. Given that terms of probation automatically contained the requirement that the youth "shall keep the peace and be of good behaviour" (sec. 23(1)(a)), and that the requirement could include "such other reasonable conditions set out in the order as the court considers desirable, including conditions for securing the good conduct of the young person and for preventing the commission by the young person of other offenses" (sec. 23(2)(g)), it is not surprising that youths frequently are brought to court for failing to comply with dispositions.

What we see in figures 6.15 through 6.17 is that the rate (per 100,000 youths) at which these cases are brought in court (see fig. 6.15), the rate at which the accused are found guilty (see fig. 6.16), and the rate at which they are sentenced to custody (see fig. 6.17) is higher for boys than girls. Boys have consistently been brought to court, found guilty, and sentenced to custody at a higher rate than girls. Moreover, for both boys and girls, these rates increased slightly during the later 1990s and early 2000s until 2003–4, at which point there was a noticeable decline, especially in the rate at which offenders were sentenced to custody (see fig. 6.17).

As with the trends regarding violation of a valid court order in the United States, looking at the rates tells one story, while looking at the youth court caseload for boys and girls tells quite a different one. While more boys than

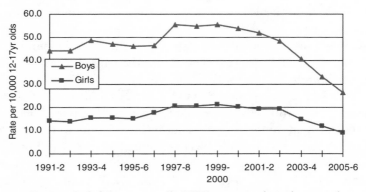

Figure 6.15. Rate at which failing-to-comply (FTC) cases were brought to youth court

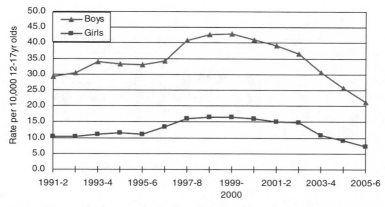

Figure 6.16. Rate at which accused were found guilty of failing to comply (FTC) in youth court

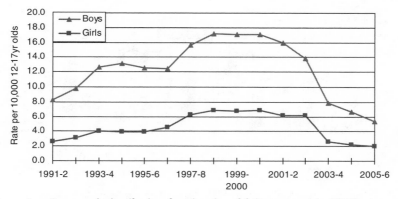

Figure 6.17. Rate at which offenders found guilty of failing to comply (FTC) were sentenced to custody

girls are brought into court, found guilty, and sentenced to custody, these failing-to-comply cases actually constitute a larger proportion of the girls' youth court caseload than the boys'—at every stage of the proceedings. Looking at the proportion of cases brought to court in which failing to comply was the most serious charge, one notices two things. First, these cases consistently account for a slightly larger proportion of the girls' youth court caseload (see fig. 6.18). Second, these cases accounted for slightly increasing proportions—for both boys and girls—until the early 2000s.

Looking next at the proportion of guilty cases in which failing to comply was the most serious conviction, slightly more pronounced gender differ-

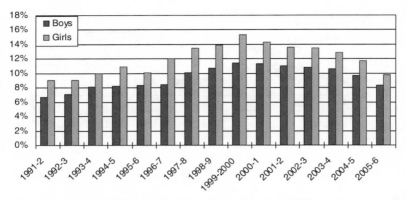

Figure 6.18. Proportion of all cases brought to court in which FTC was the most serious charge

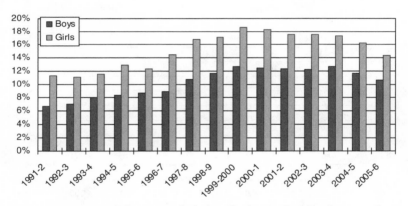

Figure 6.19. Proportion of all cases in which the offender was found guilty in youth court and in which failing to comply (FTC) was the most serious conviction
Note: "All cases" include Criminal Code traffic and other federal statutes.

ences and increases present themselves (see fig. 6.19). These cases account for a slighter larger proportion of the girls' court caseload. Instead of accounting for, on average, about 12 percent of the girls' caseload, as these cases did during the 2000s at the brought-to-court stage, they account for, on average, about 17 percent of the girls' caseload at the found-guilty stage. Boys see less change between these two youth court stages, with these cases accounting for around 10–12 percent of their caseload at either the brought-to-court stage or the found-guilty stage.

The most dramatic gender differences appear in the use of custody for these failing-to-comply cases (see fig. 6.20). In the earlier stages of youth court processing the difference between boys and girls was anywhere from 3 percent to 5 percent. At the sentencing-to-custody stage, however, the differences grew to up to 17 percent. For example, in 1999–2000, around 34 percent of girls' custodial sentences were for failing to comply, whereas these cases only accounted for around 17 percent of boys' custodial sentences. Also interesting to note—and similar to the United States—is that these cases account for a larger proportion of both the boys' and girls' caseload at this stage than at earlier stages.

The similarity between the Canadian youth court processing of a failing-to-comply violation and the U.S. youth court processing of a valid-court-order violation is quite striking. Figure 6.21 summarizes the data for 2005–6 in Canada. Two things stand out in it. First, at each stage these cases account for a larger proportion of girls' cases than boys'. Second, the deeper into the system one goes, the more of these cases there are, especially for girls. Figure 6.22 shows the same trends with the charge of obstructing justice (predominantly violating a court order) in the United States in 2004. These cases start out accounting for around 13 percent of the girls' caseload and by the sentencing-to-custody stage account for close to a third (see fig. 6.22). In Canada, these cases start out accounting for around 10 percent of the girls' caseload and by the sentencing-to-custody stage account for around 26 percent of the caseload (see fig. 6.21). For whatever reason, in both Canada and the United States, these relatively minor offenses are not being screened out as much as other offenses are as they move through the system.

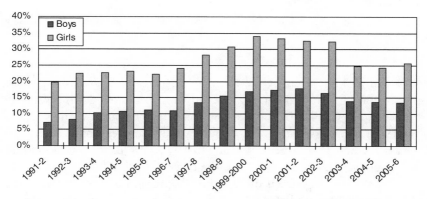

Figure 6.20. Proportion of all cases in which the offender was sentenced to custody and in which failing to comply (FTC) was the most serious conviction
Note: "All cases" include Criminal Code traffic and other federal statutes.

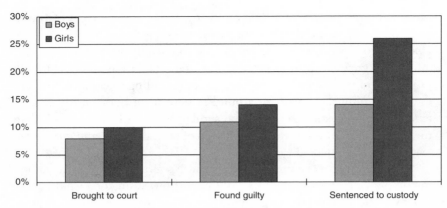

Figure 6.21. Proportion of failing-to-comply (FTC) cases at each stage of youth court processing (Canada, 2005–6)

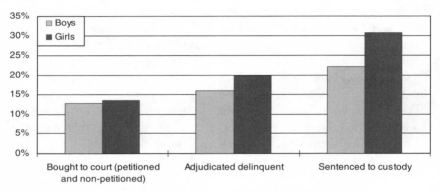

Figure 6.22. Proportion of obstructing-justice cases at each stage of youth court processing (United States, 2004)

When looking at either the rate (per ten thousand youths) or at the proportion of failing-to-comply cases in which the offender is sentenced to custody in Canada in 2003–4, one sees a rather dramatic one-year decrease (in comparison to 2002–3), followed by smaller declines over the next two years. That decrease was due to new youth justice legislation that was implemented on April 1, 2003, the first day of that fiscal year. One of the YCJA's explicit goals, as discussed in chapter 4, was a reduction in the use of court and custody for minor offenses. It contained clearer directions for police to divert and at the sentencing stage required proportionality in sentencing, so that the severity of the sentence should reflect the seriousness of the offense and degree of responsibility of the offender. These cases, then, were generally targeted in the legislation for removal from the youth justice system. The final blow to the use of custody for these offenses came with the sentencing provisions, which outlined the requirements for an offender to be eligible for a custodial sentence. As we mentioned in chapter 4, a youth was no longer automatically eligible for a custodial sentence the first time he or she failed to comply with a sentence. Under the YCJA, a youth could be given a custodial sentence for a failure to comply only if there were at least two previous instances where the youth had failed to comply, and a sentence of custody is not required even then. The result was a rather striking reduction in sentencing offenders in these cases to custody.

It is not clear why custody is used so much for these failing-to-comply cases. Figure 6.23 shows the proportion of these cases (found guilty) that received a custodial sentence. Throughout the 1990s and early 2000s the offenders in close to 40 percent of these cases, both boys and girls, were sentenced to custody. It is not until 2003–4, with the YCJA, that one sees a rather substantial decrease, resulting in only around a quarter of the offenders in these cases receiving custody.

There are a number of different explanations for the relatively high use of custody for these cases, especially prior to 2003–4. It could be that these cases are seen as quite serious—that failing to comply is, in effect, failing to respect the court—and thus a relatively harsh punishment is necessary.

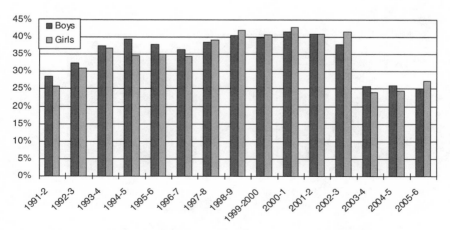

Figure 6.23. Proportion of FTC cases with guilty verdicts in which the offender was sentenced to custody

Indeed, under the YOA offenders in these types of cases were more likely to receive custody than those who had been charged with serious violence, even when criminal record is controlled for (Sprott, 2006). Another possibility is that these cases are simply status offenses in disguise, and the high use of custody reflects the desire to intervene and "help"—a desire most profoundly felt when dealing with girls. Although no data are available to directly test these various hypotheses, there are some data that can help determine whether these cases represent, in effect, simple attempts to control youths.

As already mentioned, these failing-to-comply cases are largely breaches of probation. One can therefore look at the number of failing-to-comply cases in the context of the number of probation sentences handed down in a given year. Using probation sentences as measure of the population or the denominator of cases that are eligible for a charge of failing to comply with a disposition, one can then calculate the proportion receiving a charge of failing to comply. This is, of course, not an ideal calculation, because it is not longitudinal—(tracking the proportion of failing-to-comply charges from the probation sentences handed down). Rather, it is a rather fuzzy one-year snapshot of probation sentences and failing-to-comply charges. What one sees is that of all probation sentences handed down, girls have a larger proportion of failing-to-comply cases (see fig. 6.24).

Figure 6.25 shows the proportion of failing-to-comply cases in which the offender was sentenced to custody out of all probation sentences handed down. This analysis, like the previous one, helps to control for the fact

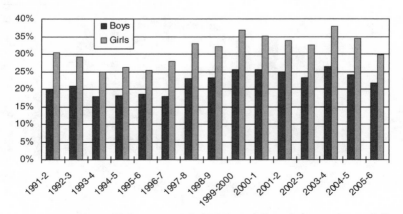

Figure 6.24. Proportion of failing-to-comply (FTC) cases (brought to court) out of all probation sentences handed down (that same year)

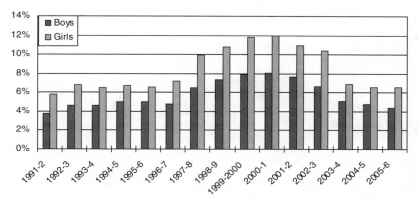

Figure 6.25. Proportion of failing-to-comply (FTC) cases in which the offender was sentenced to custody out of all probation sentences handed down that same year

that girls simply receive a higher proportion of probation sentences than do boys, given their less serious offenses and offending histories. Here one notices, as in the previous graph, that of all probation sentences handed down, girls have a larger proportion of failing-to-comply cases in which they were sentenced to custody.

Custodial Populations

From the available data, it appears that in Canada, as in the United States, the proportion of youths in custody who were girls was dramatically greater than the proportion of adult prisoners who were women. Figure 6.26 shows the proportion of those in youth and adult custody who were girls and women in 1969. While girls constituted almost 30 percent of the youth custodial population, women made up only 3 percent of the adult prison population. These data are similar to those in the United States in 1971. As we suggested in chapter 5, the ratio of women to men in the adult system seems to reflect, in large part, differences in the offending patterns of men and women. One might surmise, therefore, that a substantial portion of the "additional" portion of girls in the youth custody population would, be the result of the interventionist aim of the JDA.

Unfortunately, Canadian provinces do not routinely report custodial counts of youths by gender. This is not terribly surprising, because some custodial facilities—particularly those for younger youths—were mixed gender, and therefore even administratively required counts for each institution would not necessarily capture data relevant for us.

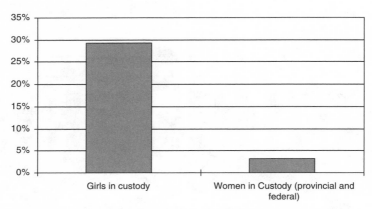

Figure 6.26. Proportion of girls and women in correctional institutions: Canada, 1969

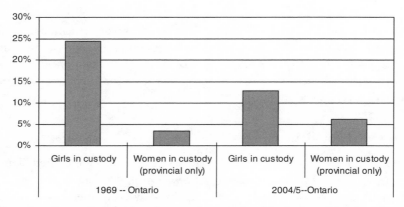

Figure 6.27. Proportion of girls and women in correctional institutions: Ontario, 1969 and 2004–5

For a more recent picture of the relative number of girls and women in Canadian custodial counts, we turn to data from Ontario—Canada's largest province (see fig. 6.27). In 1969 the proportion of girls in custody in Ontario was slightly lower (24 percent) than that for Canada in total (29 percent). The proportion of women overall was the same in Ontario and Canada (roughly 3 percent).[3] However, in 2004–5, the proportion of girls in custody in Ontario had decreased to 13 percent, while the proportion of women in custody had increased to 6 percent (see fig. 6.27). Regardless of the decrease for girls in Ontario, they were still more likely to be in custody than women.

When one looks in detail at the relative rates of imprisonment of girls and women as compared to those of boys and men, we see a pattern different in some perspectives from that which we saw in the United States, but quite similar in more important ways. The rates and ratios are presented in table 6.1.

Looking first at the data from 1969 in Canada and Ontario, we see that

Table 6.1. Rates (per 10,000 girls/women or boys/men in the population) of boys and girls in public custodial institutions (and percentage of custodial population)

Canada, 1969	Girls or women	Boys or men	Ratio (girls/women)	Ratio (boys/men)
Youths in training schools	6.17 (29.2%)	14.35 (70.8%)	7.09	0.53
Adults in prisons and penitentiaries*	0.87 (3.2%)	26.97 (96.8%)		

Ontario, 1969, 1998–89, and 2004–5	Girls or women	Boys or men	Ratio (girls/women)	Ratio (boys/men)
1969: Youths in training schools*	6.31 (24.4%)	18.66 (75.6%)	7.09	0.79
1969: Adults in prison*	0.89 (3.5%)	24.94 (96.5%)		
1998–99: Youths in prison (open + secure)	5.31 (13.6%)	31.89 (86.4%)	5.30	1.85
1998–99: Adults in prison	1.0 (5.8%)	17.25 (94.2%)		
2004–5: Youths in custodial facilities	1.30 (13.0%)	8.26 (87.0%)	1.32	0.53
2004–5: Adults in prison**	0.98 (6.2%)	15.50 (93.8%)		

* For the 1969 figures (Canada and Ontario), local jails were not included (largely holding remand populations). Thus the 1969 figures might be artificially lower than those for other years.

** Excludes penitentiaries (sentences of two years or more); see chapter 6, note 3.

Note: For Canada, 1969: "Youths" = age 10–17; "Adults" = age 18+. For Ontario, 1969: "Youths" = age 10–16; "Adults" = 17+. For Ontario, 1998–99 and 2004: "Youths" = age 12–17; "Adults" = age 18+.

the rates of imprisonment of girls were considerably higher than the rates for women (see table 6.1). The ratios of the rates of girls to those of women in prison were 7.09 for both Canada and Ontario. This means, in effect, that the imprisonment rate for girls was 7 times that of women. Boys, however, were imprisoned (in Canada and more specifically in Ontario) at lower rates than men (ratios of 0.53 for Canada and 0.79 for Ontario). This suggests that girls, in 1969, were being incarcerated at a higher frequency than one would expect.

The Ontario data from 1998–89, similar to those from the United States in the mid-1990s, saw a decrease in the ratio of the rates of girls to women in prison. There were around 5 girls for every 1 woman in prison (a ratio of 5.30). The decreased ratio was due in part to a slight increase in women's imprisonment and a slight decrease in girls' imprisonment. This is similar to the United States, though the United States saw rather substantial declines in the rate of girls imprisoned coupled with substantial increases in the rate of women imprisoned. Thus, while the ratio of girls to women in prison was smaller in 1997 in the United States (a ratio of 1.28; see table 5.2) than in 1998–89 in Ontario (5.30; see table 6.1), one has to keep in the mind the reason for the smaller ratio in the United States: it was due, in part, to a relatively large increase in women's imprisonment. When looking at rates of girls in prison in 1997 in the United States (9.0 per ten thousand; see table 5.2) and 1998–89 in Ontario (5.31 per ten thousand; see table 6.1), one sees a lower rate in Ontario. However, the rate decrease from decades earlier (1969 in Ontario and 1977 in the United States) was about the same in both countries. Interestingly, in the late 1990s in Ontario, the ratio of the rates of boys to men was 1.85, meaning that for every 1 man in prison there were close to 2 boys in prison.

By 2004–5, however, the imprisonment data for Ontario looked quite different. The imprisonment rate for boys dropped dramatically, in part because of the impact of the Youth Criminal Justice Act. Hence, in 2004, the rate of imprisonment of adult men was about twice that of boys (a ratio of 0.53). The rates of imprisonment for girls had also dropped dramatically. The result was that in 2004 the rates of imprisonment for women and girls were such that the numbers of incarcerated girls were only slightly higher compared to women (a ratio of 1.32). Thus, it would appear that girls were still disadvantaged when one compares their imprisonment relative to women's, and to boys' imprisonment relative to men's. At the same time, however, when this ratio is compared to the ratio of the custody rates of girls and women 35 years earlier, girls in 2004–5 were clearly not being incarcerated at a rate comparable to the earlier one.

With respect to this analysis, then, the use of custody for girls would appear still to be disproportionate to that of boys and women, but less so than it had been 35 years earlier. And although the United States, in 2006, for the first time saw a ratio of 0.93 (lower rates for girls than women), that came at a cost: a rather substantial increase in the number of women in prison.

Summary

As in the United States, the story in Canada of the youth justice system's treatment of girls is, in large part, the story of the shifts in sensibilities and legislation. But the story is different in important ways, in large part because the structure of the Canadian federation does not encourage swift changes in the laws relating to youth justice of the kind the United States enacted in 1974. Canada's story is also interesting in comparison with the United States because Canada has not experienced frequent legislative changes— indeed, there have been only three major changes in youth justice legislation during the 20th and 21st centuries. Thus, it is perhaps easier to see effects of legislative changes in Canada than in the United States, where the various states change their youth justice laws rather frequently. Canada is also interesting to compare with the United States because Canada did not see the explosive changes in adult incarceration rates that the United States did. This relative stability of the broader context of incarceration makes it easier to see and understand Canadian trends in incarcerating girls.

Structure of the Canadian Federation

As we pointed out in chapter 4, the federal government in Canada has responsibility for criminal law (including, in Canada's case, youth justice law), though the provinces are responsible for the administration of this law. Canada's original youth justice law, which governed youth justice until 1984, celebrated the necessity of using the criminal law to control sexually active girls. At around the same time that due-process concerns were being injected into the juvenile justice system in the United States in the 1960s, Canadians were beginning to question whether such broadly defined activities as "sexual immorality" or some ill-defined "similar form of vice" were specific enough to warrant intervention under criminal legislation such as the JDA. In 1965, as we noted in chapter 4, the first of many documents involving proposed changes to Canada's delinquency legislation recommended that the criminal law (including the law dealing with young offenders) not be used for welfare purposes. The legislative proposals first discussed in the late 1960s and introduced into Parliament in 1970 did not become law until much later. But unlike that of the United States, Canada's federal government had the power to change—at least officially—the manner in which noncriminal behavior by youths was dealt with by the entire country. The most dramatic legal change came in 1984, when the scope of youth offending was limited to behaviors that fell into the category of federal offenses (largely criminal code and drug offenses, since relatively few youths have the opportunity to commit other federal offenses such as evading income taxes). The next legal change occurred in 2003, when the youth justice law was again replaced.

Changes in the Administration of the Law

What we see from the Canadian context is that changes in the administration of law tend to occur before formal legislative changes. For example, it appears that criminalizing the sexual behavior of young girls was falling out of favor decades before the Parliament of Canada got around to changing the law. Though part of this change may have come about as a result of changes in social views of acceptable sexual behavior for teenage girls, it seems likely that the administration of justice in the provinces also reflected the attitudes expressed in the 1965 Department of Justice committee, which recommended removing such vague offenses from the criminal law for children. Nevertheless, by the end of the 1960s girls were still more likely than boys to be in court and in custody because of sexual immorality.

As in the United States, however, all status offenses in Canada were not created equal. The rate at which girls and boys were brought into court for being incorrigible did not decline in the same way that sexual immorality cases did during this period. Indeed, it is interesting to note that although the rates at which cases of incorrigibility were brought to court were slightly higher for girls than for boys, the difference between the genders was trivial as compared to the difference that we saw for sexual immorality. We suspect that being incorrigible was associated with child welfare, or with family conflict that would tend—more than sexual immorality—not to be highly correlated with gender. If these incorrigibility cases were related to family conflict, it may have been harder to keep them out of court. And if these cases also involved issues of child welfare, it might have taken changes in provincial legislation (largely in the 1970s) to shift these cases out of the youth (criminal) justice system and into the (provincially controlled and run) child welfare system. Not surprisingly, until about 1963, the majority

of incorrigibility cases resulted in custody for girls and boys alike. Even in the late 1960s, in close to half of incorrigibility cases in which the accused was adjudicated delinquent, the offender was sentenced to custody. Sexual immorality cases, on the other hand, almost certainly because of changing views about what should be criminalized, became less likely to result in sentences of custody in the 1950s through the 1960s, especially for girls.

More generally, it also appears that in the Canadian context the shine was beginning to wear off the use of custody for other offenses, and especially for girls in the 1950s and 1960s. The proportion of ordinary cases (other than sexual immorality or incorrigibility) that resulted in a custodial sentence decreased quite considerably—especially for girls. This change, once again, appeared long before the law actually changed in the 1980s. By the end of the 1960s, the likelihood of a case's ending in a sentence of custody was more or less the same for girls and boys. Given the relatively minor nature of most offending by girls compared to offending by boys, however, this does *not* imply equal treatment. To the extent that custodial sentences might be expected to be associated with more serious cases, an equal likelihood of receiving a custodial sentence would almost certainly mean that girls were receiving custodial sentences at a higher rate than were boys for equally serious cases.

Though we do not have data for the 1970s and 1980s, it would seem fair to infer, from the legislative changes which occurred with respect to incorrigibility and the decline in the use of charges for sexual immorality, that much of the disproportionate use of status offenses with girls disappeared during this period.[4] That does not mean, however, that the use of the courts for social welfare interventions for girls disappeared. We have already seen that, relative to women, girls were dramatically overrepresented in correctional institutions in Canada in 1969.

Canada experienced concerns with failing to comply with a disposition similar to those experienced in the United States when it developed the provision that those in violation of a valid court order could be placed in custody without losing federal funding. Throughout the 1990s the rates at which both boys and girls were brought into court and sentenced to custody for this offense grew. Also as in the United States, these cases always accounted for a larger proportion of the girls' caseload than the boys, especially the deeper into the system one went.

There were further concerns in Canada about using custodial dispositions more generally for child welfare purposes, though these concerns were almost never expressed in gendered terms. As discussed in chapter 4, when a 1995 sentencing amendment prohibited the use of custody for welfare purposes, the provision, as far as we can tell, spurred almost no debate, perhaps partly because it was included in a bill that also created "presumptive transfers" of youths to adult court and increased the maximum sentence for those found guilty of murder in youth court. These other, more dramatic changes appeared to have attracted all the attention, even though, predictably, they had no impact on the processing of cases (Doob and Sprott, 2004).

The concern about the overrepresentation in custody of those found guilty of failure to comply with a disposition obviously was important to the framers of the youth justice legislation that went into effect in April 2003. In that legislation, only if a youth had failed to comply with a disposition more than once could the failure justify placing the youth in custody. Once again, however, to the extent that this section got any attention, it was not discussed in terms of its effect on girls in particular.

Girls' Incarceration in Canada and the United States

What one sees with the legislative change in 2003 is a dramatic reduction in the use of custody for these failing-to-comply cases. Instead of seeing a slow decrease over the years, as one did with sexual immorality, one sees a dramatic one-year reduction, which demonstrates the power of legislative change. More generally, looking at the data that are available on girls, boys, men, and women, one sees general declines in the use of custody with girls. The data, however, are limited—only those for the largest province (Ontario) are available, and they cover only a few specific years—and thus it is impossible to know what the broader Canadian trends might be. Regardless, one sees, as in the United States, a slight reduction in the rate at which girls were sentenced to custody between 1969 and 1998–89 (see table 6.1).

The similarly slight declines in the rate of girls in custody in Canada and the United States between the 1960s–70s and the 1990s are especially notable with respect to the United States. Given that the United States was experiencing enormous increases in incarceration more generally, that there was a reduction in the use of custody for girls reflects a trend counter to that occurring with boys and adults. Had the United States not seen such a high use of imprisonment generally, one might have expected the decline in imprisonment of girls to be even larger. What sets Canada apart from the United States is the effect of the implementation of new legislation in 2003. After that legislative change, one sees an enormous reduction in the rates at which both girls and boys were sentenced to custody (see table 6.1).

Looking across the three time frames for which we have data for Ontario, one sees—as for the United States—that the numbers of girls relative to those of women and boys in custodial facilities decreased, though in the United States they had decreased more. The reason for the larger decrease in the ratios in the United States, however, was because of a relatively large increase in imprisoned women. The reason for the decreased ratio of girls to women in Canada was instead due to a relatively large decrease in incarceration rates for girls from 1998 to 2004. However, the ratios of girls to women and boys to men still show that there are more girls in custodial settings than would be justified by their offenses (relative to their male counterparts).

Chapter 7

Continuity and Change
in Justice for Girls

Female juvenile offending and the justice system's response to girls are under-studied topics in most developed nations, and these topics have never been the subject of transnational comparative assessment. The aim of this monograph was to review the social and legal developments in two countries to assess whether there were shared or different histories and whether the comparative approach helped in unraveling the puzzles of girl crime and justice.

Our comparative examination found some interesting similarities as well as differences between these two countries. The first part of this chapter identifies four basic similarities, followed by three smaller but significant differences between the past generation of reform in the United States and Canada. The second section discusses the value and limits of comparative study. We believe that, among other uses of the comparative data developed in this study, recent experiences in Canada can be used to estimate the potential impact of a status offender policy in the United States, had the United States not seen enormous increases in the use of incarceration for everyone else. The more wholehearted recent legislative efforts in Canada have had at least twice the impact of their American parallels in reducing girls' imprisonment rates.

The United States and Canada: Similarities
in the Treatment of Girls

Historical Development of Juvenile Justice

As every student of American juvenile justice knows, the first formal separate juvenile court in the United States opened for business in Chicago in 1899. By 1920, 46 of the then 48 states had created juvenile courts. And Canada, which had juvenile courts in place in some locations in the latter part of the 19th century, established in federal law a separate juvenile justice law in 1908. Not surprisingly, given that there was a fair amount of communication between the American and Canadian juvenile justice leaders of the time (perhaps more than there is now), the goals of these systems were very similar: to separate youths from adults and to intervene in the lives of troubled and troublesome youths in order to rehabilitate them. The similarity was not, however, because of "policy transfer" from one country to another, in the same sense in which it is discussed in the early part of the 21st century (see, for example, Jones and Newburn, 2007). The systems were similar in large part because the concerns and values that shaped the development of the separate justice systems in the two countries were similar (compare, for example, the description of the development of the Juvenile Delinquents Act in Canada provided by Leon, 1977, with the description of the development of the Chicago juvenile court written by Tanenhaus, 2002).

The systems that evolved in each country had broad mandates and aimed simultaneously to divert youths from the adult system and to provide services to help "reform" or "rehabilitate" them. Girls did not feature in the rhetoric relating to the founding of the juvenile courts. Yet, in both countries a disproportionate number of girls were brought into the system and sentenced to custody for noncriminal or status offenses. The stated goal of this treatment, however, was not punishment: each country justified the inclusion of status offenses as a mechanism by which to rehabilitate a wayward youth. The judge, acting as a benevolent parent, would help, aide and guide the youth, usually by means of a prison sentence. Although boys were much more likely to cause trouble in the community, girls, for most of the first two-thirds of a century of juvenile justice, appeared to be the special targets of rehabilitative interventions in both the United States and Canada.

Reforms after 1970: Chipping Away at Status Offenses

In Canada and the United States, those involved in juvenile justice matters eventually began to be concerned about the broad mandate of the juvenile courts. These concerns had been expressed from time to time in the early part of the 20th century. But by the 1960s it was clear that those who expressed concerns could expect to have an audience for their views. Though girls did not feature as the focus of these due-process concerns, the broader ungendered concerns about due process and the use of custody for status offenses more generally began to be discussed openly in polite company in the 1960s.

In Canada, given the federal government's role of being responsible for juvenile justice (criminal) law but not for the law's administration, it is not surprising that the first official recognition of the rights problem in the juvenile justice system came from a federal body: a committee set up by the federal Department of Justice in 1961. In the United States, the first important statements about the issue of rights also came from a federal body: the landmark Supreme Court decisions of the 1960s. Issues of rights and issues of intervention are, of course, quite separate matters. But the wholesale dominance of the interventionist purpose of the juvenile justice system and the manner in which interventions were taking place was a concern. It became clear in both countries that ignoring issues around the rights of children who were targets of these interventions could not survive the winds of change that blew across these two countries in the 1960s.

Throughout the 1960s, then, it became less and less acceptable to place youths in custody for status offenses. In Canada, the 1965 report from the federal Department of Justice's Committee on Juvenile Justice expressed concern about the term "juvenile delinquent," essentially suggesting that it implied that the youth had a broadly defined delinquent character rather than that he or she had simply committed an offense (MacLeod, 1965). Indeed, according to the committee's 1965 report, "a recommendation that was urged repeatedly on the Committee is that the term 'juvenile delinquent' should be abandoned for purposes of legal characterization" (MacLeod, 1965: p. 36, para. 81). More important, the committee made a number of recommendations that broadly might be considered to relate to "rights" (these related to, e.g., statements to the police, appeals of court decisions, and maximum lengths of custodial sentences). Furthermore, the committee explicitly recommended that "conduct now variously described as incorrigibility, unmanageability, being beyond the control of a parent or guardian, or being in moral danger, should not be included within the offence provisions of the federal Act" (MacLeod, 1965: Recommendation 15, p. 285). The committee was apparently ahead of its time: though its report was released in 1965, status offenses were not removed from federal youth justice legislation in Canada for another 19 years. The goal in Canada—proposed federally in 1965 and made law in 1984—was to remove status offenses completely from the jurisdiction of the legislation.

Although certain rights issues were addressed by the U.S. Supreme Court in the 1960s, the first federal legislative change relating to status offenses in the United States was made in the mid-1970s with the enactment of the

Juvenile Justice and Delinquency Prevention Act. Unlike the Canadian proposal in 1965 and the law that went into effect in 1984, each of which had the goal of removing status offenses from the jurisdiction of the youth court, one of the key goals in the American act in 1974 was simply to reduce the use of custody for status offenses.

As we have seen, however, both countries found it difficult to avoid intervening in the lives of troubled and troublesome children. During the final quarter of the 20th century, both countries developed mechanisms to ensure that youths could be placed in custody if they violated orders of the court. Offenses were created—in the United States, violating a valid court order (which could have been originally imposed for noncriminal behavior), and in Canada, failing to comply with a disposition (in which a youth originally had to have been found guilty of an actual offense for which a normal sentence was imposed). Each of these had the effect of allowing youths to be incarcerated for normal youthful behavior: violating the edicts of their elders (in this case judges).

Gaps between Perceived and Actual Trends in Criminality by Girls

While those concerned with rights and those who believed that youths should be found to have committed a criminal offense before being incarcerated focused on the problem of status offenses in the two countries, others focused their attention on what they saw as an increasing tendency in girls toward violence. This concern appears to arise from time to time when unusual events—serious violence committed by girls—hit the press. It is conceivable that some would argue that an increase in real violence by girls justifies special interventions in the lives of girls. People might argue, as we noted in chapter 2, that unless special attention is given to girls who offend, sugar and spice will morph into snips and snails and puppy-dog tails.

We looked at arrest and court trends in both countries as well as self-reported offending and victimization in the United States to obtain a picture of what was happening. Though neither data source—official (administrative) statistics and self-reported behaviors—is ideal, together they paint pictures of girl crime trends very different from the picture painted by those who think they see a wave of girl crime clouding the horizon. We came to the conclusion that although the view may be widespread in both countries that crime—violent crime especially—is increasing among girls, to the extent that they are becoming "just like boys," in neither country could we find any convincing evidence to support such a claim.

When looking at both countries there seemed to be a proclivity to take the statistics out of context. Thus, if one were looking for a girl crime wave, one would undoubtedly find evidence of it (e.g., increases in arrest rates for certain offenses such as minor assaults). However, in looking carefully at the research to date, it appears that the most prudent conclusion is that there is no evidence of an expansion in serious violent crime among girls. Instead, in both countries there appears to be relative stability. For the United States especially, the trends appear relatively clear—there have been few, if any, changes in self-reported offending by girls or in victimization rates. The increases that have been seen tend to be focused on arrests for minor offenses, which are very likely due to changes in policy or policing rather than changes in the behavior of girls. And in Canada, the increase appears more to be an artifact of changes in boys' behavior: as rates of police apprehension of boys decrease, girls become an increasingly high proportion of all young offenders. In both countries, we suggest, an observer looking out at a roomful of young offenders, would see a higher proportion of girls now than they would have seen a few decades ago. There is no evidence, however, that rates of offending for girls have increased.

A Justice Policy Problem for Girls and Young Women: Status Offenses

In both countries we see that there is still some evidence that what are, in effect, status offenses still exist and are being used somewhat disproportionately with girls. Thus, the primary justice problem for girls remains what it has always been: minor offenses and status offenses pushing girls into the justice system. The majority of the crimes that girls commit are minor, and it is these minor offenses, such as stealing and minor assaults, along with failing to comply with a disposition in Canada or violating a valid court order in the United States (e.g., not obeying a curfew, running away, or family conflict), that tend to drive crime rates for girls. Indeed, one might argue that family conflict is what actually drives many of the status-type offenses in both Canada and the United States. No detailed data exist on what youths are brought into court for when they either fail to comply or violate a valid court order. Hence there is obviously, at this point, no way to test this theory. However, a recent Canadian case illustrates how family conflict may indeed play a role in the offenses that bring youths into contact with the courts.

In early 2007, a 16-year-old girl (M. B.) hit the limits of her parents' tolerance, as well as that of the youth court judge who eventually met her in his courtroom. The girl had obviously been a problem to her parents. Indeed, at the time of her offense, she was subject to two probation orders (one as a result of being found guilty of biting her mother) that required her to "keep the peace and be of good behaviour." The court found that in addition to doing damage to her own bedroom in her parents' house (the criminal offense of "damage to property"), the girl's misbehavior constituted something other than keeping the peace and behaving well, so he found her guilty of failing to comply with a disposition under section 137 of the Youth Criminal Justice Act. She was refused bail and held in detention for eight days prior to her youth court hearing. She had also been required to attend school and had failed to do so on six occasions in the previous month. Perhaps most important, the girl had a history of failing to comply with her mother's rules. And to make matters even worse, she had come home intoxicated on at least one previous occasion.

The new offense of damaging her room obviously triggered another court appearance and involved the charge of damage to property as well as charges of failing to comply with the previous disposition (the probation order that required her to behave herself). According to the judge, the girl's youth worker "indicated that things have 'deteriorated' at home between M. B. and her parents and M. B. is 'beyond parental control.' Her latest report card indicates that she is doing poorly in every subject she is taking. [Her] youth worker recommended that a period of open custody should be imposed."

Under section 39 of the YCJA, there are specific hurdles to the use of imprisonment. Broadly speaking, the youth must either have committed a violent offense, or have committed a relatively serious offense and been sentenced on two or more previous occasions, or have failed to comply with noncustodial sentences. The girl, in this case, could not be given a custodial sentence on the basis of normal criminal behavior, because a custodial sentence for the crime of messing up her room (damage to property) is not an option. In sentencing the girl, the court noted that it "has the authority to impose a custodial sentence upon M. B. for each of the [failure to comply with a disposition] . . . offenses committed by her, but it does not have the authority to do so for the Criminal Code offense committed by her [damage to property]" (*R. v. M. B.,* 2007: para. 24).

Nevertheless, M. B. was given the maximum possible custodial sentence for this offense—six months in custody—as well as yet another probation order. To put this lengthy sentence in context, only 7% of *all* custodial sentences for all youths in Canada exceeded six months in length. Hence, even though policy dictated that her actual criminal offense of damaging her bedroom did not, in law, justify a custodial sentence, violating her parents' and the judge's orders did.

The court clearly reversed the statutory preference given to proportionality over rehabilitation in asserting that the sentence "length is sufficient and necessary to promote M. B.'s rehabilitation and it is proportionate to the offenses she has committed," though it is rather difficult to figure out how the learned judge calculated proportionality.

Offenses such as those committed by M. B. are obviously not major threats to society; rather, it is apparently either the court (because the girl failed to follow judicial orders) or the family (because she did not follow the rules of the house) that feels most threatened. As long as these problems within the family exist, so perhaps will the state's desire to intervene. Indeed, even in Canada, where criminal legislation explicitly prohibits the use of custody for welfare purposes,[1] there are cases in which youths are sentenced to custody for just such purposes. Our presumption, then, is that in both countries these minor offenses and failing to comply/violating a valid court order will likely remain the center of gravity for juvenile justice with respect to girls.

The United States and Canada: Differences in the Treatment of Delinquent Girls

Levels of Government Responsible for Juvenile Justice

The constitutional differences between the United States and Canada make the comparison between the two countries certainly more complex but potentially more interesting than might otherwise be the case. The federal government in the United States obviously plays a relatively limited role in developing or reforming juvenile justice legislation. In the United States, juvenile justice legislation is a state, not a federal, responsibility. Thus, the first federal piece of legislation that was developed in the United States, in the mid-1970s, could only urge states to keep status offenders out of custody. Because gentle persuasion was unlikely to be sufficient on its own, though, the U.S. federal government used other tools at its disposal: the distribution of money to the states for complying with federal law. The imprisonment rates of status offenders were thus slow to change. Changes had to be made in each state individually, and although money talks, its voice is softer than the voice of the law.

Furthermore, in the United States, state youth justice laws are seen more as civil procedures rather than as criminal legislation. Thus there is no strong argument for not bringing certain types of cases in the court or not using certain types of sentences. The individual states did not have a standard (e.g., the behaviors that are criminalized for adults) against which to judge its juvenile justice laws. Thus, the conflicting goals of "diversion" and "intervention" could coexist more easily than in a jurisdiction in which the youth justice law was unambiguously criminal law. Although the United States tended, after the Supreme Court cases in the 1960s and the JJDPA in the 1970s, to attempt to restrict the paternalistic nature of the youth justice system, the state could intervene or respond to the needs of the youth, regardless of the offense, and still be consistent with the overall purpose of the juvenile delinquency legislation. This approach tended disproportionately to involve girls.

Canada's youth justice legislation, on the other hand, was always based on the federal government's criminal-law jurisdiction. Hence, even in 1908, when the definition of the (criminal) offense of delinquency was very broad, the law was ultimately based on criminal-law principles. The provinces have the responsibility of administering the law—as they do with adult criminal law—and thus there are still substantial differences across provinces in the use of court and custody to respond to youth offending. It appears to us, however, that this jurisdictional variation understandably is considerably less in Canada. When the Supreme Court of Canada said in the early 1990s that current legislation allowed courts to hand down a long custodial sentence if youths come from dysfunctional families,[2] that case was binding everywhere in Canada. But when the government of Canada legislated this possibility away a few years later, the effect—in theory—was also binding in all parts of the country. This is not to suggest that variation in the administration of justice is not important in Canada. Nor is it to suggest that judges invariably follow the law. It means only that the starting point in the policies that relate to girls and boys in youth justice all start in one place: the Canadian Parliament. Moreover, the criminal-law orientation made it more difficult to justify the use of the court or of custody solely on the basis of the needs of the youth.

In Canada, criminal-law principles and protections can never be far from policy makers' thoughts. The same is not necessarily true for the United States. For example, Szymanski (2008) notes that 31 of the 51 American jurisdictions deny juvenile delinquents the right to a jury trial, a decision that is consistent with the U.S. Supreme Court's decision in *McKeiver v. Pennsylvania*, 404 U.S. 528 (1971). In Canada, this simply would not have been possible: youths in Canada—because the law is unambiguously based in criminal law—have the same rights to a jury trial as do adults—but only if they are in jeopardy of being imprisoned for five years or more. This condition led, for a short time in the early 1990s, to the otherwise inexplicable maximum sentence of "five years less a day" for a youth found guilty of murder in youth court. Had a youth been in jeopardy of a sentence of five years or more (as became law in the mid-1990s), he or she would have had the right to choose to be tried by a judge and jury in youth court (under sec. 11(f) of the 1982 Charter of Rights and Freedoms). In 1996, when the maximum sentence in youth court for murder increased, the possibility of a jury trial was integrated into the Canadian youth court for the first time.

Policy Changes and Stabilities That Influenced Juvenile and Criminal Justice

In the United States, though the federal role in juvenile justice is much weaker than in Canada, there is no question that the 1974 JJDPA was an important development. It was the first formal federal attempt to direct the states' responses to status offenses. The Supreme Court cases of the 1960s were also important, because they were the first official recognition that intervention or rehabilitation through the youth justice system might not be as beneficial as all the rhetoric claimed. Moreover, these cases firmly asserted the need for certain due-process rights for youths who found themselves within the youth justice system. However, the real changes were likely seen more at the state level, as each state changed its juvenile justice laws to comply with the federal act and the Supreme Court cases. Keeping up with the states' changes is obviously difficult, for an enormous number of them occur in any given year. Indeed, there are so many changes in juvenile justice legislation that the National Center for Juvenile Justice has created a "Snapshot" series of bulletins outlining the changes and variations in juvenile justice legislation across the states.

Canada, on the other hand, has had only three distinct pieces of youth justice legislation since 1908. In addition, during this first century of having a separate youth justice system, there were only four occasions—once each in the 1920s and 1980s, and twice in the 1990s—on which the legislation then in place was substantively changed. Only one of these changes—the amendment in 1986 creating the youth offense of failing to comply with a disposition—had any measurable impact on youth justice. When Canada amended its juvenile justice laws in 1984 to focus only on criminal offenses and to incorporate due-process rights, supported by all political parties represented in the Canadian Parliament, these important legal changes were not seen as particularly surprising. Although the Canadian federal government had claimed jurisdiction over youth justice matters in 1908 by creating, for youths, the criminal offense of delinquency, it was only one relatively small additional step to limit what is defined as criminal for youths to those same acts that are criminal for adults. Indeed, a number of reports relating largely to (adult) criminal law in the 1970s and early 1980s (see Webster and Doob, 2006: p. 332) had urged restraint in the use of the criminal law. One form of restraint, of course, is restraint in defining annoying behaviors as criminal. An important example of such a statement of restraint came in 1982, when the minister of justice, Jean Chrétien (subsequently prime minister from 1993 until 2003), released a booklet setting out "the policy of the Government of Canada with respect to the purpose and principles of criminal law" (Government of Canada, 1982: preface). The *first* principle "to be applied in achieving [the] purpose [of the criminal law]" was that "the criminal law should be employed to deal only with that conduct for which other means of social control are inadequate or inappropriate, and in a manner which interferes with individual rights and freedoms only to the extent necessary for the attainment of its purpose." Although it is hard to argue that Canada has followed this principle in the development of its criminal law (we expect, for example, that few other countries have criminalized water skiing at night), such thinking almost certainly would have some influence on the manner in which youths were being dealt with.

Canada's most recent legislation—the 2003 Youth Criminal Justice Act—went one step further and made it clear that an overriding goal of the law was to reduce the use of the youth court and custody, noting in the preface to the law that one goal was to [reduce] "the over-reliance on incarceration for non-violent young people." The goal of sentencing was to hold youths accountable for their offenses by crafting a sentence that is "proportionate to the seriousness of the offense and the degree of responsibility of the young person for that offense" (YCJA, 2003: sec. 38(2)(c)). Rehabilitation was a secondary goal and could be accomplished only within the constraint of a proportionate sentence. The explicit prohibition against the use of custody for welfare purposes ("A youth justice court shall not use custody as a substitute for appropriate child protection, mental health or other social measures"—sec. 39(5)) that was first introduced into Canadian youth justice law in the mid-1990s was also incorporated into the new law.

Net Impact of Reforms on Girls in the Two Nations

Given the different levels of government responsibility for youth justice legislation (predominantly the states in the United States and the federal government in Canada), it is perhaps not surprising to find more dramatic changes in Canada than in the United States in the early years of the

21st century, when Canada's new youth justice law came into effect. Until that point, what we saw in Canada and the United States was general similarity—slight declines in the rates at which girls were incarcerated. But looking at the treatment of girls in the youth justice systems in isolation ignores one of the strengths and complexities of a comparative analysis. There were dramatic differences between the two countries in what was happening to adults in the criminal justice system and, to some extent, what was happening to boys in the youth justice systems.

Figures 7.1 and 7.2 show the change in imprisonment rates for girls and boys for the United States and Ontario (Canada), respectively, over three time periods, using 1977 as the baseline for the United States and 1969 as the baseline for Ontario (Canada).[3] The base year of 1977 is used in figure 7.1 for the United States because that year both public and private facilities for youths were surveyed. Compared to 1977, the 1997 imprisonment rate for girls declined slightly, while that for boys increased. In 2006 the imprisonment rate was again lower than in 1977 for girls and somewhat higher for boys, though not as high as it was in 1997.

Figure 7.2 shows that the trends in Ontario appear to be very similar to those in the United States until 2003. Relative to the base year of 1969, the imprisonment rate in 1998–89 for girls declined slightly (by almost exactly the same amount as in the United States), while boys' imprisonment rate increased. That the United States saw declines in the rate of girl imprison-

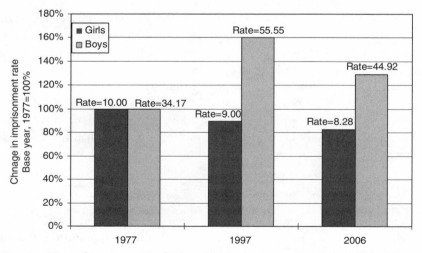

Figure 7.1. Rate of imprisonment of girls and boys using 1977 as the standard: United States
Note: Rates for youths based on ages 10–17.

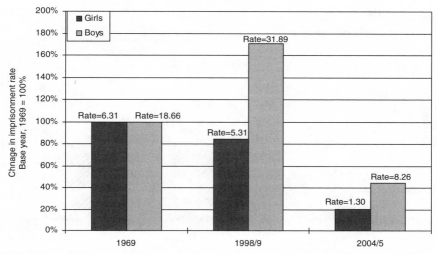

Figure 7.2. Rate of imprisonment of girls and boys using 1969 as the standard: Ontario
Note: Rates for youths based on ages 10–16 in 1969 and 12–17 in 1998–99 and 2004.

ment that were similar to those in Ontario is remarkable, given the broader enormous increases in imprisonment among boys, men, and women in the United States. If the imprisonment policies for girls are influenced by broader policies of imprisonment for boys and adults, then had the United States not seen these increases in imprisonment one might have expected the decline in imprisonment of girls to be even larger. What really sets Canada apart from the United States is what happened after April 1, 2003, when Canada's new youth justice legislation, the Youth Criminal Justice Act, came into effect. There was an enormous reduction, for both girls and boys, in 2004 in Ontario compared to 1969 (see fig. 7.2).

Comparisons between Canada and the United States

Similarities and differences aside, Canada provides an important comparison for the United States. Since the 1970s the United States has seen remarkable growth in the imprisonment of men, women, and boys. The fact that there has been no such growth in the rate of imprisonment of girls is remarkable. What is unclear, however, is how that happened. Were changing sentiments—that the state should no longer be incarcerating youths for noncriminal behavior—responsible for this change? Or was it the effect of the JJDPA and its financial incentives for deinstitutionalization of status offenders? The lack of increase in the incarceration of girls has to be

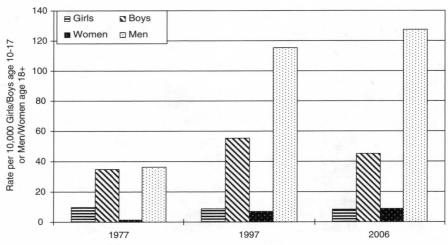

Figure 7.3. Rate of girls/boys (detained/committed) in public/private facilities and men/women sentenced prisoners under state/federal control: United States, 1977, 1997, 2006.

understood in the criminal justice context of increased incarceration of just about everyone else. Figure 7.3 shows the rates of youths and adults in prison over three different time periods. This figure does *not* include jail populations (for youths or adults), which are obviously, for adults, a nontrivial number of people, especially from the 1980s on. Thus, the total imprisonment rates are higher than what we have presented here. Nevertheless, one sees the enormous increase in the male imprisonment rate. The increase in the rate of boys' imprisonment was smaller than that in the men's rate, but still noteworthy. Imprisonment of women also increased, though their numbers are small. Incarceration of girls, on other hand, declined very slightly.

One wonders what might have happened to imprisonment rates for girls in the United States had there not been the influence of the broader explosion in incarceration of everyone else. Looking north to Canada helps provide such a comparison. With relative stability in incarceration for at least the past 50 years (Webster and Doob, 2006), one can more clearly see the impact of legal change. Figure 7.4 shows the incarceration rates for Ontario across three time periods. In 1969 Ontario local jail populations were likely undercounted in the custodial counts, so the figures for 1969 might be lower than for other years. Regardless, one sees relative stability in Ontario for men and women across all three time periods. The similar declines in the United States and Ontario in girls' incarceration rates suggests that perhaps the great success of the JJDPA was in keeping girls' incarceration rates relatively stable. Had the explosion in imprisonment not happened, the reductions in girls' imprisonment might have been even more impressive.

Interestingly, one sees a rather substantial increase in boys' incarceration rates in Ontario in 1998–89, while the rate for girls declined slightly, just as they did in the United States. That girls did not experience the same increase in imprisonment as boys did is interesting. Girls in Canada may have also been swimming against the tide of increased incarceration rates, though it was only boys who were increasingly imprisoned, unlike in the United States, where rates for men and women were also increasing. Perhaps the removal of status offenses from the federal youth justice legislation kept girls' rates stable. And it was likely the increase in the rate of incarceration among boys that drove the government's concern about overusing custody and thus led to the development of the Youth Criminal Justice Act.

In 2004 in Ontario there was an enormous reduction for both boys and girls in the use of custody. This reduction is clearly due to the new legislation. However, one could see evidence of changes even before any legal changes occurred. What happened in the last few years of the 20th century and the first couple of years of this one had happened decades earlier. For

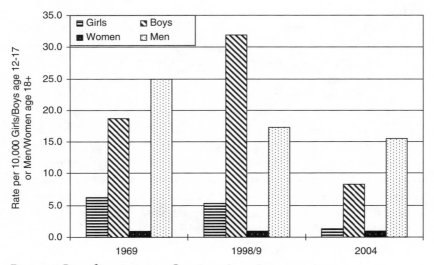

Figure 7.4. Rate of imprisonment: Ontario, 1969, 1998–99, 2004
Note: For 1969 the youth population for the denominator was 10–17.

example, decades earlier the decision to bring youths—largely girls—to court for sexual immorality and sentencing girls convicted of such offenses to custody had begun to decline long before the law changed. However, one sees the most dramatic changes when the prevailing mood coincides with a change in law. The reductions in the use of custody under the YCJA in Ontario in 2004 were larger than those in any other year.

In both countries, then, there are still concerns about the use of custody for girls. In Ontario in 2004, the ratio of the rate of incarceration of girls to women in custody was around 1.3. Although lower than it was previous years, this ratio still means that more girls than women are in custody. Given that the ratio of boys to men in custody is below 1 and that girls commit more minor offenses and have less extensive criminal histories than boys, girls should not be seen in custody as much as they are if the only reasons for incarcerating them are their offense and their criminal record. The United States has also seen many changes in the rate of incarceration of girls, but there is no question that girls are still more likely than boys to be incarcerated for very minor offending. The problem may be that girls still bring paternalistic concerns to the forefront, and thus custody may be seen as "necessary" in order to rehabilitate them.

The Value and Limits of These Comparisons

This study has used three types of comparisons to explore the significance of historical data regarding the offenses and systemic treatment of young girls. The first set of comparisons (for both Canada and the United States) was across the gender line—comparing the crimes and dispositions of young girls and young boys. A second set of comparisons controlled for gender but contrasted age, analyzing the difference in outcomes for young girls and women and contrasting the effects of age difference for females with those for males. The third set of contrasts was across national boundaries.

Each of these comparisons provided distinctive information. The gender contrast showed the persistence of protectionist motives for young females as well as the continued dominance of male juveniles in all serious crime categories. The difference across ages for females showed the enormous difference that protectionist motives made in the level of confinement for young girls in both Canada and the United States a generation ago. The trends in the incarceration of girls versus those for women also give some indication of the extent to which changing laws and values have reduced the differential incarceration of young girls for protective motives.

The values added by comparing patterns in Canada and the United States were also considerable. The two-nation comparison shows that the persistence of protectionist incarceration over time is a strong element in both countries, despite the policy efforts to reduce such incarceration and the obvious progress made. Until quite recently, there was no clear difference between the progress made by Canada and that made by the United States in eliminating protective incarceration, but the Canadian legislation of 2003 has created a quite substantial Canadian advantage.

The allocation of political responsibility for juvenile justice to the individual states means that federal legislation in the United States that has an impact equivalent to that of the Canadian reforms of 2003 is not possible, but state systems in the United States could produce similar changes with similar impacts. And the data from Canada show both the magnitude of change that could be achieved with this type of reform and the policy mechanisms that generate such dramatic impact. The Canadian trends suggest that United States systems could more than double the decarceration of girls in relatively short order by implementing Canadian-style reform strategies cast in the mold of the 2003 changes.

Why was the 2003 Canadian legislation such a success? One reason was the broad mandate it announced: a general preference for reductions in custodial sentences. Our study showed how narrow status-offense initiatives can be undermined by the creation of exempt categories such as offenses based on violation of a valid court order or failing to comply with a court order. The across-the-board mandate for noncustodial dispositions in the 2003 legislation provided much broader momentum for the reduction of protective incarceration. In addition, it is perhaps important to remember that Canada has not only distanced itself from the high-imprisonment policies of the United States, but also has tended to be suspicious generally (for adults and for youths) of claims of benefit from high-imprisonment policies (Doob and Webster, 2006). The success of broad efforts to decarcerate young offenders in Canada since 2003 suggests one important limit on the efforts to protect status offenders from locked custody in the United States: the lack of any broad anti-incarceration sentiments at the policy level, combined with U.S. imprisonment policies, has limited the capacity of the system to find other ways of dealing with those deemed to be status offenders. The effort to combat this one form of secure confinement in the United States has been fighting against a tide of increased incarceration for other types of juvenile offenders as well as adults.

There appear to be limits on the abilities of systems to fine-tune nonsecure outcomes for specific types of youths when the overall rate of youth confinement is on the increase. Perhaps the mixed policy motives in the United States, even more than the diffusion of the power to reform, that has limited the power of status-offender reforms to establish a juvenile justice system for girls and young women that focuses more on their actions than on their status.

Appendices

Appendix A: Comparisons of Charges in Arrests of Boys and Girls

To illustrate that comparisons of charges can be presented in many different ways, we will use Adler's starting point: numbers of boys and girls reported as having been arrested for index violent and property offenses in the United States in 1972 compared to 1960. Row A1 in table A.1 shows these numbers and the percentage increases (306 percent for girls and 82 percent for boys).

One could also control for population changes over this 12-year period and express these data as rates per ten thousand in the population. Row A2 shows these calculations. It is important to note that these numbers, when expressed as rates per ten thousand youths, result in values quite different from percentage increases and in quite different ratios of those percentage increases. Instead of a 306 percent increase for girls, it's a 209 percent increase; and for boys, instead of an 86 percent increase, it's a 37.1 percent increase. Also, the increase for girls, using rates, results in an increase 5.63 times that of boys. This stands in contrast to the raw arrest numbers, which resulted in girls seeing an increase that was 3.75 times that of boys (compare row A1 with row A2).

Another quite plausible way of demonstrating the closing of the gap between boys and girls would be to calculate the number of boys arrested for index violence and property offenses for every girl arrested for the same class of offenses. As shown in row B, this decreased from 10.6 boys for every girl in 1960 to 4.5 boys for every girl in 1972. Similarly, as shown in row C,

Table A.1. Arrests of those under 18 years of age for index violent and property offenses

Method	Girls				Boys			Result
	1960	1972	Change or comparison		1960	1972	Change or comparison	
A1. Adler method: Increase in number of arrests for index violent and property offenses between 1960 and 1972 (for each gender)	16,311	66,244	306.1% increase from 1960 to 1972		171,036	310,620	81.6% increase from 1960 to 1972	Increase for girls between 1960 & 1972 was 3.75 times that of boys
A2. Percentage increase in rate between 1960 and 1972	13.06 per 10,000 girls	40.36 per 10,000 girls	209% increase from 1960 to 1972		132.79 per 10,000 boys	182.12 per 10,000 boys	37.1% increase from 1960 to 72	Increase for girls between 1960 and 1972 was 5.63 times that of boys
B. Ratio of boys to girls in each year	13.06 per 10,000 girls	40.36 per 10,000 girls	1960: 10.2 boys for each girl arrested		132.79 per 10,000 boys	182.12 per 10,000 boys	1972: 4.5 boys for each girl arrested	Ratio of boys to girls decreased by 56%
C. Proportion of offenders who are girls	13.06 per 10,000 girls	40.36 per 10,000 girls	1960: Girls are 9% of offenders		132.79 per 10,000 boys	182.12 per 10,000 boys	1972: Girls are 18% of the offenders	Proportion of total group of offenders who are girls doubled.

Table A.1. Arrests of those under 18 years of age for index violent and property offenses (continued)

Method	Girls			Boys			Result
	1960	1972	Change or comparison	1960	1972	Change or comparison	
D. Actual increase in rates between 1960 and 1972	13.06 per 10,000 girls	40.36 per 10,000 girls	1960 to 1972: 27.3 per 10,000 increase	132.79 per 10,000 boys	182.12 per 10,000 boys	1960–72: 49.33 per 10,000 increase	Increase for *boys* was 20.03 per 10,000 larger (or 81% larger) than for girls.
E. Difference in rates of offending for girls and boys	13.06 per 10,000 girls	40.36 per 10,000 girls	1960: 119.73 difference in rates for girls and boys	132.79 per 10,000 boys	182.12 per 10,000 boys	1972: 141.76 difference in rates for girls and boys	Difference in rates for boys and girls was *greater* in 1972 than it had been in 1960.

the proportion of all offenders who were girls doubled during this 12-year period, from accounting for 9 percent of all offenders arrested for these offenses in 1960 to 18 percent in 1972. It would seem, then, that the evidence of a relatively large increase in violent crime by girls shows up clearly and unambiguously in these four different types of comparisons (rows A1–C).

Row D, however, suggests something quite different. The actual *increase* in the rate of violent arrests for girls was considerably smaller than it was for boys. Girls saw a rate increase of 27.3 from 1960 to 1972, to while boys saw a rate increase of 48.33. Thus, the increase was 20.03 (or 81 percent) larger for boys than it was for girls.

Finally, the actual size of the gap between girls' rates and boys' rates was *larger* in 1972 than it was in 1960. In 1960 there was a rate difference between boys and girls of 119.73 (boys' rate in 1960 of 132.79 minus the girls' rate in 1960 of 13.06). In 1972, however, the difference grew to 141.76.

So, with respect to the more serious index offenses, have there really been more substantial increases overall in girls than in boys? Our conclusion is simple: Because percentage increases from different base rates are inherently deceptive, the only sensible thing to do is to look at actual changes expressed as numbers or rates, not percentage changes. These allow everyone to understand what the data look like.

Appendix B: Relative Involvement in Serious Crime by Girls and Boys

As has been demonstrated throughout this chapter, girls are less likely to be in youth court than boys, especially for the more serious offenses. Table B.1 shows the breakdown for both boys and girls of violent and property offending in 2004 in the United States. For all groupings of offenses, the estimated number of cases involving boys vastly outnumbers the number involving girls. More important, girls constitute a higher proportion of the less serious cases than of the more serious cases. For example, 29.6 percent of the accused in simple assaults were girls, compared to 23.7 percent of the accused in aggravated assaults. Girls constituted 31.1 percent of the youths adjudicated delinquent for larceny-theft but only 9.5 percent of the youths adjudicated delinquent for burglary.

In Canada, as in the United States and other countries, girls are much less likely to be involved in youth court than boys, especially when looking at serious offenses. Table B.2 shows the breakdown of violent, property, drug, and "other" offending for girls and boys at the "found guilty" stage.

Table B.1. Estimated number of cases adjudicated delinquent and proportion of cases for which girls are responsible: United States, 2004

	Girls	Boys	Proportion committed by girls
Aggravated assaults	5,200	16,700	23.7%
Simple assaults	27,400	65,200	29.6%
All other violence (everything except aggravated assaults and minor assaults)	4,000	29,700	11.9%
Total violence	36,600	111,600	24.7%
Burglary	5,300	50,300	9.5%
Larceny-theft	25,000	55,500	31.1%
All other property (everything except burglary and larceny-theft)	15,000	71,700	17.3%
Total property	45,300	177,500	20.3%
Drug law violations	13,400	62,800	17.6%
Other	46,200	135,200	25.5%
Total delinquency	141,600	487,000	22.5%

Totals may not add up because values of N are estimates and are rounded to the nearest 100th.

Similar to the United States, offending by girls is concentrated in the less serious offenses. For example, while 34 percent of the minor assaults involve girls as offenders, only 21 percent of the more serious assaults involve girls as offenders. With property offenses also, girls are much more likely to be involved in minor offending than they are to be involved in the most serious property offenses. For example, in 25 percent of the theft cases, girls were the offenders. In contrast, girls were the offenders in only 9 percent of the cases in which a youth was found guilty of break-and-enter.

Appendix C: Findings from the GAO Reports, 1983 and 1991

In the five-state study in the 1983 GAO report, the data appeared to show a reduction in the number of status offenders detained. Although the sample of detention facilities (and cases within facilities) in each state was not

Table B.2. Number of cases found guilty and proportion of cases for which girls are responsible: Canada, 2005–6

	Girls	Boys	Proportion committed by girls
Assault levels 2 and 3	433	1,609	21%
Assault level 1	1,157	2,256	34%
All other violence (everything except assault levels 1, 2 and 3)	465	2,819	14%
Total violence	2,055	6,684	24%
Break-and-enter	316	3,364	9%
Thefts	933	2,862	25%
All other property (everything except break-and-enter and thefts)	714	3,552	17%
Total property offenses	1,963	9,778	17%
Drug offenses	199	1,497	12%
All other offenses*	944	4,178	18%
Total offenses (including drug offenses)	5,161	22,137	19%

* The "all other offenses" category does not include traffic or other federal statutes.

random, and therefore not a representative of any one state, there were decreases in the number of detained status offenders in all five of the states that were studied (GAO, 1983). There was, however, considerable variability. For example, the report noted that Massachusetts actually decriminalized status offenses and made the Department of Public Health responsible for them, while in another state "over 36 percent of the sampled [detained] juveniles . . . were accused of status offenses or were not accused of any offense at all" (GAO, 1983: p. 10). In addition, while there were decreases in the number of detained status offenders, girls were still far more likely than boys to be detained for such offenses. For example, in the 713 cases from selected facilities within the chosen five states, 168 of the offenders were girls and 545 were boys. Of the 168 detained girls, 72 (43 percent) were detained for status offenses (as the most serious offense), whereas only 56 (10 percent) boys were detained for status offenses (GAO, 1983: p. 51). In other words, not only did status offenses make up a much higher proportion of the caseload for girls, but the absolute number of girls detained for status offenses outnumbered that of boys.

The GAO report did not differentiate public from private detention facilities. There had been concern, a few years earlier, that the decrease in the numbers of youths being detained for status offenses in public institutions might be accompanied by increases in detained status offenders in private institutions. Lerman (1980) examined trends in the use of custody and noted that there "have been significant reductions in long-term correctional handling of youths in trouble, but there have also been offsetting changes in the use of private correctional settings" (p. 281). He also noted that data from the GAO reports which showed decreases were usually only from public institutions. In the end, he argued that "the movement to take status offenders out of public correctional institutions has often been accompanied by a transfer of legal responsibility from probation and correctional authorities to public child welfare officials" (p. 285). Although having someone other than a youth court judge sentence a youth to custody for behavior such as sexual promiscuity or incorrigibility might stigmatize the youth less, he or she would still be in custody. Others were concerned about what they saw as simply a relabeling of status offenders—calling them "persons in need of supervision" (PINS)—and having a different branch of the government (child welfare or public health) incarcerate them (see, for example, Gilman, 1976; and Stiller and Elder, 1974).

The 1991 GAO report noted, with data from all of the states this time, that "thirty-eight of the 50 participating states have reduced status offender detention by at least 75 percent since they entered the grants program" (GAO, 1991: p. 20). Of course, there was still remarkable variability. States chose a base year and then examined how their detained population had changed between that year and 1988. Some states reduced their detained status offender population substantially (e.g., Iowa and Alabama), while others saw increases in their detained status-offender population (e.g., Kentucky and Georgia). Generally, however, the vast majority of states saw decreases in the detention of status offenders.[1]

Appendix D: Limitations to Custody Data

The data for youths in custody come from the Children in Custody survey, which began in 1971. It obtained information on youths who were in publicly operated detention centers, training schools, shelters, halfway houses, and group homes. Initially only public institutions were surveyed; however, in 1974 some private institutions were added to the sample. The data obtained were one-day counts of all youths in the sampled institutions on a specific day who were either detained (pre-adjudication) or sentenced (post-adjudication). Because each year that we present contains different data—in terms of both the institutions sampled (public, private, types of facilities, etc.) and the types of youths sampled (detained vs. sentenced)—we caution against year-to-year comparisons. Differences across years may reflect sampling changes rather than changes within jurisdictions.

As with all other data on this topic, the decisions made on what data to collect and how these data should be presented varied across years. For example, whether or not populations in public and private institutions are kept separate and whether detained populations are presented separately from sentenced populations varies across years. Even though the available data vary somewhat from year to year, we felt it was best to present the most complete set of data available.

Appendix E: Obstructing Justice

Table E.1. Obstructing-justice cases: rate increases and rate differences between boys and girls, 1985 and 2004

	Rate increase from 1985 to 2004		Rate difference between boys and girls (boys' rate minus girls' rate)	
	Boys	Girls	1985	2004
Obstructing-justice cases brought to court	56.4	24.8	21.7	53.2
Obstructing-justice cases in which accused was adjudicated delinquent	27.0	10.8	11.9	28.1
Obstructing-justice cases in which offender was sentenced to custody	6.5	1.8	5.8	10.4

Appendix F: Disorderly Conduct

Table F.1. Rate increases and rate differences between boys and girls in disorderly-conduct cases, 1985 and 2004

	Rate increase from 1985 to 2004		Rate difference between boys and girls (boys' rate minus girls' rate)	
	Boys	Girls	1985	2004
Disorderly-conduct cases in which offender was brought into court	23.0	17.8	16.1	21.4
Disorderly-conduct cases in which offender was adjudicated delinquent	9.5	5.2	2.5	6.8
Disorderly-conduct in which offender was cases sentenced to custody	1.0	0.5	0.5	1.1

Appendix G: Custodial Counts and Population Estimates

Table G.1. Counts in public institutions and population estimates, 1971

	Girls/women	Boys/men	Total
Youths in public facilities (committed)	9,975	38,075	48,050
Adults sentenced to state/ federal institutions	6,329	191,732	198,061
Population, 10–17	16,272,667	16,896,492	33,169,159
Population, 18+	71,863,887	65,988,376	137,852,263

Note: Adult state/federal incarceration includes only those people who are physically in state/federal custodial institutions. Later definitions (post-1977) were broadened to include those "under jurisdiction." See Sourcebook for Criminal Justice Statistics for more details.

Source for sentenced adult prisoners: Sourcebook, 2006: table 6.28, http://www.albany.edu/sourcebook/pdf/t6282006.pdf.

Source for youths in custody: Sourcebook, 1974: table 6.5, p. 419.

Population estimates: U.S. Census Bureau, http://www.cecnsus.gov/popest/archives.

Table G.2. Counts in public institutions and population estimates, 1977

	Girls/women	Boys/men	Total
"Residents"* (youths) in public facilities	7,175	36,921	44,096
Adults sentenced to state/federal institutions	11,044	267,097	278,141
Population—10–17	15,860,900	16,508,844	32,369,744
Population—18+	80,858,265	73,918,022	154,776,287

* It is not clear whether the definition of "residents" includes detained youths.
Source for sentenced adult prisoners: Sourcebook, 2006: table 6.28, http://www.albany.edu/sourcebook/pdf/t6282006.pdf.
Source for youths in custody: Sourcebook, 1980: table 6.6, p. 481.

Table G.3. Counts in public and private institutions and population estimates, 1977

	Girls/women	Boys/men	Total
"Residents"* (youths) in public and private facilities	15,858	57,308	73,166
Adults sentenced prisoners under state/federal jurisdiction	11,044	267,097	278,141
Population—10–17	15,860,900	16,508,844	32,369,744
Population—18+	80,858,265	73,918,022	154,776,287

* It is not clear whether the definition of "residents" includes detained youths.
Source for sentenced adult prisoners: Sourcebook, 2006: table 6.28, http://www.albany.edu/sourcebook/pdf/t6282006.pdf.
Source for youths in custody: Sourcebook, 1980: table 6.6, p. 481.

Table G.4. **Counts in public and private institutions and population estimates, 1987**

	Girls/women	Boys/men	Total
Youths "in"* public and private facilities	19,035	72,611	91,646
Adult sentenced prisoners under state/federal jurisdiction	26,822	533,990	560,812
Population, 10–17	13,437,169	14,136,537	27,573,706
Population, 18+	93,563,386	85,669,363	179,232,749

* It is not clear whether "in" includes detained and committed youths.
Source for adults under state/federal correctional authorities: Sourcebook, 2006: table 6.28,http://www .albany.edu/sourcebook/pdf/t6282006.pdf.
Source for youths in custody: Sourcebook, 1988: table 6.8, p. 595.

Table G.5. **Counts in public and private institutions and population estimates, 1997**

	Girls/women	Boys/men	Total
Youths in public and private facilities (committed)	8,956	66,450	75,406
Youths in public and private facilities (detained)	4,810	23,230	28,040
Adult sentenced prisoners under state/federal jurisdiction	73,794	1,120,787	1,194,581
Population, 10–17	15,289,227	16,144,763	31,433,990
Population, 18+	104,610,079	97,116,162	201,726,241

Source for adults under state/federal correctional authorities: Sourcebook, 2006: table 6.28, http://www .albany.edu/sourcebook/pdf/t6282006.pdf.
Source for youths in custody: Author's analysis of OJJDP's Census of Juveniles in Residential Placement 1997 (machine-readable data files).
Reference: Sickmund, M., Sladky, T. J., and Kang, W. (2008). Census of Juveniles in Residential Placement Databook. http://www.ojjdp.ncjrs.gov/ojstatbb/cjrp.

Table G.6. Counts in public and private institutions and population estimates, 2006

	Girls/women	Boys/men	Total
Youths in public and private facilities (committed)	8,886	55,672	64,558
Youths in public and private facilities (detained)	4,691	21,653	26,344
Adult sentenced prisoners under state/federal jurisdiction	103,104	1,399,075	1,502,179
Population, 10–17	16,392,436	17,215,603	33,608,039
Population, 18+	115,885,477	109,777,445	225,662,892

Source for adults under state/federal correctional authorities: Sourcebook, 2006: table 6.28, http://www
.albany.edu/sourcebook/pdf/t6282006.pdf.
Source for youths in custody: Author's analysis of OJJDP's Census of Juveniles in Residential Placement
2006 (machine-readable data files).
Reference: Sickmund, M., Sladky, T. J., and Kang, W. (2008). "Census of Juveniles in Residential
Placement Databook." http://www.ojjdp.ncjrs.gov/ojstatbb/cjrp/.

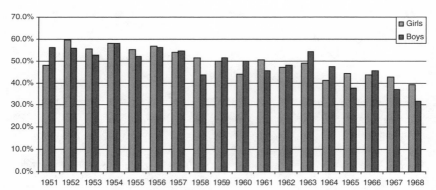

Figure H.1. Percentage of all incorrigibility cases in which the offender was adjudicated
delinquent that were sentenced to custody

Appendix H: Proportion of Adjudicated-Delinquent Incorrigibility Cases That Were Sentenced to Custody

When looking at the proportion of the adjudicated-delinquent incorrigibility cases that were sentenced to custody, one sees a relatively high use of custody (see fig. H.1). Girls and boys had similar proportions of these adjudicated-delinquent incorrigibility cases sentenced to custody. Throughout the 1950s and early 1960s, the offenders in half or more of these incorrigibility cases were sentenced to custody (for both boys and girls). There appeared to be a slight decrease in the later 1960s, such that only around 30 percent to 40 percent of the offenders in these cases were sentenced to custody.

The similar proportions of boys and girls in adjudicated-delinquent incorrigibility cases who were sentenced to custody do not necessarily mean boys and girls were treated equally. Given that girls tend to have less serious offending patterns and histories, the figures for female juvenile offenders indicate a remarkably high use of custody. Of course, during this time in Canada—as in the United States—the focus was not so much on the offense and criminal history, but on the offender.

Appendix I: Proportion of Adjudicated-Delinquent Immorality Cases That Were Sentenced to Custody

Further evidence for the decline in sentencing offenders in sexual immorality cases to custody comes from looking at the proportion of adjudicated-delinquent immorality cases that were sentenced to custody (see fig. I.1). Up

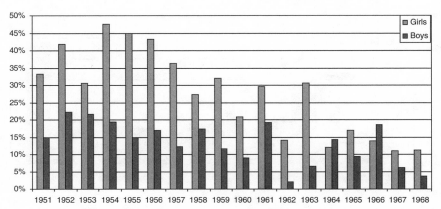

Figure I.1. Percentage of all immorality cases in which offender was adjudicated delinquent that were sentenced to custody

until 1954 the proportion of girls' cases sentenced to custody increased, to a peak of more than 45 percent. After 1954, however, there were substantial declines, such that by 1968 the girls in just over 10 percent of these cases who were adjudicated delinquent were sentenced to custody. Boys also saw declines, although, because their numbers were lower to begin with, the declines are not nearly as impressive. The rate decreases in sentencing the offenders in these immorality cases to custody, coupled with the decreases in the proportion of offenders sentenced to custody, suggests that unlike incorrigibility cases, sexual immorality cases were actually declining.

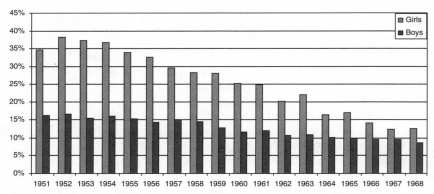

Figure J.1. Percentage of all cases in which offender was adjudicated delinquent that were sentenced to custody

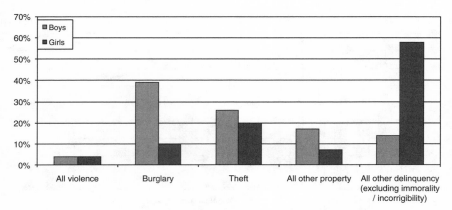

Figure J.2. Proportion of cases sentenced to custody (excluding immorality and incorrigibility cases)

Appendix J: Adjudicated-Delinquent Cases Sentenced to Custody

If one examines the proportion of all cases in which the offender was adjudicated delinquent and subsequently sentenced to custody, one sees that girls are more likely to be sentenced to custody than boys (see figs. J.1 and J.2). This is because of the increased use of custody and the relatively punitive—or at the time perhaps "rehabilitative"—response to incorrigibility and sexual immorality with girls.

Notes

CHAPTER ONE

1. Based on membership in the United Nations as of October 31, 2007.

2. Canada has ten provinces and three territories. For all practical purposes related to youth justice, the three territories, though small in population, can be considered to be provinces.

3. For various interesting but in this context unimportant reasons, the Canadian laws governing young offenders applied in Newfoundland (now Newfoundland and Labrador) only after 1984, notwithstanding the fact that Newfoundland became a province of Canada in 1949.

4. http://www.keytosaferschools.com/girlviolence.htm.

5. Index offenses include murder, nonnegligent manslaughter, robbery, forcible rape, aggravated assault, burglary, larceny/theft, motor vehicle theft, and arson.

CHAPTER TWO

1. http://www.fbi.gov/ucr/cius2006/data/table_37.

2. http://www.fbi.gov/ucr/cius2006/data/table_42.

3. It is worth noting that direct comparisons across Canada and the United States in the rates of crime or subsets of crime are typically problematic. In Canada, there is a single (federal) set of criminal laws that are under the sole jurisdiction of the federal government. Though the provinces (and territories) administer the law and provide "counts" of crimes to the federal statistical agency (Statistics Canada), the definitions of offenses and so on are uniform. Typically, the provinces and territories' reporting to the federal statistical agency is complete and uniform. In the United States, in contrast, index offenses are a subset of all possible criminal offenses and other measures of crime, such as those used by the National Center for Juvenile Justice, are an attempt to get comparability on the basis of differing

definitions and sometimes incomplete data. The differing definitions across states, and between the various states and Canada, are important enough that comparisons on rates other than homicide are problematic. Most notably, comparisons of the absolute levels of index crime rates in the United States to overall crime rates in Canada are, for the most part, meaningless.

4. http://www.fbi.gov/ucr/cius2006/data/table_37.

5. http://www.fbi.gov/ucr/cius2006/data/table_37.

6. Aside from any considerations about comparability of offenses, U.S. rates are calculated using an estimate of the overall number of 10-to-17-year-olds, notwithstanding the fact that this is not, inevitably, the age range of juvenile courts in all states, and notwithstanding the fact that the number of youths dealt with in adult courts (by way of statutory exclusion from juvenile court or direct file statutes) is nontrivial in the United States. Canadian rates, on the other hand, are calculated using 12-to-17-year-olds because 12 is the youngest age at which a youth can be brought to court in Canada. There have not been many transfers to adult court in Canada—typically fewer than 100 per year in the country with about 2.5 million youths. Since April 1, 2003, transfers to adult court have not been legally permitted in Canada.

7. Because figures for motor vehicle thefts and arsons were not easily available, we could not create a similar property offense index for Canada.

8. To use a simple example, imagine that at time 1 the rate for boys was 8 and the rate for girls was 1. At time 2, imagine that the rate for boys increased to 10 and the rate for girls increased to 2. At time 1, the ratio of the rate of girls to boys was 0.125, and at time 2 the ratio increased to 0.20. While boys saw a rate increase of 2 and girls saw a rate increase of only 1, and while at time 1 the rate difference between girls and boys was 7 and at time 2 the rate difference increased to 8, the ratio of girls' rates to boys' rates nevertheless increased because proportionately girls saw a larger increase (100 percent) than did boys (25 percent).

CHAPTER THREE

1. We focus our attention primarily on the development of the courts and court proceedings for youths. As others have acknowledged, the "corrections" part of the system began much earlier (see Steinberg and Schwartz, 2000).

2. In both jurisdictions, there are various words that have been used, at various times in history, to avoid the implication that youths are "sentenced" in a manner that in any way resembles the manner in which adults who have been found guilty are sentenced. In Canada, for example, under the Young Offenders Act, we were supposed to talk about "dispositions" rather than sentences. Similarly, youths are sometimes "placed" in custody, rather than "sentenced" to custody. To avoid con-

fusion, we will generally be using the term "sentence" (and its derivatives) rather than the various other terms that have been used during the past century.

3. Because the original 1925 report is not easily available, it is not clear how much, if any, notice was taken of the findings of differences in treatment between girls and boys. Given the title of the report, however, it is likely safe to assume that little concern was raised about the treatment of girls. For those who are interested, the report is P. Kasius (1925), "Venereal Disease Aspects of Delinquency," in *The Development of Juvenile Courts and Probation: Annual Report and Proceedings of the Nineteenth Annual Conference of the National Probation Association* (New York: National Probation Association).

4. The definition of a "wayward minor" was provided in Title VII-A of the New York Code of Criminal Procedure, Section 913-a (1943): "Any person between the ages of sixteen and twenty-one who either (1) is habitually addicted to the use of drugs or intemperate use of intoxicating liquors, or (2) habitually associates with dissolute persons, or (3) is found of his or her own free will and knowledge in a house of prostitution or assignation or ill fame, or (4) habitually associates with thieves, prostitutes, pimps or procurers or disorderly persons, or (5) is willfully disobedient to the reasonable and lawful commands of parent, guardian or other custodial and is morally depraved or is in the danger of becoming morally depraved may be deemed a wayward minor." Though there were five different categories, and two more were added in 1944, Tappan (1947) noted that in practice only subsection 5 of the statute was used, in part because there were difficulties in securing sufficiently specific proof for the other four provisions. After sex offenses, the other most common complaints brought before the court were "truancy, resistance to authority, keeping late hours, running away from home, or staying away over night—the sort of charge upon which delinquency is commonly found by the Children's court" (Tappan, 1947: p. 158).

5. In February 1967 the President's Commission on Law Enforcement and Administration of Justice issued a publication titled *The Challenge of Crime in a Free Society*, which encompassed all aspects of the justice system, including special categories of offenses (e.g., organized crime, drug offenses, etc.). Chapter 3 included recommendations for the operation of the juvenile justice system. Another volume, *Juvenile Delinquency and Youth Crime*, elaborated on the recommendations in chapter 3, provided additional background on the recommendations, and had a more lengthy discussion of some of the history. We use information from both reports in this chapter.

6. The other mandate was sight-and-sound separation of juveniles from adults in detention and correctional facilities (see Snyder and Sickmund, 2006: p. 96).

7. Initially states had two years in which to deinstitutionalize status offenders,

but later amendments extended the deadline and defined "substantial compliance" as a reduction of 75 percent of incarcerated status offenders (see Sweet, 1991).

CHAPTER FOUR

1. In 1857 the Parliament of the Province of Canada, in an Act for the More Speedy Trial and Punishment of Juvenile Offenders (1857), attempted to expedite trials for some youths. There was also concern, at this time, over imprisoning youths with adults. An Act Establishing Prisons for Young Offenders (1857) was passed that year to encourage the separation of youths and adults (Trépanier, 1999; and Gagnon, 1984).

2. For example, Quebec in 1868 passed provincial legislation that established certified reform schools for young offenders. The federal law regarding the incarceration of juveniles was then amended in 1869 in order to facilitate the use of these reform schools. Specifically, an Act Respecting Juvenile Offenders within the Province of Quebec (1869) allowed youths to be sentenced to a reform school instead of, or in addition to, a common jail. Also at this time, Quebec created a new class of delinquents: the incorrigibles. These were youths who would not obey the rules of the newly established reform schools: "The Lieutenant-Governor may at any time, on the report of one of the inspectors of prisons for the Province of Quebec, order any offender undergoing sentence in any certified reformatory school . . . to be removed as incorrigible; and . . . imprisoned in the penitentiary for the remainder of the term of his sentence" (Act Respecting Juvenile Offenders within the Province of Quebec, 1869, sec. 4). Youths who willfully neglected or refused to follow the rules of the reform school could also be imprisoned for three months with hard labor (sec. 6). Following this legislation, Montreal—the largest city in Quebec at the time—opened both a reform and an industrial school for girls in 1870 and a reform school for boys in 1873.

3. The then-current definition of a juvenile delinquent was anyone under the age of 16 "who violates any provision of *The Criminal Code,* chapter 146 of the Revised Statutes, 1906, or any Dominion or provincial statute, or of any by-law or ordinance of any municipality, for which violation punishment by fine or imprisonment may be awarded, or who is guilty of sexual immorality or any similar form of vice, or who is liable by reason of any other act to be committed to an industrial school or juvenile reformatory under the provisions of any Dominion or provincial statute." An amendment was introduced at this time to remove the words "for which violation punishment by fine or imprisonment may be awarded," presumably to broaden the definition of a juvenile delinquent.

4. It should be noted that discrimination on the basis of age did not become a formal civil-liberties issue until 1985, at which point Canada's Charter of Rights and Freedoms generally prohibited discrimination on the basis of age.

5. Since 1998 the Canadian Centre for Justice Statistics has used three different definitions of "case." For our purposes here, the variation is not important. In this instance, a "case" consists of one or more charges against a single individual that begin the court process in the same court on the same day.

6. The definition of "case" referred to here (in a data set created for us in 2005) is one or more charges against an individual that complete the court process on the same day.

CHAPTER FIVE

1. These analyses for the United States, and the analogous one for Canada in chapter 6, should be seen as suggestive and tentative rather than definitive. The most obvious reason is that the data are clearly incomplete on a number of dimensions. First of all, we do not have custody data broken down by gender for a wholly adequate number of years. For both the United States and Canada, the interest in gender among the custodial data collectors over the past 35 years appears to have been somewhat inconsistent. Second, as will be noted, there are sometimes serious difficulties in assessing what the data mean. At times it is not clear, for example, whether the data consistently included remand populations. Third, in some instances, there are sampling problems (e.g., different institutions sampled in different years) that might account for at least some of the observed differences. Fourth, notwithstanding our best efforts as well as those of a research assistant, we were not able to find certain data for certain years (e.g., the proportion of those in Canada's penitentiaries, broken down by gender, who were sentenced in particular provinces). This last problem is analogous to the U.S. problem of not being able to know which state the prisoners in federal correctional facilities were sentenced in. In addition, even when there were some data, we could not always get data from the same years from both countries. We present the data that are contained in this and the following chapters, however, because they appear to be consistent with other findings that we present in this book. It is equally important to keep in mind that the exact values of some of the ratios depends, in many instances, on which ratio one presents. For this reason, we have presented the actual imprisonment rates (for girls, boys, men, and women) so that the causes of the changes in ratios can be fully understood.

2. As discussed in chapter 3, the VCO was created so that states, if they wished, could incarcerate a youth for not following an order of the court—even if the initial offense for which the court order was given was a status offense—without losing federal funding for being out of compliance with the JJDPA and its deinstitutionalization mandate.

3. Appendix G contains the raw number of custodial counts and population estimates for those with ratio fetishes who would like to calculate additional indexes.

4. Unfortunately, the corrections-data breakdown of race or ethnicity did not match the manner in which available population data were broken down. In the corrections data there appeared to be a category for Hispanics that was mutually exclusive with respect to whites, blacks, American Indians, and Asians. However, in the population data that we located, there was no such mutually exclusive category available. Thus, because the denominator available to us for Hispanics was likely to be inappropriate given our numerator, we felt that it would be deceptive to present those rates.

5. On the other hand, one could argue that it is equally plausible that the imprisonment of girls may have little to do with broader criminal justice policy trends. Girl crime may be driven in large part by rehabilitative goals and low-level offending, and thus the high-imprisonment policies targeted at boys and adults fail to capture many girls.

CHAPTER SIX

1. The law is not gendered. Consensual sex with people of either sex is prohibited in situations in which one consenting partner is under 16 and the other is more than five years older than the younger partner.

2. Not surprisingly, data in Canada are available in inconsistent ways over the time period of interest to us. We have therefore presented what data we could find. As best we could determine, data for time periods not included here are either unavailable or available only in forms that would not be meaningful for our purposes.

3. This does not include penitentiary populations—those sentenced to two years or more in Canada. Penitentiary populations—and indeed adult prison populations overall—have been quite constant in Canada since the early 1960s (Doob and Webster, 2006). In addition, women are vastly underrepresented in Canadian penitentiaries, typically constituting about 2–3 percent of that more serious (longer-sentenced) group during the past 25 years (Gartner, Webster, and Doob, in preparation).

4. The lack of data concerning the characteristics of offenders in prison is remarkable but may reflect a broad policy assumption in Canada either that it doesn't matter who is in prison or that we would prefer not to know. This issue is much broader than simply the lack of data on the gender of child prisoners for two decades starting in the late 1960s. In the first part of the 21st century, one cannot routinely find publicly available data on the average custodial count for adult men and women in most provincial prisons (which account for about 60 percent of the overall imprisoned adult population). Similarly, the criminal justice system data collectors apparently do not collect and certainly do not disseminate information about the race or skin color of those apprehended or before the courts for

criminal offenses or incarcerated. A number of principled arguments have been made about this (see Doob, 1991; and Wortley, 1999). Indeed, even though it is publicly acknowledged that Aboriginal offenders are vastly overrepresented in Canada's prisons and are overrepresented as victims and offenders in homicides (Doob, Grossman, and Auger, 1994), information about the Aboriginal status of homicide victims and offenders is no longer available. Apparently the official position on these sensitive issues is that if the Canadian public can see no evil, the politicians will hear no evil. Whether the lack of information about gender is a result of the same kind of government sensitivity is, of course, anyone's guess. We suspect that the lack of information reflects both a desire to avoid controversy and a general lack of concern about who is actually brought into the criminal justice systems for both youths and adults.

CHAPTER SEVEN

1. "A youth justice court shall not use custody as a substitute for appropriate child protection, mental health or other social measures" (sec. 39(5) of the Youth Criminal Justice Act); and "A youth justice court judge or a justice shall not detain a young person in custody prior to being sentenced as a substitute for appropriate child protection, mental health or other social measures" (sec. 29(1) of the Youth Criminal Justice Act).

2. *R. v. M. (J. J.)* (1993), 2 Supreme Court Reports 421, 81 Canadian Criminal Cases (3d) 487.

3. National data for these comparisons were not available. Our best proxy was Ontario data, which, on many criminal justice measures, including incarceration rates, is more or less representative of the country as a whole

APPENDIX

1. The GAO report cautions that their exact numbers may not be correct because of differences across states in what constitutes a status offense. That is, some states characterize status offenses as delinquent offenses, which may lead to under- or overreporting. Moreover, the data were reported by detention facility administrators and were not verified, and there were concerns about trends in public versus private institutions.

References

Legislation and Legal Cases

An Act Respecting Arrest, Trial and Imprisonment of Youthful Offenders. S.C. 1894, 57–58 Vic. C. 58.

An Act Respecting Juvenile Delinquents. S.C. 1908, 7–8 Ed. VII c. 40.

An Act Respecting Juvenile Delinquents. S.C. 1929, 19–20 Geo. V c. 46.

Canadian Charter of Rights and Freedoms (Being Part I of the Constitution Act, 1982).

Young Offenders Act. R.S.C. 1985, c. Y1.

Youth Criminal Justice Act. S.C. 2002, c. 1, in force April 1, 2003.

R. v. Frost (1977). 37 C.C.C. (2d). 65 (Prov. Crt.).

R. v. M. (J. J.) (1993). 2 S.R.C 421 (S.S.C.).

R. v. M. B. (2007). N.J. 61 (Prov. Crt.).

R. v. Tomlin (1977). 2 W.W.R. 277.

Attorney-General of British Columbia v. Smith (1967). 32 C.C.C. (1d) 244 (S.C.C).

Publications

Acoca, L. (1999). Investing in girls: A 21st century challenge. *Juvenile Justice 6*, 3–13.

Adler, F. (1975). *Sisters in Crime: The Rise of the New Female Offender.* New York: McGraw-Hill.

Ageton, S., and Elliott, D. S. (1978). *The Incidence of Delinquent Behavior in a National Probability Sample of Adolescents.* Boulder: University of Colorado, Behavioral Research Institute.

American Bar Association and National Bar Association (2001). *Justice by Gender:*

Lack of Appropriate Prevention, Diversion, and Treatment Alternatives for Girls in the Juvenile Justice System. Washington, D.C.: American Bar Association and National Bar Association.

Attorney-General of British Columbia v. Smith. (1969). Canadian Criminal Cases, vol. 1, p. 244.

Austin, R. (1982). Women's liberation and increases in minor, major, and occupational offenses. *Criminology,* 20, 407–30.

Balkan, S., and Berger, R. J. (1979). The changing nature of female delinquency. In C. Kopp (ed.), *Becoming Female: Perspectives on Development.* New York: Plenum.

Bartollas, C. (1993). Little girls grown up: The perils of institutionalization. In C. Culliver (ed.), *Female Criminality: State of the Art.* New York: Garland Press.

Beattie, K. (2005). Adult correctional services in Canada, 2003/4. *Juristat,* 25(8), 1–31.

Belknap, J., Winter, E., and Cady, B. (2001). *Assessing the Needs of Committed Delinquent and Pre-Adjudicated Girls in Colorado: A Focus Group Study.* A Report to the Colorado Division of Youth Corrections, Denver: Colorado Division of Youth Corrections.

Berger, R. (1989). Female delinquency and the emancipation era: A review of the literature. *Sex Roles,* 21(5–6), 375–99.

Bottoms, A. (2002). The divergent development of juvenile justice policy and practice in England and Scotland. In M. K. Rosenheim, F. E. Zimring, D. S. Tanenhaus, and B. Dohrn (eds.), *A Century of Juvenile Justice.* Chicago: University of Chicago Press.

Braithwaite, J. (1989). *Crime, Shame and Reintegration.* Cambridge: Cambridge University Press.

Breed, A. (1976). *Task Force Report on Juvenile Justice and Delinquency Prevention.* Washington, D.C.: National Advisory Committee on Criminal Justice Standards and Goals.

Bruck, C. (1975). Women against the law. *Human Behavior,* 4, 24–33.

Calverley, D. (2006). Youth custody and community services in Canada, 2003/4. *Juristat,* 26(2), 1–21.

Canada (1938). *Report of the Royal Commission to Investigate the Penal System of Canada.* Joseph Archambault, chairman. Ottawa: King's Printer.

Canadian Centre for Justice Statistics (2004). *Canadian Crime Statistics, 2003.* Ottawa: Statistics Canada.

Canadian Centre for Justice Statistics (2006). Special data request. Ottawa: Statistics Canada.

Canadian Parliament. House of Commons (1908). *Debates,* 10th Parliament, 4th Session, 1907–8, July 8, 1908. Ottawa: Canadian Government.

Canadian Parliament. House of Commons (1924). *Debates,* 14th Parliament, 3rd Session, 1924, June 23, 1924. Ottawa: Canadian Government.

Canadian Parliament. House of Commons (1929). *Debates,* 16th Parliament, 3rd Session, 1929, May 16, 1929. Ottawa: Canadian Government.

Canter, R. (1982). Sex differences in self-report delinquency. *Criminology,* 20(3/4), 373–93.

Chesney-Lind, M. (1973). Judicial enforcement of the female sex role. *Issues in Criminology,* 8, 51–70.

Chesney-Lind, M. (2001). Are girls closing the gender gap in violence? *Criminal Justice,* 16(1), 18–23.

Chesney-Lind, M. (2002). Criminalizing victimization: The unintended consequences of pro-arrest policies for girls and women. *Criminology & Public Policy,* 2(1), 81–89.

Chesney-Lind, M., and Irwin, K. (2008). *Beyond Bad Girls: Gender Violence and Hype.* New York: Routledge.

Chesney-Lind, M., and Paramore, V. (2001). Are girls getting more violent? Exploring robbery trends. *Journal of Contemporary Criminal Justice,* 17(2), 142–66.

Chesney-Lind, M., and Shelden, G. R. (2004). *Girls, Delinquency and Juvenile Justice.* 3rd ed. Belmont, CA: Thomson Wadsworth.

Children's Bureau and U.S. Department of Health, Education and Welfare, in cooperation with the National Probation and Parole Association and the National Council of Juvenile Court Judges (1954). *Standards for Specialized Courts Dealing with Children.* Washington, D.C.: Government Printing Office.

Conway, J. (1992). Female young offenders, 1990–91. *Juristat* Service Bulletin. *Canadian Centre for Justice Statistics,* May, 12(11).

Datesman, S., and Scarpitti, F. (1977). Unequal protection for males and females in the juvenile court. In T. N. Ferdinand (ed.), *Juvenile Delinquency: Little Brother Grows Up.* Newbury Park, CA: Sage.

Datesman, S., and Scarpitti, F. (1980). The extent and nature of female crime. In Datesman and Scarpitti (eds.), *Women, Crime and Justice.* Oxford: Oxford University Press.

DeKeseredy, W. (2000). *Women, Crime and the Canadian Criminal Justice System.* Cincinnati, OH: Anderson.

Deming, R. (1977). *Women: The New Criminals.* Nashville, TN: Thomas Nelson.

Department of the Solicitor General (1967). *First Discussion Draft: An Act Respecting Children and Young Persons.* Ottawa: Department of the Solicitor General.

Doob, A. N. (1991). *Workshop on Collecting Race and Ethnicity Statistics in the Criminal Justice System.* Toronto: Centre of Criminology, University of Toronto.

Doob, A. N. (2001). *Youth Court Judges' Views of the Youth Justice System: The Results of a Survey.* Report to the Department of Justice Canada.

Doob, A. N., Grossman, M. G., and Auger, R. (1994). Aboriginal homicides in Ontario. *Canadian Journal of Criminology,* 36(1), 29–62.

Doob, A. N., and Meen, J. M. (1993). An exploration of changes in dispositions for young offenders in Toronto. *Canadian Journal of Criminology,* 35(1), 19–29.

Doob, A. N., and Sprott, J. B. (1998). Is the "quality" of youth violence becoming more serious? *Canadian Journal of Criminology,* 40(2), 185–94.

Doob, A. N., and Sprott, J. B. (2004). Changing models of youth justice in Canada. In M. Tonry and A. N. Doob (eds.), *Crime and Justice: A Review of Research,* vol. 31. Chicago: University of Chicago Press.

Doob, A. N., and Webster, C. M. (2006). Countering punitiveness: Understanding stability in Canada's imprisonment rate. *Law and Society Review,* 40(2), 325–68.

Federal Bureau of Investigation (2006). *Crime in the United States, 2004.* Uniform Crime Reports. Washington, D.C.: FBI, Department of Justice.

Federal-Provincial-Territorial Task Force on Youth Justice (1996). *A Review of the Young Offenders Act and the Youth Justice System in Canada.* Ottawa: Department of Justice.

Fergusson, D. M., and Harwood, L. J. (2002). Male and female offending trajectories. *Development and Psychopathology,* 14, 159–77.

Figueria-McDonough, J. (1984). Feminism and delinquency. *British Journal of Criminology,* 24, 325–42.

Flicker, B. (1982). Standards for juvenile justice: A summary and analysis. In Institute of Judicial Administration and American Bar Association, *Juvenile Justice Standards: Standards Relating to Noncriminal Misbehavior,* 2nd ed. Cambridge, MA: Ballinger.

Fox, R. (1977). Young persons in conflict with the law in Canada. *International and Comparative Law Quarterly,* 26(2), 445–67.

Fox, R., and Spencer, M. (1971). The young offenders bill: Destigmatizing juvenile delinquency. *Criminal Law Quarterly,* 14, 172–19.

Gagnon, D. (1984). *History of the Law for Juvenile Delinquents.* Ottawa: Minister of the Solicitor General of Canada.

Garbarino, J. (2006). *See Jane Hit: Why Girls Are Growing More Violent and What We Can Do About It.* New York: Penguin Press.

Gartner, R., Webster, C., and Doob, A. N. (in preparation). *Trends in the Imprisonment of Women in Canada.*

General Accounting Office (1978). *Removing Status Offenders from Secure Facilities: Federal Leadership and Guidance Are Needed.* Washington, D.C.: General Accounting Office.

General Accounting Office (1983). *Improved Federal Efforts Needed to Change Juvenile Detention Practices.* Washington, D.C.: General Accounting Office.

General Accounting Office (1984). *Better Monitoring and Record Keeping Systems Needed to Accurately Account For Juvenile Justice Practices.* Washington, D.C.: General Accounting Office.

General Accounting Office (1991). *Noncriminal Juveniles: Detentions Have Been Reduced but Better Monitoring Is Needed.* Washington, D.C.: General Accounting Office.

General Accounting Office (1995). *Juvenile Justice: Minimal Gender Bias Occurring in Processing Non-Criminal Juveniles.* Washington, D.C.: General Accounting Office.

Gibbons, D., and Griswold, M. J. (1957). Sex differences among juvenile court referrals. *Sociology and Social Research,* 42, 106–10.

Gilman, D. (1976). How to retrain jurisdiction over status offenses: Change without reform in Florida. *Crime and Delinquency,* 22(1), 48–51.

Giordano, P., and Cernkovich, S. (1979). On complicating the relationship between liberation and delinquency. *Social Problems,* 26(4), 467–81.

Gold, M., and Reimer, D. (1975). Changing patterns of delinquency behavior among Americans 13 to 16 years old, 1967–1972. *Crime and Delinquency Literature,* 7, 483–517.

Government of Canada (1982). *The Criminal Law in Canadian Society.* Ottawa: Government of Canada.

Grant, I. (1984). The "incorrigible" juvenile: History and prerequisites of reform in Ontario. *Canadian Journal of Family Law,* 4(3), 293–318.

Grygier, T. (1968). Juvenile delinquents or child offenders: Some comments on the first discussion draft of an act respecting children and young persons. *Canadian Journal of Corrections,* 10(3), 458–69.

Hurst, H. (1975). Juvenile status offenders. Speech delivered to the New Mexico Council on Crime and Delinquency, Albuquerque, June 20.

Institute of Judicial Administration and American Bar Association (1982). *Juvenile Justice Standards: Standards Relating to Noncriminal Misbehavior.* 2nd ed. Cambridge, MA: Ballinger.

Isaacs, J. L. (1963). The role of the lawyer in representing minors in the New York family court. *Buffalo Law Review,* 12, 501–21.

James, J., and Thornton, W. (1980). Women's liberation and the female delinquent. *Journal of Research in Crime and Delinquency,* 17, 230–44.

Jones, T., and Newburn, T. (2007). *Policy Transfer and Criminal Justice: Exploring US Influence over British Crime Control Policy.* Maidenhead: Open University Press,

Junger Tas, J. (1984). *Recent Trends in Juvenile Delinquency and Reactions of the Juvenile Justice System.* The Hague: Research and Documentation Centre, Ministry of Justice.

Juvenile justice experts should focus on girls' unique needs. (January 7, 2000). *Psychiatric News.* www.psychiatricnews.org/pnews/00–01-07/girls.html.

Ketcham, O. (1965). Legal renaissance in the juvenile courts. *Northwestern University Law Review,* 60(5), 585–98.

Knupfer, A. M. (2001). *Reform and Resistance: Gender, Delinquency, and America's First Juvenile Court.* New York: Routledge.

Kotsopoulos, S., and Loutsi, Z. (1977). Trends in juvenile delinquency in Greece. *International Journal of Offender Therapy and Comparative Criminology,* 21(3), 270–78.

LeBlanc, M., and Biron, L. (1980). Status offenses: A legal term without meaning. *Journal of Research in Crime and Delinquency,* 17(1), 114–25.

Lenroot, K. F. (1923). The evolution of the Juvenile Court. *Annals of the American Academy of Political and Social Science,* 105, 213–22.

Leon, J. (1977). The development of Canadian juvenile justice: A background for reform. *Osgoode Hall Law Journal,* 15(1), 71–106.

Lerman, P. (1980). Trends and issues in the deinstitutionalization of youths in trouble. *Crime and Delinquency,* 26(3), 281–98.

Lindsey, E. (1914). The juvenile court movement from a lawyer's standpoint. *Annals of the American Academy of Political and Social Science,* 52, 140–48.

Lou, H. H. (1927). *Juvenile Courts in the United States.* Chapel Hill: University of North Carolina Press.

MacLeod, A. (1965). *Juvenile Delinquency in Canada: The Report of the Department of Justice Committee on Juvenile Delinquency.* Ottawa: Minister of Justice and Attorney-General of Canada.

Mawby, R. (1980). Sex and crime: The results of a self-report survey. *British Journal of Criminology,* 31(4), 525–43.

McManaman, J. (1905). The juvenile court. In Board of Commissioners of Public Charities, *Eighteenth Biennial Report.* Springfield, IL: State Journal, State Printers.

Mulvihill, O., Tumin, M., and Curtis, L. (1969). *Crimes of Violence.* Vol. 12. Washington, D.C.: Government Printing Office.

Murphy, J. P. (1929). The juvenile court at the bar: A national challenge. *Annals of the American Academy of Political and Social Science,* 145, 80–97.

National Center for Juvenile Justice (2006). *National Juvenile Court Data Archive: Juvenile Court Case Records, 1985–2003* [machine-readable data files]. Pittsburgh, PA: NCJJ.

National Council of Juvenile and Family Court Judges (1980). Evaluation standards. *Juvenile and Family Court Journal,* 31(2), 3–13.

National Council on Crime and Delinquency. (1975). Jurisdiction over status offenses should be removed from the juvenile court: A policy statement, 22 October 1974. *Crime and Delinquency,* 21(2), 97–99.

Nettler, G. (1974). *Explaining Crime.* New York: McGraw-Hill.

Odem, M. E. (1995). *Delinquent Daughters: Protection and Policing Adolescent Female Sexuality in the United States, 1885–1920.* Chapel Hill: University of North Carolina.

Office of Juvenile Justice and Delinquency Prevention (1985). *Runaway Children and he Juvenile Justice and Delinquency Prevention Act: What Is the Impact?* Washington, D.C.: U.S. Government Printing Office.

Office of Juvenile Justice and Delinquency Prevention (1986). *America's Missing and Exploited Children.* Washington, D.C.: U.S. Government Printing Office.

Parker, G. (1970). The appellate court view of juvenile court. *Osgoode Hall Law Journal,* 7(2), 155–76.

Parmelee, M. (1918). *Criminology.* New York: MacMillan.

Pastore, A., and Maguire, K. (2004). *Sourcebook of Criminal Justice Statistics, 2003: Bureau of Justice Statistics.* Washington, D.C.: U.S. Government Printing Office.

Perkins, F., and Lenroot, K. (1934). *Juvenile Court Standards: United States Department of Labor and Children's Bureau.* Washington, D.C.: U.S. Government Printing Office.

Pike, L. (1876). *A History of Crime in England.* London: Smith, Elder.

Pope, C., and Feyerherm, W. (1982). Gender bias in juvenile court dispositions. *Social Service Research,* 6, 1–16.

President's Commission on Law Enforcement and Administration of Justice. (1967a). *Task Force Report: Juvenile Delinquency and Youth Crime; Report on Juvenile Justice and Consultants' Papers.* Washington, D.C.: U.S. Government Printing Office.

President's Commission on Law Enforcement and Administration of Justice (1967b). *The Challenge of Crime in Free Society.* Washington, D.C.: U.S. Government Printing Office.

Prothrow-Stith, D., and Spivak, H. R. (2005). *Sugar and Spice and No Longer Nice: How We Can Stop Girls' Violence.* San Francisco: Jossey-Bass.

Puzzanchera, C., Finnegan, T., and Kang, W. (2007). *Easy Access to Juvenile Populations.* http://www.ojjdp.ncjrs.gov/ojstatbb/ezapop/.

Puzzanchera, C., and Kang, W. (2007). *Juvenile Court Statistics Databook.* http://ojjdp.ncjrs.gov/ojstatbb/jcsdb/.

Reitsma-Street, M. (1993). Canadian youth court charges and dispositions for females before and after the implementation of the Young Offenders Act. *Canadian Journal of Criminology,* 35(4), 437–58.

Report of the Department of Justice Committee on Juvenile Delinquency (1965). *Juvenile Delinquency in Canada.* Ottawa: Government of Canada.

Roberts, J. (1998). The evolution of penal policy in Canada. *Social Policy and Administration,* 32(4), 420–37.

Rosenblatt, E., and Greenland, C. (1974). Female crimes of violence. *Canadian Journal of Criminology and Corrections,* 16, 173–80.

Sanders, W. (1970). *Juvenile Offenders for a Thousand Years: Selected Readings from Anglo-Saxon Times to 1900.* Chapel Hill: University of North Carolina Press.

Shain, I. J., and Burkhart, W. R. (1960). *A Study on the Administration of Juvenile Justice in California (Part II): Prepared for the Governor's Special Study Commission on Juvenile Justice.* Sacramento: Government of California.

Shelden, G. R. (1981). Sex discrimination in the juvenile justice system: Memphis, Tennessee, 1900–1917. In M. Q. Warren (ed.), *Comparing Male and Female Offenders.* Newbury Park, CA: Sage.

Shoemaker, D. (1994). Male-female delinquency in the Philippines: A comparative analysis. *Youth and Society,* 25(3), 299–329.

Sickmund, M., Sladky, T. J., and Kang, W. (2008). *Census of Juveniles in Residential Placement Databook.* http://www.ojjdp.ncjrs.gov/ojstatbb/cjrp/.

Sickmund, M., Sladky, T. J., Kang, W., and Puzzanchera, C. (2008). *Easy Access to the Census of Juveniles in Residential Placement.* http://ojjdp.ncjrs.gov/ojstatbb/ezacjrp/.

Smith, D. (2005). The effectiveness of the juvenile justice system. *Criminal Justice,* 5(2), 181–95.

Snyder, H. (1999). The overrepresentation of juvenile crime proportions in robbery clearance statistics. *Journal of Quantitative Criminology,* 15, 151–61.

Snyder, H., and Sickmund, M. (2006). *Juvenile Offenders and Victims: 2006 National Report.* Washington, D.C.: U.S. Department of Justice, Office of Justice Programs, OJJDP.

Solicitor General of Canada (1975). *Young Persons in Conflict with the Law: A Report of the Solicitor General's Committee on Proposals for New Legislation to Replace the Juvenile Delinquents Act.* Ottawa: Solicitor General of Canada.

Solicitor General of Canada (1977). *Highlights of the Proposed New Legislation for Young Offenders.* Ottawa: Solicitor General of Canada.

Solicitor General of Canada (1979). *Legislative Proposals to Replace the Juvenile Delinquents Act.* Ottawa: Solicitor General of Canada.

Sprott, J. B. (2006). The use of custody for failing to comply with a disposition cases under the Young Offenders Act. *Canadian Journal of Criminology and Criminal Justice,* 48(4), 609–22.

Sprott, J. B., and Doob, A. N. (2003). It's all in the denominator: Trends in the processing of girls in Canada's youth courts. *Canadian Journal of Criminology and Criminal Justice,* 45(1), 73–80.

Sprott, J. B., Doob, A. N., and Jenkins, J. (2001). Problem behaviour and delinquency in children and youth. *Juristat,* 21(4), 1–13.

Stahl, A., Finnegan, T., and Kang, W. (2006). *Easy Access to Juvenile Court Statistics: 1985–2003.* http://ojjdp.ncjrs.gov/ojstatbb/ezajcs/.

Standing Committee on Justice and Legal Affairs (1997). *Reviewing Youth Justice.* Thirteenth Report of the Standing Committee on Justice and Legal Affairs. Ottawa: House of Commons.

Steffensmeier, D., and Cobb, M. (1981). Sex differences in urban arrest patterns, 1934–79. *Social Problems, 29,* 37–50.

Steffensmeier, D., and Kramer, J. (1979). Sex differences in delinquency: An analysis of juvenile court statistics, 1970–76. *Pepperdine Law Review, 6,* 751–66.

Steffensmeier, D., Schwartz, J., Zhong, H., and Ackerman, J. (2005). An assessment of recent trends in girls' violence using diverse longitudinal sources: Is the gender gap closing? *Criminology, 43*(2), 355–405.

Steffensmeier, D., and Steffensmeier, R. (1980). Trends in female delinquency: An examination of arrest, juvenile court, self-report and field data. *Criminology, 18*(1), 62–85.

Steffensmeier, D., Zhong, H., Ackerman, J., Schwartz, J., and Agha, S. (2006). Gender gap trends for violent crimes, 1980–2003: A UCR-NCVS comparison. *Feminist Criminology, 1*(1), 72–98.

Steinberg, L., and Schwartz, R. (2000). Developmental psychology goes to court. In T. Grisso and R. Schwartz (eds.), *Youth on Trial: A Developmental Perspective on Juvenile Justice.* Chicago: University of Chicago Press.

Stiller, S., and Elder, C. (1974). PINS: A concept in need of supervision. *American Criminal Law Review, 12*(1), 33–60.

Sutton, J. R. (1988). *Stubborn Children: Controlling Delinquency in the United States, 1640–1981.* Berkeley: University of California Press.

Sweet, R. J. (1991). Deinstitutionalization of status offenders. *Pepperdine Law Review, 18,* 389–415.

Szymanski, L. (2008). Juvenile Delinquents' Right to a Jury Trial (2007 Update). NCJJ Snapshot, 13(2), February. Pittsburgh, PA: National Center for Juvenile Justice.

Tanenhaus, D. S. (2002). The evolution of juvenile courts in the early twentieth century: Beyond the myth of immaculate construction. In M. K. Rosenheim, F. E. Zimring, D. S. Tanenhaus, and B. Dohrn (eds.), *A Century of Juvenile Justice.* Chicago: University of Chicago Press.

Tappan, P. (1947). *Delinquent Girls in Court: A Study of the Wayward Minor Court of New York.* New York: Columbia University Press.

Tappan, P. (1949). *Juvenile Delinquency.* New York: McGraw-Hill.

Teitelbaum, L. (2002). Status offenses and status offenders. In M. K. Rosenheim, F. E. Zimring, D. S. Tanenhaus, and B. Dohrn (eds.), *A Century of Juvenile Justice.* Chicago: University of Chicago Press.

Thornton, W., Voigt, L., and Doerner, W. (1987). *Delinquency and Justice.* 2nd ed. New York: Random House.

Tonry, M., and Doob, A. N. (2004). Youth crime and youth justice. In M. Tonry and A. Doob (eds.), *Crime and Justice: A Review of Research,* vol. 31. Chicago: University of Chicago Press.

Trépanier, J. (1999). Juvenile delinquency and youth protection: The historical foundations of the Canadian Juvenile Delinquents Act of 1908. *European Journal of Crime, Criminal Law and Criminal Justice,* 7(1), 41–62.

Trépanier, J. (2004). What did Quebec not want? Opposition to the adoption of the Youth Criminal Justice Act in Quebec. *Canadian Journal of Criminology and Criminal Justice,* 46(3), 273–99.

U.S. Department of Justice (1972). *Crime in the United States, 1972.* Uniform Crime Reports. Washington, D.C.: Government Printing Office.

U.S. Department of Justice and Office of Juvenile Justice and Delinquency Prevention (1980). *Standards for the Administration of Juvenile Justice: Report of the National Advisory Committee for Juvenile Justice and Delinquency Prevention.* Washington, D.C.: U.S. Government Printing Office.

U.S. Department of Labor and Children's Bureau (1934). *Juvenile Court Standards.* Bureau publication 121. Washington: Government Printing Office.

U.S. Government (November 18, 1980). Proceedings and debates of the 96th Congress (2nd ed.). *Congressional Record,* 126(162), H10919–43.

U.S. House of Representatives (1992). *Hearings on the Reauthorization of the Juvenile Justice and Delinquency Prevention Act of 1974.* Hearings before the Subcommittee on Human Resources of the Committee on Education and Labor. 102nd Congress. Serial No. 102–125. Washington, D.C.: Government Printing Office.

Waite, E. (1921). How far can court procedure be socialized without impairing individual rights? *Journal of the American Institute of Criminal Law and Criminology,* 12(3), 339–47.

Wallace, M. (2004). Crime statistics in Canada, 2003. *Juristat,* 24(6), 1–26.

Wattenberg, W., and Saunders, F. (1954). Sex differences among juvenile offenders. *Sociology and Social Research,* 39, 24–31.

Webster, C. M., and Doob, A. N. (2007). Punitive trends and stable imprisonment rates in Canada. In M. Tonry (ed.), *Crime and Justice: A Review of Research,* vol. 36. Chicago: University of Chicago Press.

Wilson, N. (1981). The masculinity of violent crime: Some second thoughts. *Journal of Criminal Justice,* 9(2), 111–23.

Wortley, S. (1999). A Northern taboo: Research on race, crime and criminal justice in Canada. *Canadian Journal of Criminology,* 41(2), 261–74.

Zimring, F. (2005). *American Juvenile Justice.* Oxford: Oxford University Press.

Index

Aboriginal people, 4, 92–93, 197n4
Ackerman, J., 25–26, 28–29
Acoca, L., 28
acts, early, in Canada, 194n1
Adler, Freda, 13–17, 175–76
African American girls, and custody, 53
age: of consent, 129; maximum, for
    juvenile court jurisdiction, 79, 83,
    86–87; range, for juvenile courts,
    192n6
age discrimination, 194n4
Ageton, S., 17
Agha, S., 25–26, 29
American Bar Association, 64, 72
American Indians, 123–24
appeal, right to, in youth court, 49,
    80, 83, 87, 160. See also due process,
    in juvenile court
apprehension rates, 10
Archambault Commission, 80
arrest data, 10–11, 13, 15–17, 26–29, 33,
    43, 100–101
arrest rates: national, 17, 25, 28; for
    women and girls, 13, 162
arrest trends, 29–30, 99, 161
arson, 31, 192n7

Ashbrook, John, 67–68
assault, 21–23, 26, 29–31, 34–35, 38, 41,
    55, 162, 178–79; sexual, 34
Auger, R., 197n4
Austin, R., 13, 17
Ayelsworth, A. B., 76

Balkan, S., 13, 17
Bartollas, C., 28
Beattie, K., 20
Becca's Law, 69
Belknap, J., 28
Berger, R. J., 13, 17
Biron, L., 20
Braithwaite, John, 19
breaking and entering, 24, 36, 179
Breed, A., 64
Bruck, C., 13
burglary, 10, 23, 31–32, 41, 55, 139,
    178
Burkhart, W. R., 58

Cady, B., 28
Calverley, D., 20
Canadian Centre for Justice Statistics,
    195n5

Canadian Charter of Rights and Freedoms, 87

Canter, R., 17, 20

case, definition, 29, 195n6

caseloads, in youth court, 104–5, 109–10, 131–33, 138, 142–44, 155

Cernkovich, S., 17

Chesney-Lind, M., 5, 13, 17, 20, 28, 44, 47, 66, 69–70, 72, 120

Children in Custody survey, 113, 181

Children's Aid Society (Ontario), 75

Children's Bureau of Philadelphia, 48–49, 57

child welfare, in Canada, 76, 88, 93, 129, 154–55, 181

Chrétien, Jean, 167

civil liberties, 67, 95

Cobb, M., 17

Committee on Delinquency (Canada), 85

Committee on Juvenile Justice, 160

consensual sex, 57, 129, 196n1. *See also* age: of consent

constitutionality, of juvenile court laws, 49–50

Conway, J., 90

court data, 17, 29–30, 43, 101–2

court referrals, 16

court trends: Canadian, 34–38, 40, 161; U.S., 29–33, 38, 161

crime rates, direct comparisons between the U.S. and Canada, 191n3 (chap. 2); for girls, 14

crime wave, involving girls and women, viii, 1, 3–4, 25, 28, 161–62

criminology texts, early, 11

culture, changing, 8–9

curfew violations, 17, 101, 162

Curtis, L., 12

custodial counts, tables, 183–86

custodial policy, viii

custodial populations: in Canada, 130, 149–53; in the U.S., 99–101, 113–24, 170

custodial sentences, 88, 93–94, 106, 114, 127, 135, 138, 145, 155, 160, 163

custody, use of, 53, 62–63, 65–68, 87, 89, 92, 94, 96, 134–42, 144–48, 155, 165, 167, 171–72, 181, 187, 189; for girls, 56–57, 90–91, 106, 150, 153, 156, 172; for status offenses, 101, 117, 126, 159–61; for welfare purposes, 88, 93, 155–56, 164, 167

custody data, by gender, 195n1

cyberluring, 129

data, difficulties in assessing, 195n1

Datesman, S., 17, 120

deinstitutionalization, 63, 69–70, 72, 98, 169

DeKeseredy, W., 9

delinquency, defined, in Canada, 75–77, 79–81, 84–85, 92, 166. *See also* juvenile delinquent

Deming, R., 13

detention facilities, special, for juveniles, 45, 68, 113, 193n6

disobedience, 17

disorderly conduct, 101, 107–10, 112, 127, 183

diversion. *See* juvenile justice system, justifications for a separate system

Doerner, W., 17

Doob, A. N., 20, 89–90, 93, 95, 156, 167, 170, 173, 196n3, 197n4

drinking, 13, 16

drugs and drug use, 16–17, 25, 33–34, 37–39, 42, 61, 154, 178, 193n5

due process, in juvenile court, 51–53,

58–59, 61–63, 67, 81, 83, 87, 96, 98, 128, 153, 159, 166; for girls, 54, 57

Elder, C., 181
Elliott, D. S., 17
ethnicity, lack of data, 4–5, 123–24, 196n4 (chap. 5)

failure to comply, 130, 141–49, 156, 161–64, 166, 173
family conflict, 28, 154, 162
family issues, vii–viii, 12, 51
Federal-Provincial-Territorial Task Force, 91
feminist movement. *See* women's movement
Fergusson, D. M., 20
Feyerherm, W., 120
Figueria-McDonough, J., 17
Finnegan, T., 123
Flicker, B., 64
Fortas, Abe, 62
foster home, 69, 75
Fox, R., 83
freedom, for women, and affect on crime, 1, 9–12, 18
funding, and youth justice policy, 3, 71–72, 164

Gagnon, D., 80, 83, 194n1
gang culture/gang activity, 7, 13, 26
GAO reports, 70–71, 179–81, 197n1 (appendix)
Garbarino, James, 9–10
Gartner, R., 196n3
Gault, Gerald, 62
gender disparity, 69, 83, 85–86
gender-neutral language, 93
gender-specific services, 71–72, 91
Gibbons, D., 56, 120

Gilman, D., 181
Giordano, P., 17
Gold, M., 17
Google, 8
Graham, George Perry, 77
Grant, I., 138
Greenland, C., 13
Griswold, M. J., 56, 120
Grossman, M. G., 197n4
Grygier, T., 83

Harwood, L. J., 20
Hispanics, 196n4 (chap. 5)
homicide, 20–26, 30, 34, 90, 156, 166, 192n3, 197n4
Hurst, Hunter, 66

incarceration: protective, 173; rates of, 115, 127, 153, 158, 168–72, 197n3
incorrigibility, 1, 17, 28, 44, 46, 55–56, 65, 82, 128, 130–36, 138–41, 154–55, 160, 181, 187–89, 194n2
index offenses, 14–16, 175, 178; listed, 191n5
industrial schools (training schools), in Canada, 74, 82, 84, 128, 181, 194n2
infanticide, 21, 90
Institute of Judicial Administration, 64
intervention, 98–99, 112, 120, 132, 149, 153, 155, 159–60, 166; special, for girls, 161. *See also* juvenile justice system, justifications for a separate system
Irwin, K., 5, 28, 72
Isaacs, J. L., 58

James, J., 17
Jenkins, J., 20
Johnson, Lyndon, 58

Jones, T., 159

Junger Tas, J., 20

juvenile court, vii, 3; early history, Canada, 74–75; early history, U.S., 45–46; founding of, 159; statistics, 25

juvenile delinquent, 71, 75–77, 80, 160, 165, 194n3

Juvenile Delinquents Act (Canada), 75–85, 88, 128, 130, 141, 149, 153, 159

juvenile justice, goals for, 165; historical development, 158–59. *See also* juvenile court: early history, Canada; juvenile court: early history, U.S.

Juvenile Justice and Delinquency Prevention Act of 1974 (JJDPA), 3, 63, 65, 67, 69–72, 95–96, 98, 114, 120, 126–27, 141, 161, 165–66, 169, 171, 195n2; grant programs, 71

juvenile justice system, justifications for a separate system, 51–52, 55, 58, 76–77, 80–81

Kang, W., 29, 102, 122–25, 185–86

Kent v. United States, 62

Ketcham, O., 57–58

Kildee, Dale, 68

Knupfer, A. M., 1, 44, 47, 53

Kotsopoulos, S., 20

Kramer, J., 16

Labrador, and Canadian law governing young offenders, 191n3 (chap. 1)

Lancaster, Edward, 76–77

Lapointe, Ernest, 78–79

larceny, 23, 26, 31, 33, 37, 55, 178

LeBlanc, M., 20

legal representation, for youths, 77, 80–81, 83, 87

Lenroot, Katharine, 49

Leon, J., 159

Lerman, P., 181

liberation theory (liberation hypothesis), 9, 11–13, 16–17

Lindsey, Benjamin B., 77

Lindsey, Edward, 46, 48–50, 52

liquor-law violations, 25–26

Lou, H. H., 45

Loutsi, Z., 20

MacLeod, A., 81–83, 160

Maguire, K., 20

marijuana, 25–26, 38, 42

Martínez, Matthew, 70

Massachusetts Bay Colony, 47

Mawby, R., 20

McGibbon, Peter, 80

McLellan, Anne, 92

McManaman, John, 48

media depiction of girl violence, 5–7, 9–10, 13, 161

Meen, J. M., 89

Meighen, Arthur, 77–78

Miller, George, 68

Monitoring the Future, 26, 28

motor vehicle theft, 31, 192n7

Mulvihill, O., 12

murder. *See* homicide

Murphy, J. Pretence, 48–50, 52

National Advisory Committee on Criminal Justice Standards and Goals, 64–65

National Bar Association, 64, 72

National Center for Juvenile Justice, 29, 66, 101, 166, 191n3 (chap. 2)

National Council of Juvenile and Family Court Judges, 57, 66

National Council on Crime and Delinquency, 63–64

National Crime Victimization Survey, 26–28
National Probation and Parole Association, 48, 57
National Youth Risk Behavior Survey, 26, 28
Nettler, G., 13
Newburn, T., 159
Newfoundland, and Canadian law governing young offenders, 191n3 (chap. 1)
New York Family Court Act (1963), 59

obstructing justice, 101–7, 110–12, 126, 182
Odem, M. E., 120
Office of Juvenile Justice and Delinquency Prevention, 69–70, 72
organized crime, 193n5

Paramore, V., 28
parens patriae, 53, 58, 62
Parker, G., 85
Parmelee, M., 5
Pastore, A., 20
penitentiary populations, 196n3. *See also* custodial populations
Perkins, F., 49
petty theft, 16
Pike, L., 11
police, role of, 38, 55, 60, 65–66, 69, 74, 97, 146, 160, 162
policy transfer, 159
Pope, C., 120
pregnancy, out of wedlock, 61, 66
President's Commission on Law Enforcement and Administration of Justice, 58
private hearings, hallmark of early juvenile courts, 45

probation, 46, 54, 62, 88–89, 91–92, 141–42, 148–49, 163
probation officers, hallmark of early juvenile courts, 45
property crime (property offenses), 17, 21–24, 26, 31, 36, 38, 41, 55–56, 178–79, 192n7
prostitution, 21, 46, 93
Prothrow-Smith, Deborah, 10–11
public health issues, 38, 181
Puzzanchera, C., 29, 102, 123–25

race, lack of data, 4–5, 123–24, 196n4 (chap. 5), 196n4 (chap. 6)
racial tension, 7
Railsback, Tom, 68
rape, 26, 30
recidivism, 47
reformatory, in the U.S., 46–47
reform school (juvenile reformatory), in Canada, 74–75, 84, 194n2
Regnery, Al, 69
rehabilitation: of girls, 44; for juveniles, 47, 51, 62–63, 75, 164, 166–67
Reimer, D., 17
Reitsma-Street, M., 89–90
Reno, Janet, 10
Research Triangle Institute, 72
robbery, 28, 30, 34
Roberts, J., 95
Rock, Allan, 90
Rosenblatt, E., 13
runaways, 21, 25–26, 56, 65, 68–70, 101, 162

Saunders, F., 55
Scarpitti, F., 17, 120
schools, reporting violence, 8–9
Schwartz, J., 25–26, 28–29
Schwartz, R., 192

self-report data, versus official data, 10, 16, 25, 29, 43, 106, 139, 161–62

sentencing, 56, 87–88, 93–94, 100, 106, 167, 192n2; maximum lengths for custodial sentences for youths, 90, 156, 160, 166; options for juveniles in Ontario, 74–75; prison or penitentiary, 20

sex offenses, 56

sex roles (gender roles), vii, 8–9

sexual behavior, 55, 57, 95

sexual immorality, 1, 44, 77–79, 81–82, 84–85, 91, 96, 128–41, 153–56, 172, 187–89, 194n3

sexual intercourse, categorized as delinquency, 78–79

sexual promiscuity, 53–54, 66, 181

sexual revolution, of the 1960s, 138

Shain, I. J., 58

Shelden, G. R., 14, 17, 20, 44, 47, 66, 69–70, 120

Shoemaker, D., 20

shoplifting, 10, 142

Sickmund, M., 20, 30, 33, 62, 116, 122–25, 185–86, 193n6

Sladky, T. J., 116, 122–25, 185–86

Snyder, H., 10, 20, 30, 33, 62, 193n6

Spencer, M., 83

Spivak, Howard R., 10–11

Sprott, J. B., 20, 89–90, 148, 156

standards, 3, 12, 64, 80, 98; for juvenile court, 65–66, 164; published, 49, 57

Standing Committee on Justice and Legal Affairs, 91

status offender policy, in the U.S., 158

status offenses, vii–viii, 16–17, 20, 25, 28, 46–47, 50, 52–55, 56–61, 65, 68, 73, 85–87, 89–90, 94–97, 98, 100, 112, 114, 120–24, 180–81; and gender, 70–72; and girls, 60–61,

64, 141, 162; removed from juvenile court jurisdiction, 63–67, 81, 96, 99, 160–61, 171

Steffensmeier, D., 16–17, 25–26, 28–29

Steffensmeier, R., 16–17, 25–26

Steinberg, L., 192

Stiller, S., 181

superpredator scare, of the 1990s, 25

Supreme Court, decisions of the 1960s, 3, 52, 61–63, 98, 160, 165–66

Sutton, J. R., 47

Sweet, R. J., 47, 194n7

Szymanski, L., 165

Tanenhaus, D. S., 45, 48, 159

Tappan, P., 46–47, 52–55, 60, 62, 193n4

Teitelbaum, L., 47

television, increase in violence in shows, 7, 9

theft, 23–26, 31–33, 37, 41–42, 178–79

Thornton, W., 17

Toews, Vic, 129

training schools. *See* industrial schools (training schools), in Canada

transfer, of youths to adult court, 3, 62, 89–90, 156, 192n6

Trépanier, J., 194n1

trial by jury, for youths, 49, 77, 80, 165–66. *See also* due process, in juvenile court

truancy, 17, 55, 61, 69, 85

Tumin, M., 12

ungovernable conduct, 56

Uniform Crime Reports (Canada), 21, 26

Uniform Crime Reports (United States), 21–23, 26–27, 29

U.S. Violent Crime Index, 34

valid court orders (VCOs), 67–70, 72–73, 95–96, 101–2, 106–7, 130, 141–42, 161–62, 164, 173, 195n2
vandalism, 59
vice, 77–78, 84, 91, 128, 153, 194n3
victimization, 16, 43, 161–62
violence: by girls, 4–9, 17, 161; trends, 26; by youth, 11, 139, 148
violent crime, 21–24, 26, 30–31, 38, 41; by girls, 178
Virk, Reena, 5–7
Voigt, L., 17

Waite, Edward, 48–49, 52
Wallace, M., 20
Wattenberg, W., 55
wayward minor, definition, 193n4
Wayward Minor Court, 54
weapons, use by girls, 6–7
Webster, C. M., 95, 167, 170, 173, 196n3
Wilson, N., 17
Winter, E., 28
women's liberation, 10
women's movement, 8, 11, 17

working mothers, effect on delinquency, 12
Wortley, S., 197n4

Young Offenders Act, 83, 87–90, 92, 96, 128, 141, 148, 192n2
youth court processing, 100–101, 129
youth crime data, versus self-reported offending, 19–20
Youth Criminal Justice Act (YCJA), viii, 34–35, 37–38, 42, 92–94, 96, 146–47, 152, 163, 167, 171–72
youth justice data, 5, 100
youth justice processing, 19, 41, 111–12
youth justice system (juvenile court): gender discrimination, 1–2, 4, 71; operation over time, 100; ratio of girls to boys, 40; scope of, 48, 50; state versus federal administration, 3; U.S. compared to Canada, 2, 94–97

zero-tolerance policing, 28
Zhong, H., 25–26, 28–29
Zimring, F., 25, 48, 51–52, 55, 113